The Annual of the American Institute of Graphic Arts

Graphic Design USA

Written by Steven Heller, Sharyn O'Mara,
and Ellen Shapiro
Designed by Beth Crowell, Cheung/Crowell Design
Jacket/cover designed by Louise Fili, Louise Fili Ltd
Managing Editor: Marie Finamore

Distributed to the trade by Watson-Guptill Publications,
1515 Broadway, New York, NY 10036.

ISBN: 0-8230-7233-9

First printing, 1999.

Distributed outside of the United States and Canada by
Hearst Books International, 1350 Avenue of the
Americas, New York, NY 10019.

Printing: Syl, Barcelona, Spain
Color Separation: Syl, Barcelona, Spain
Paper: Creator Silk 135 gsm
Page layouts were composed in Adobe QuarkXpress
3.32r.5 on a Power Macintosh 8100/80.
Typefaces: Bembo, Frutiger, and Univers

The Annual of the American Institute of Graphic Arts

1998 Medalists

1998 Design Leadership Award

1997-1998 Award Exhibitions

Visiting Exhibitions and Conferences

Lou Danziger.
One of a small pack of postwar pioneering Modernist American designers,
Lou designed a world of
signs + symbols;
colors and
textures.
Asymmetrically balanced forms banished
static symmetry from his dynamic
graphic space.
Trails
were blazed, conventions were flaunted,
design and America were expanded
& enriched.

●

April Greiman
            marches to the beat
                        of a different drummer.
She follows her eyes and feelings,
            even when they lead
                        off the edge of territory
                                    she only recently
                                                charted.
Taking risks,
            she never looks back or
                        back tracks.
March on,
            April.   We'll try to catch up.

●

In the 1950s
when paper promotions featured gilded scripts and elegantly clichéd images,
Champion Paper had the imagination
to let designers stretch
to their limits with ink on paper.

For almost half a century,
Champion showed designers,
                        clients,
                                    and printers
what was possible.

Champion,
            thank you for believing in design;
            thank you for the legacy.

— PHILIP MEGGS

The medal of the AIGA, the most distinguished in the field, is awarded to individuals in recognition of their exceptional achievements, services, or other contributions to the field of graphic design and visual communications. The contribution may be in the practice of graphic design, teaching, writing, or leadership of the profession. The awards may honor designers posthumously.

Medals are awarded to those individuals who have set standards of excellence over a lifetime of work or have made individual contributions to innovation within the practice of graphic design.

Individuals who are honored may work in any country, but the contributions for which they are honored should have had a significant impact on the practice of graphic design in the United States.

The Design Leadership Award recognizes the role of perceptive and forward-thinking organizations that have been instrumental in the advancement of design by applying the highest standards, as a matter of policy.

The AIGA's 1998 awards committee was chaired by Paula Scher and included Katherine McCoy, Philip Meggs, Michael Vanderbyl, Jilly Simons, and Lucille Tenazas. Committee member Philip Meggs offers the poems on the opposite page as insights into the 1998 medalists.

Louis Danziger

Work, Think, Feel

By Steven Heller

A few years ago a publisher asked Lou Danziger to give advice to art students. He offered these words — "Work. Think. Feel." — and elaborated thus: *Work:* "No matter how brilliant, talented, exceptional, and wonderful the student may be, without work there is nothing but potential and talk." *Think:* "Design is a problem-solving activity. Thinking is the application of intelligence to arrive at the appropriate solution to the problem." *Feel:* "Work without feeling, intuition, and spontaneity is devoid of humanity."

These sentiments are not, however, applicable only to students. Rather, they underscore Danziger's own half-century career as a graphic designer, design consultant, educator, and one of the most prolific of America's late Modern practitioners — the generation that came imme- diately after Paul Rand, Alvin Lustig, Will Burtin, and others.

Born into the generation for whom design was a mission to give order, beauty, and utility (often cut with wit) to a crassly commercial world, Danziger stood on the shoulders of pioneer Modernists, yet extended the reach of Modernism through his own achievements. Although Danziger is reluctant to be tied to any dogma, insisting, "No matter what I do, I want to do it well," his design exemplifies the diversity of Modernism and his teaching promotes the diversity of design. Danziger is a "designer's designer and an educator's educator," states Katherine McCoy, former co-chair of Cranbrook Academy, about the man for whom designing and teaching are two distinct but decidedly unified disciplines. Indeed, he has significantly affected many design genres — including advertising, corporate work, and the design of books, periodicals, museum catalogues, and exhibitions — and influenced the hundreds of students who attended his classes at Chouinard, CalArts,

ABOVE: "Russian Avant Garde" exhibition catalogue cover, Los Angeles County Museum of Art (1980).

an "E." And she wants to be a secretary. Johanna would like to enter the business world.

DANZIGER, LOUIS
2925 Matthews Avenue. Stage Crew, Oriole Art Staff, Poster Sq. His art shows up with infinite grace. He's always sketching all over the place. Commercial artist.

DASHOW, AARON
346 East 173rd Street. History Dept. Sq.,

Harvard University, and the Art Center College of Design, where he currently teaches.

Twenty years ago Danziger "retired" from designing per se (although he continues to consult for Microsoft and others) and devoted himself almost entirely to teaching. Yet his print work from the '50s, '60s, and '70s is not Modernist nostalgia. Certainly the advertisements, brochures, catalogues and posters that fill his extensive oeuvre reveal certain formal, architectonic, and conceptual characteristics of their times, but they also stand as testaments to his individuality. In Danziger's hands Modernism was not simply the cold, formulaic template developed to unify corporate messages; rather, each of his problems demanded and received appropriate, unique, and often inspired solutions. His commonsense approach to the needs of business demanded that at all times he seek the elegant solution, which he defines as "taking a minimal amount of material and a minimal amount of effort — nothing wasted — to achieve maximum impact." Although his work promoted a time-sensitive product or idea, Danziger used a timeless design intelligence — a true universality that defies the parameters of the period — when he ensured that the page or pages he designed were structurally sound, piqued the audience's interest, imparted a message, and left a mark. Danziger's work challenges the notion that all graphic design is ephemeral. Though the message may eventually be obsolete, like a classic painting or sculpture, the formal essence of his work is as fresh as the day it was composed.

Louis Danziger was born in 1923 and raised in the Bronx, New York. At eleven, he was interested in letterforms and was an avid browser of the German language design magazine *Gebrauchsgraphik*,

THIS PAGE, CLOCKWISE FROM ABOVE CENTER: Magazine cover for *Western Apparel Industry* magazine (1952). Yearbook entry and cover, Evander Childs High School, Bronx, New York (1941). OPPOSITE PAGE, CLOCKWISE FROM CENTER LEFT: Call for entries, annual show of the Art Directors Club of LA (ADLA) (1952). *Photo:* Louis Danziger and Marvin Rand. Trademark, Flax Artist's Materials (1949). Package label, One-Coat Rubber Cement, Flax's Artist's Material (1952). Announcement card, front and back, Lightrend company (1952). Inside spread, ADLA call for entries (1952).

F

M. Flax Artists Materials, 10846 Lindbrook Drive, L.A. 24, Calif.

F

FLAX

1

one-coat rubber cement

8 **ADLA**

ART DIRECTORS CLUB OF LOS ANGELES

Invites your participation in the 8th Annual

West Coast Exhibition of Advertising Art

February 25 to March 11

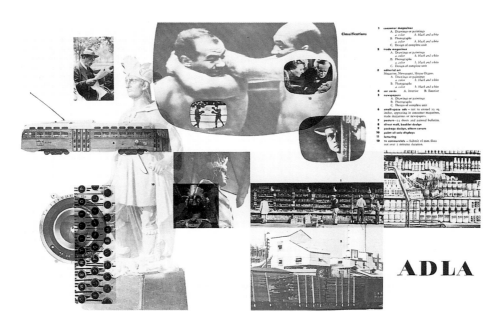

ADLA

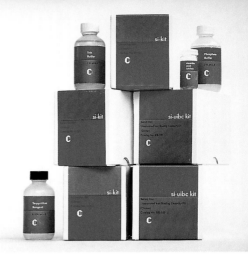

CLOCKWISE FROM TOP LEFT: Packaging for Clinton Laboratories diagnostic reagents: Urinary Ketokit (1959), Serum Iron Kit (1964), Chemtrol (1959), and Glucose Reagent (1962). "Crossroads" announcement card, Aspen Design Conference (1955). Exhibition design, Art Directors Show, ADLA (1952).

In Aspen 1955   June 13 to 18

INTERNATIONAL DESIGN CONFERENCE

Five thought-provoking days of Design talk with
many of the most distinguished thinkers from
all parts of the world.
For full details write to:
International Design Conference
220 South Michigan Avenue
Chicago 4, Illinois

which he found in the public library. "I discovered that the
Germans were doing the most interesting things with book jackets
and posters," he says about these early inspirations, which led him
to become an art major at Evander Childs High School. "Although
most Americans at that time were either hostile to or ignorant of
modern art," he says, "in my high school… all the art majors were
given student memberships to the Museum of Modern Art."
Commercial art was offered as a viable profession for the artistically
inclined and, although his parents were less than sanguine about
his becoming a commercial artist, Danziger decided to follow this
path. After high school, he served in the Army in the South Pacific
(New Guinea, the Admiralties, the Philippines, and Japan) from 1943
through 1945 and designed the occasional poster. After being dis-
charged, he moved to California — escaping New York's cold
weather — and attended Art Center School on the G.I. Bill.

Postwar California did not have the media industries that supported modern graphic design in the same way that New York did,
but it was a burgeoning hotbed of contemporary design thinking.
Other East Coast designers had already trekked to the City of Angels,
none having a greater effect on Danziger's life than Alvin Lustig
(posthumous recipient of the AIGA Lifetime Achievement Award),
who was teaching graphic and industrial design classes at Art Center.
Danziger remembers his first encounter with Lustig in 1947 as accidental: "I didn't like school at all, because it was very rigid at that
time. But one day I heard this voice coming out of a classroom talking about social structure, religion, and the broadest implications of
design. So I stuck my nose in the door and saw that it was Lustig.
From then on I sat in on every class." Lustig connected design to the
worlds of art, music, and literature and instilled in students a belief
that design was socially and culturally important.

Danziger became part of the Design Group, like-minded designers who had been students of Lustig and were "opposed to mindless,

Preview & Museum Association reception, Tuesday, February 23rd at 8 p.m.

Recent
Sculpture
U.S.A.

Please present this card for admission.

TOP: "Talk Balloons" announcement card for Aspen Design
Conference (1955). BELOW: "Recent Sculpture U.S.A." exhibition
announcement card, Los Angeles County Museum of Art (1954).

NGLE MYSTERY

sentimental, nostalgic commercial design." In turn, he and his peers
aspired to promote attitudes about design that were loftier than
the profession itself. He became friends with Saul Bass, Rudolph de
Harak, and Charles Eames (who introduced him to Buckminster
Fuller's book *Nine Chains to the Moon*) and recalls the palpable excitement among them that they were missionaries of progressive design.
"But I don't think we talked about our work in the philosophical
or theoretical terms that are discussed today," he says. "We were talking about very practical matters."

Danziger and his colleagues vied for what little work was available at that time. "This was the problem," he explains. "Any client
that had any money went to an advertising agency. Annual reports
in those days were designed by printing firms. So the only clients that
were really interested in modern work were essentially furniture and
lighting manufacturers that advertised in architectural magazines."
Although Danziger did some striking early identity and advertising
for Flax Artist's Materials (including a trademark that is used today),
General Lighting, Steelbuilt, Inc., and Fraymart Gallery, he was
disenchanted with the provincialism of Los Angeles and referred to it
as a "hick town." He returned to New York, working briefly with
Alexander Ross, a graphic designer who specialized in pharmaceutical
products, and then taking a job at *Esquire* magazine, where he sat in
the art department next to Helmut Krone (later the chief art director
for Doyle Dane Bernbach). At the time, Krone so admired Paul
Rand that his work area, covered with Rand's tearsheets, was like a
shrine. Danziger used to hang reproductions of Egyptian and Chinese
artifacts at his desk and recalls saying to Krone, "If you want to be
as good as Rand, don't look at Rand; look at what Rand looks at."

Since the *Esquire* job offered him little chance to do good work,
Danziger took refuge in Alexey Brodovitch's legendary "Graphic
Journalism" night class at the New School. On the very first evening
when the students were asked to bring in their portfolios, Danziger
recalls that Brodovitch, who was not given to parceling out praise,
"spent much of the evening favorably discussing my work."
Brodovitch taught Danziger to believe in his own uniqueness. "He
instilled the idea that you cannot do good work unless you have guts
to do something you have not seen before," Danziger says. He
also learned to have "a proper disrespect for design." Unlike Lustig,
Brodovitch did not need to attach world-shaping significance to design.

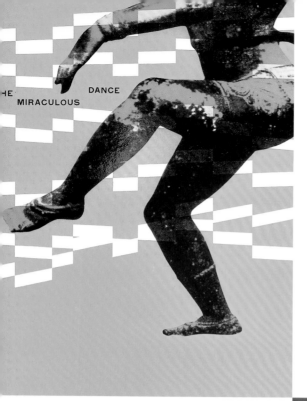

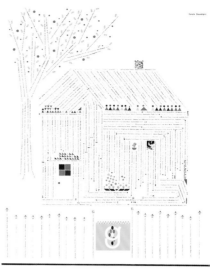

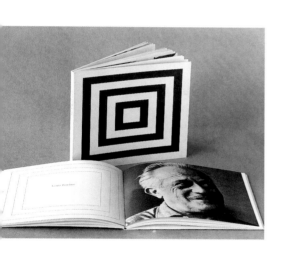

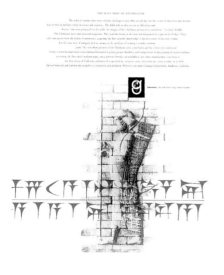

OPPOSITE PAGE: "Jungle Mystery" advertisement for Gelvatex Coatings Corporation (1956). THIS PAGE, CLOCKWISE FROM TOP LEFT: Print advertisement series for Gelvatex Coatings Corporation, all designed in 1956: "The Miraculous Dance," "Type House and Tree," an ad composed of the names and addresses of hundreds of paint dealers, "The Gay Walls of Pompeii," and "The Wise Men in Vermillion." Center left: "Four Abstract Classicists" exhibition catalogue, Los Angeles County Museum of Art (1959).

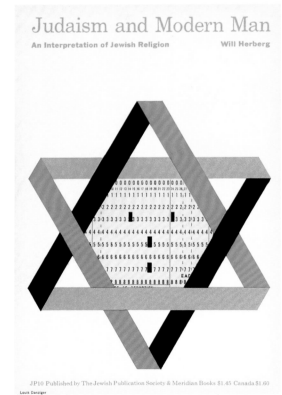

Samuel Taylor Coleridge on language and the mind

"Language is the armory of the human mind;
and at once contains the trophies of its past,
and the weapons of its future conquests."*

Container Corporation of America

CCA

(Biographia Literaria, XVI, 1817)   *Great Ideas of Western Man . . . one of a series*   *Artist: Louis Danziger*

The
Light
Touch

Judaism and Modern Man

An Interpretation of Jewish Religion   Will Herberg

JP10 Published by The Jewish Publication Society & Meridian Books $1.45 Canada $1.60
Louis Danziger

Ketokit, a kit for the simple, rapid, test-tube determination of urinary 17-ketosteroids! Contact your dealer.

A new product from CLINTON LABORATORIES 6010 Wilshire Boulevard, Los Angeles 36, California

"I always felt that it was the contradictions between my two masters that allowed me to form my own point of view," Danziger adds.

After finishing the course with Brodovitch, the peripatetic Danziger went west again, this time to study architecture, which he thought was more socially meaningful. At the newly founded and short-lived California School of the Arts, he resumed his studies with Lustig, as well as with architect Raphael Soriano and engineer Edgardo Contini. It was here that he embraced Buckminster Fuller's principle of "de-selfing." "Most young designers are very much concerned about being present in their work," Danziger explains. "And Bucky Fuller's idea was that you are invisible — everything is objective. And a very important thing was the idea of doing a great deal with very little — maximum performance with minimal means." Danziger was also influenced by Paul Rand's book *Thoughts on Design* because it clarified issues that had been running through his mind, "particularly where he talked about symbols and metaphors," he says. "Finding something that stands for something else. Being able to encapsulate ideas in a single image." For Danziger, it was equally important to be astutely analytical enough to understand the essence of what needed to be communicated. "You can always find the appropriate symbol for the wrong message," he cautions.

Danziger never became an architect but imbued effective architectonic structure into the scores of magazine covers, booklets, catalogues, packages, and advertisements he was then producing for a growing roster of architectural, cultural, and entertainment clients. He was also becoming expert at the difficult art of conceptualization. At the time, "the big idea," the introduction of wit and metaphor through a marriage of visual and textual means, had gained momentum in mass advertising and design, and Danziger was one of its

OPPOSITE PAGE, CLOCKWISE FROM CENTER LEFT: "Foot and Egg" and "Sledgehammer and Egg" advertisements, The Dreyfus Company (1956). Ad for Container Corporation of America, part of "Great Ideas of Western Man" series (1958). Book cover, *Judaism and Modern Man*, Meridian Books (1959). Urinary Ketokit ad, Clinton Laboratories (1959). THIS PAGE, FROM CENTER DOWNWARD: "Birds" advertisement, Container Corporation of America (1961). Trademark for Jaylis Draperies (1960).

leading proponents. Danziger further analyzed every aspect of his problem and then relied on certain tools to refine his solution. For example, he preferred photography over drawings because, he says, "by and large photographs are more believable, more persuasive than drawings, which are perceived as contrived." At first he did not shoot his own photography, but finding he was often dissatisfied with the work of freelance photographers, he acquired the skill to do his own.

This particular component of his design, the combining of type and photography, was influenced by Italian designers at the time, notably the work of Studio Boggeri in Milan. Danziger was so taken by the Italians that in 1957 he moved to Italy, where he was hired by Boggeri himself. Although he loved the work of the studio, they did not have some of the tools that he was used to: "They lacked electric pencil sharpeners and layout pads and had ways of working which were unfamiliar to me. I was used to American efficiency and was impatient with the laid-back Italian methods," he relates. He left Boggeri after a week, but remained in Europe for another nine months.

This penchant for picking up stakes did not seem to interfere with Danziger's success. In fact, during the height of the counterculture '60s, when he was forty-five, he decided to take a year off, though he was at the peak of his career. At the time many professionals were dropping out and reevaluating their lives, and Danziger was no exception. He determined how much money he needed to maintain his life-style, consulted one day a week for (long-time client) the Los Angeles County Art Museum to earn that sum, and also taught one day a week, refusing all other jobs. Ostensibly he dropped out, spending most of his time "shooting pool with the lowlifes in the pool room." At the conclusion of this hiatus, he decided to go into teaching full time.

Throughout his career Danziger has been something of a maverick. He persistently resisted opening an office. "It has to do with my personality," he says. "I don't like to shave and dress, and what I liked about California in those early days is that one could succeed professionally without having to wear a tie." He also argues that with a big staff and overhead he would never have been able to retain as much of his earnings. Nor would he have been able to do as much of the work himself, which he prefers. "By doing everything myself,"

he adds, "I didn't have to do as much work in order make a good living." As it turns out, he made a very good living, enough so that he commissioned a young architect named Frank Gehry (one of the first patrons to do so) to build an impressive building in the midst of Hollywood. Danziger lived and worked there for thirty years until the neighborhood deteriorated, as is the case in many urban centers, and became too unsavory to endure.

At its height, his vast practice included Clinton Laboratories, many aerospace companies (System Development Corporation, TRW, Norair, and so on), the Dreyfus Company, Heliodyne Corporation, Meridian Books, UCLA Art Council, and the design of countless catalogues, brochures, and posters for the Los Angeles County Museum of Art. But teaching has been his true calling. In 1952, Alvin Lustig relocated to New York and recommended that his former pupil take over his class at the California School of the Arts. From then on, Danziger taught every Friday until that school closed its doors, then moved on to Art Center, followed by Chouinard, to teach visual communications and advertising design. In 1972 he was hired by Victor Papanek, then the chair at California Institute of the Arts, and shortly thereafter Danziger became the director of its graphic design program. "I went from being a designer who taught to a teacher who designed," he says. Education was as much of a mission as it had been during his early years as a designer. And taking on the full-time load allowed him to spend more time with students and have greater responsiveness to their needs. For Danziger, teaching was art and craft. "Teaching is an intuitive thing," he says. "Some students have to be kissed and some have to be kicked, and you just have to have a feel for that." Above all his commitment was to contribute something to enhancing their lives. "I know I can't teach them everything, but as long as they're better when they leave me, then I've done a good job."

Danziger's pedagogy has been praised by teachers and students alike. Stan Jones, who studied with him in the '50s, once said, "Lou was the one who taught me what an idea was... and how to find a solution that is inherent in the problem." Kathie Mouslie Levenson, an early '60s student, stated: "He introduced a moral sense into graphic design. It was right and important that we design well." Much of Danziger's success with students lay in his unwillingness to be stuck in an ideological quagmire. He willingly bends to the

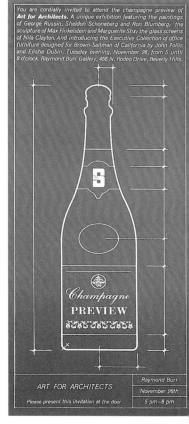

American Paintings from The Metropolitan Museum of Art

Los Angeles County Museum of Art   Lytton Gallery   June 3 - July 31, 1966

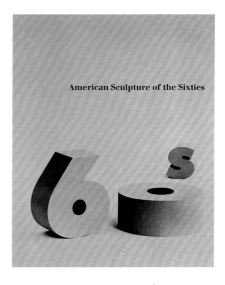

American Sculpture of the Sixties

Gerhard Marcks

Acknowledgements.

The University of California, Los Angeles, wishes to express its gratitude to the Federal Republic of Germany for making possible this catalogue in its present form. Its thanks go to the lenders of two casts of *Seeman Turm Murzistor*, Mrs. James D. Platt and Mrs. Harry Lynch Bradley; and especially to Mrs. Rudolf Hoffmann, for the loan of all other sculptures, and the drawings and prints.

The UCLA Art Galleries are indebted to Dr. Werner Hofmann, Director of the Staatliche Museen in Berlin, for his highly personal appreciation of Gerhard Marcks; and to Dr. Eugene Anderson, Professor Emeritus of the Department of History, UCLA, for his perceptive essay on his friend; and for the recollections penned this last spring by the late Walter Gropius. Dr. and Mrs. Anderson translated the essay by Werner Hofmann.

needs of each student. And he continues to teach today because he values what he learns from his perpetually younger undergrads. As for his method, he does not ever follow a syllabus: "The creative part of teaching is inventing the problem," he explains. "If I go into a room of students and I feel that, for example, as a group the people are not very imaginative, I don't give them a talk about imagination. What I do is design a new problem — a design assignment for which they have no choice but to be imaginative."

Danziger fervently believes that students should be exposed to every valid point of view so that they can form their own opinions. This was his philosophy as teacher and director of the Cal Arts program (which, given its administrative chores, was not his favorite job) and at his annual summer class at Harvard University's Carpenter Center for Visual and Environmental Studies. But in order to develop educated opinions, students must have a conducive teaching and learning environment. One of Danziger's most important contributions to design pedagogy was promoting and developing a course of graphic design history that did not exist in any codified form. "Just imagine teaching painting and making a reference to Picasso and the students don't know what you're talking about," he explains. "Here was an environment where you're trying to teach students who some of the important designers were, and they don't know what the hell you're talking about." So Danziger opened up his personal design library of vintage book and ephemera to Keith Goddard, a colleague who was teaching at Cal Arts at the time, helping him to make 300 slides that formed the basis of a pioneering design history class. After Goddard left Cal Arts, Danziger picked up the course and increased the number of slides to about 5,000. He lectured on historical issues and events that helped the students to "see themselves as part of something larger than themselves," he says. "All of a sudden, the work had some meaning to them. They felt they were part of the continuum."

One of Danziger's goals was to widen students' perspectives in the same way that Lustig expanded his own breadth of knowledge. Ultimately, though, he left Cal Arts in 1987 to teach at Art Center when, as he describes it, "the Cranbrook crowd moved in, not because I was opposed to the Cranbrook thing, but because I was opposed to the idea of the single view."

Throughout his teaching years Danziger struck a balance

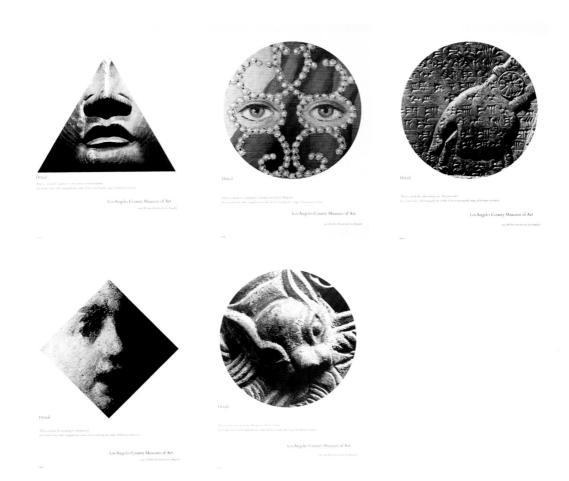

ABOVE: "Details" print advertising campaign, Los Angeles County Museum of Art (1975). BELOW: Catalogue cover, UCLA Extension (1990). OPPOSITE PAGE, TOP: Trademark for Xybion Corporation (1975), perhaps the first logo designed on a computer.

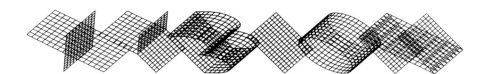

between work and academia. Though he jettisoned many of his clients when he became a full-time teacher, from 1978 to 1985, he maintained an important consultancy for Atlantic Richfield Corporation (ARCO), previously held by Herbert Bayer (who in semi-retirement still consulted on its art collection and architecture). Like Paul Rand's contributions to IBM, Westinghouse, and Cummins Engine, Danziger's tutelage over the design policy at ARCO improved the overall identity and communications systems of the chemical and petroleum company during a period of significant growth. He masterminded everything from design strategies to the company name (he lobbied for the name ARCO over Atlantic Richfield) to overseeing the quality of the work produced by the in-house design staff and others. "They had a rigid program that had been set up by Bayer," explains Danziger, "and I came to the conclusion that it was not working; that all of the emphasis on consistency was misplaced when you're in a period of history where the only reality is change. Flexibility was much more important in this business. And building appropriate structures did more good than trying to legislate design systems." For well over a decade, until recession hit the petroleum industry, forcing ARCO to make severe cutbacks, he administered one of the finest corporate design programs in the nation.

Long before the computer was widely accepted, Danziger did not hide his head in the sand as some of his peers did. Instead, he foresaw the technology revolution and took steps to understand its potential and operation. At seventy-five he knows more about the medium than many of his colleagues and some of his students. Although he does not actively design anymore, he consults with Microsoft's designers a couple of times a year and continues to teach his class every Friday. Currently, Danziger stays up on contemporary design issues and is sometimes critical of design practice and design education. He believes that there is an over-emphasis now on academic theory rather than in doing the work itself. Yet he levels his critiques not as a detached observer but as an enthusiastic participant, and his opinions are highly respected as one who for fifty passionate years has devoted his life to design and the credo "work, think, feel."

April Greiman

You Can't Fake the Cha-Cha

By Sharyn O'Mara

April Greiman was a designer in New York City in the mid-1970s when she decided to leave the comfort of a design community deeply entrenched in European tradition for an uncertain future on the opposite coast. Seeking a new spirit, she moved to Los Angeles and entered a culture that, for better or for worse, had a limited aesthetic of its own at that time. Museums and galleries were few and it was impossible to get a decent cup of coffee. But the lack of an established design practice created a unique opportunity to explore new paradigms in communications design.

Soon after she settled in Los Angeles, a friend offered to take her to the desert. "Death Valley?" she said. "Sounds pretty bleak." He dragged her along anyway, and within hours she found herself seduced by the landscape. "The desert is its own educational vehicle," she says. "While most processes occur at an invisible or microscopic level, the desert reveals its evolution in its very existence. I felt as if, for the first time, my eyes were wide open to the process of evolution, to growth, to change."

Ten years later, in 1984, the Macintosh was making an unsteady entry into the design market. Most designers were skeptical of — if not completely opposed to — the idea of integrating the computer into design practice, perhaps fearing an uncertain future wherein the tactility of the hand was usurped by the mechanics of bits and bytes. A visionary few, including April Greiman, recognized the vast potential of this new medium. An avid fan of tools and technologies since childhood, Greiman quickly established herself as a pioneer of digital communications design. "The digital landscape fascinates me in the same way as the desert," she

OPPOSITE PAGE: April Greiman, self-titled "Bullethead 1997." *Original photo:* Atila. THIS PAGE, ABOVE: U.S. postage stamp commemorating the Nineteenth Amendment (1995).

says. This fascination comes from the core of her being, a core of
perpetual curiosity and questioning that fuels her desire to explore and
inspires the cutting-edge design work that places her at the helm of
integrated design at the close of the twentieth century.

Born during the baby boom and raised in New York, Greiman
was endowed with a curious spirit from the beginning, and grew up in
a house where questioning was encouraged and adventure was a part
of life. Greiman had excellent role models in her father, mother, and
her great aunt Kitty, a strong and independent woman who had danced
with the Ziegfeld Follies and made excellence in her career a top priority. Greiman recalls her mother as a calm, grounding influence and
her father as a curious, wandering explorer who was easily distracted by
whatever interesting thing crossed his path; affectionately, they called
him "the original astronaut" because he was perpetually lost in the
space of his own imagination. Neighbors called her family "The Flying
Greimans" because they were always looking up, searching for interesting phenomena, and traveling by air.

A professional dancer with the Fred Astaire Dance School in New
York City, Renee Greiman performed on television and taught classes,
often enlisting the young April as a dance partner. As a result, April
relates, she still knows how to do the cha-cha, mambo, waltz, tango,

ABOVE: Identity and dinnerware, China Club Restaurant + Lounge (1979).
Photo: Jayme Odgers. BELOW: Folder/poster for California Institute of the
Arts (1978), designed in collaboration with Jayme Odgers (art director
and photographer).

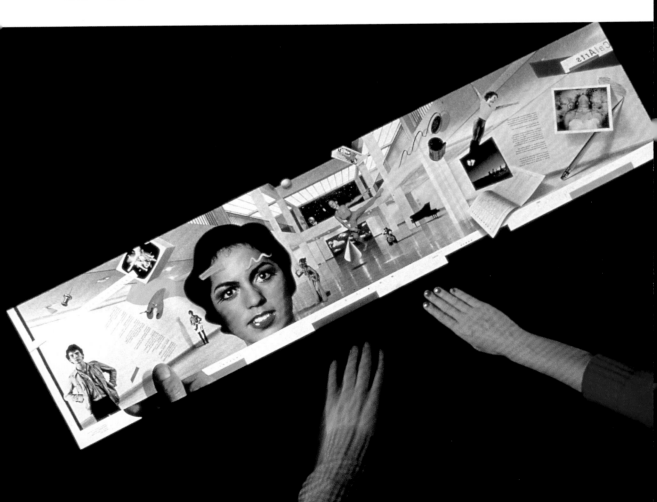

merengue, fox trot, rumba, and limbo. But perhaps her most important lesson from her mother came from her often-repeated saying, "April, you can't fake the cha-cha." From an early age, Greiman learned that integrity and immersion were critical elements in one's art.

Her formal design education began shortly after she settled on the idea of going to art school and applied to Rhode Island School of Design. Though she failed miserably on the part of the application that required her to draw a pair of old boots, the dean of admissions pointed out that her portfolio was very strong in graphics and suggested that she apply to the graphic design program at Kansas City Art Institute. Having no idea how one might define graphic design or what it meant, she nonetheless took his suggestion and was accepted into the program.

At KCAI, Greiman was introduced to the principles of Modernism by Inge Druckrey, Hans Allemann, and Chris Zelinsky, all of whom had been educated at the Basel School of Design in Switzerland. Inspired by this experience, she went to Basel for graduate school. As a student of Armin Hoffman and Wolfgang Weingart in the early 1970s, Greiman explored the International Style in depth, as well as Weingart's personal experiments in developing an aesthetic that was less reflective of the Modernist heritage and more representative of a changing, post-industrial society. Weingart introduced his students to what is now called the New Wave, a more intuitive, eclectic departure from the stark organization and neutral objectivity of the grid that sent shock waves through the design community. Wide letterspacing, changing type weights or styles within a single word, and the use of type set on an angle were explored, not as mere stylistic indulgences but in an effort to expand typographic communication more meaning-fully. Within a decade, the impact of Weingart and the students who studied with him was evident everywhere: the aesthetic had been widely co-opted and imitated, with the original intent long forgotten or known to only a few.

Greiman was one of those who remembered. In her work, she continued to explore typographic meaning and began experimenting

CLOCKWISE FROM TOP LEFT: Catalogue for California Institute of the Arts (1979). *Photo:* Jayme Odgers. Peter Shire "Swissiyaki" poster (1978). *Photo:* Jayme Odgers.

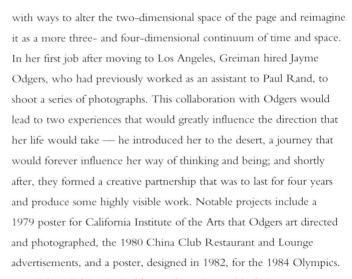

with ways to alter the two-dimensional space of the page and reimagine it as a more three- and four-dimensional continuum of time and space. In her first job after moving to Los Angeles, Greiman hired Jayme Odgers, who had previously worked as an assistant to Paul Rand, to shoot a series of photographs. This collaboration with Odgers would lead to two experiences that would greatly influence the direction that her life would take — he introduced her to the desert, a journey that would forever influence her way of thinking and being; and shortly after, they formed a creative partnership that was to last for four years and produce some highly visible work. Notable projects include a 1979 poster for California Institute of the Arts that Odgers art directed and photographed, the 1980 China Club Restaurant and Lounge advertisements, and a poster, designed in 1982, for the 1984 Olympics.

When CalArts invited her to direct its graphic design program in 1982, she committed herself to exploring design education and also gained access to state-of-the-art video and digitizing equipment. She immersed herself in being an educator as well as in the new media, spending her spare time traversing the digital terrain in a quest for image-making potential. She began using video and analogue computers to hybridize, combining different elements through the new media. Greiman knew intuitively that the field of graphic design was rapidly changing and that emerging technologies would soon be integrated into everyday design practice. In 1984 she lobbied successfully to change the department name to Visual Communications, feeling that

CLOCKWISE FROM BELOW LEFT: Identity, packaging, and hang tags for TSE Cashmere (1988). Identity, business cards, hang tags, and postcards for Vertigo (1979). Five- and ten-second station identifications for Lifetime television (1985), in collaboration with Eric Martin; post-production collaboration with Bob Engelsiepen. Di-zin logotype (1984).

the term "graphic design" would prove too limiting to future designers. Later that year, with her business booming, she decided to switch gears and become a student rather than an educator, to study the effect of technology on her own work. She returned to full-time practice and acquired her first Macintosh.

Also in 1984, Greiman also completed a poster for Ron Rezek titled "Iris Light" that was significant for its innovative use of video imagery and integration of New Wave typography with classical design elements. This work incorporated a still video image at a time when this meant shooting a traditional photograph off the monitor using a 35mm camera. "Iris Light" represented a turning point in Greiman's work: it is the first hybrid piece incorporating digital technology that Greiman felt was conceptually and aesthetically successful. Of the video image, she says, "Instead of looking like a bad photograph, the image was gestural. It looked like a painting; it captured the spirit of light." In this case, the video technology integrated with the concept of light: light from the video screen combined with light from the lamp resulted in an image wherein the form matched the content.

Greiman's California New Wave typography and mixed-media design had been rocking the Modernist boat for a few years when

CLOCKWISE FROM TOP: Jacket of the AIGA's *Graphic Design USA: 8*, produced in Quantel Graphic Paintbox (1987). "Pacific Wave" exhibition poster, Museo Fortuny, Venice (1988). Table of contents spread, front/back cover, and logo, *Workspirit* journal (1988).

THIS PAGE, BELOW LEFT: Ron Rezek "Iris Light" poster (1984). Videography: April Greiman and Claire Dishman. BOTTOM: "Graphic Design in America" exhibition poster, Walker Art Center, Minneapolis (1989). Paintbox work: Bob Engelsiepen. OPPOSITE PAGE (CLOCKWISE FROM LEFT): *Design Quarterly* #133, "Does It Make Sense?" Walker Art Center, MIT Press (1986). Exterior signage, Southern California Institute of Architecture (1993). SCI-ARC admissions brochure cover (1993).

she undertook a major assault upon the design community's sensibilities and preconceptions of what constitutes design in 1986, in an issue of *Design Quarterly*. Published by the Walker Art Center, edited by Mildred Friedman, and directed toward an international design audience, each issue of *Design Quarterly* focused on a specific theme. Greiman was not only the focus of issue #133, she was invited to design it and show her own work.

Greiman saw *Design Quarterly* #133 as an opportunity not only to present her digital work but to ask a larger question of the work and the medium: Does it make sense? Reading Wittgenstein on the topic, she identified with his conclusion: "It makes sense if you give it sense." She says, "I love this notion which exists in physics as well — that the observer is the observed, and the observed is the observer. The tools and technologies begin to dictate what and how you see something, or how the outcome is predictable. These ideas bring back the kid in me, that very pure curiosity." Greiman's piece challenged existing notions of what a magazine should be. Rather than the standard thirty-two-page sequence, she reformatted the piece as a poster that folded out to almost three by six feet. On the front is an image of Greiman's digitized, naked body amid layers of interacting images and text. On the back, colorful atmospheric spatial video images are interspersed with thoughtful comments and painstaking notations on the digital process — a virtual landscape of text and image. Beyond considering whether digital technologies made sense, the *Design Quarterly* poster seemed to embody the disillusionment of a nation deeply wounded by the Vietnam war and shaped by the growth of feminism, spiritualism, Eastern religion, Jungian archetypes, and dream symbolism. "Does It

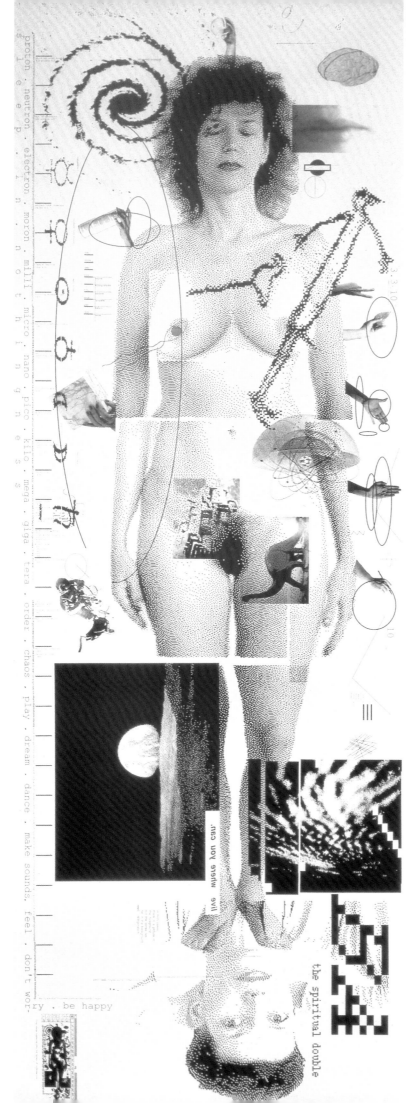

proton · neutron · electron · moron · milli · micro · nano · pico · kilo · mega · giga · tera · order · chaos · play · dream · dance · make sounds. feel · don't wor-

s l e e p e r i n n o t h i n g n e s s

where you can.

the spiritual double

don't worry · be happy

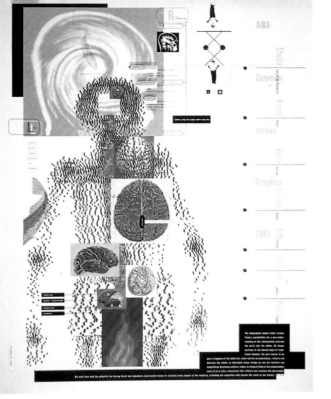

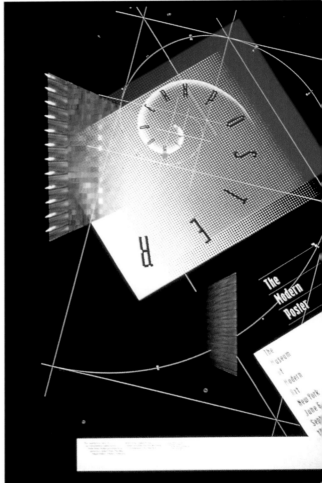

THIS PAGE, CLOCKWISE FROM CENTER LEFT: LuxCore letterhead (1996). AIGA competition poster (1993). SCI-ARC website (1995). "The Modern Poster" for the Museum of Modern Art (1989). *Paintbox work:* Bob Engelsiepen. *From the Edge,* student workbook for SCI-ARC (1991). OPPOSITE PAGE, CLOCKWISE FROM TOP LEFT: Detail and overview of tapestry designed for the Cerritos Center for the Performing Arts. *Photos:* Tim Streetporter. Exterior signage for Nicola Restaurant (1993). *Photo:* Assassi Productions. Color, finishes, and materials for the Carlson/Reges Residence, in collaboration with RoTo Architects (1996). *Photo:* Benny Chan.

Make Sense?" was also an astounding technical feat. The process of
integrating digitized video images and bitmapped type was not unlike
pulling teeth in the early days of Macintosh and MacDraw. The files
were so large, and the equipment so slow that she would send the
file to print when she left the studio in the evening and it would just
be finished when she returned in the morning. One morning, after
she had arrived and was assembling the tiled image, it was clear that
something big was missing. For some reason, her body had not printed, though everything else was there. While the technical details of
the mystery of the missing body remained unsolved, its later reappear-
ance on the pages presented another problem — Greiman didn't like
the way her right breast looked. The reproduction process had flattened
her and the light was strange. So, in what may well be the first
MacDraw breast replacement; she cloned and flopped her left breast
and placed it on the right side of her body.

Before the appearance of "Does It Make Sense?" designers
widely considered bit-mapped type and imagery not only unorthodox
but unacceptable, straying too far from the clean, crisp precision
of the International Style. The computer itself was viewed as cold and
unfriendly, wildly expensive, and a harbinger of the demise of fine
design. After the publication of *Design Quarterly* #133, many designers
felt compelled to reconsider the role of the computer in design
practice. Greiman's willingness to ask the question, and to place it at
the center of the design community, triggered countless debates about
computers, context, and creativity.

Greiman warmly recalls receiving a phone call from Massimo
Vignelli soon after he saw the poster. "I have just one question," he
said. "When do I get the other side?" A Modernist's query? Perhaps,
but more clearly an indicator of the departure Greiman had made from
the coolly classical to the intensely personal, poetic, and digital, and
in particular of the giant step that she had boldly taken into what had
been very much a man's world.

Greiman sees herself as a natural bridge between the Modernist
tradition and future generations of designers. Given her classical education at KCAI and graduate studies with Hoffman and Weingart at
Basel, she possesses the knowledge and skills of the Modernist tradition.
And yet she is a vocal advocate of the new aesthetic, defending both
the visual and conceptual aesthetics, as well as new technologies, to
skeptics. "In the tradition of graphic design in the twentieth century,

CLOCKWISE FROM CENTER LEFT: Wine label, dinnerware, stationery items, matches, dessert menu, and (ABOVE) tea service for Fresco Restaurant (1996). Summer programs poster for Southern California Institute of Architecture (1991).

you had to be either a great typographer, a great designer/illustrator, or a great poster designer. Now we are confronted with motion graphics, the World Wide Web, and interactive applications. The world has changed and the field is changing to meet it." Greiman is adamant that we must be open to new paradigms, to new metaphors, to a whole new spirit of design: "It's not just graphic design anymore. We just don't have a new name for it yet."

New paradigms emerge in Greiman's own studio including what may be a new model of the contemporary design studio, reflective of cultural shifts. Greiman acts as both a generalist and a specialist. "I don't hire graphic designers anymore. The idea of many designers working in virtual isolation is no longer relevant. I hire collaborators who are specialists in their own fields — a Web master, a researcher, a production artist — depending on the project." As a generalist, she is involved in all phases of the projects. As a specialist, the concept and design are ultimately her own. In this new studio structure, each collaborator is an expert in his or her field, with Greiman as the tie that binds. In order to expand her research into new technologies and image generation, Greiman created Greimanski Labs as a conceptual offshoot of her studio. She describes the laboratory as a place for research

CLOCKWISE FROM TOP LEFT: Greimanski Labs flame symbol and "Word/Image/Tekst" page, in *From the Center: Design Process at SCI-ARC*, published by the Southern California Institute of Architecture (1997). SCI-ARC admissions booklet/poster (1993). SCI-ARC bicycle brochure and Grand Central Station exhibition graphics (1995). Book cover, *From the Center: Design Process at SCI-ARC* (1997). SCI-ARC admissions booklet spread (1993).

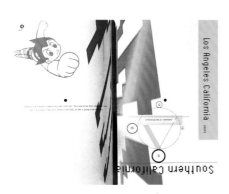

Urban Re-visions: Current Projects for the Public Realm

During the later 1980s and into the nineties, a number of significant directions have emerged in the fields of city planning and urban design that diverge sharply from patterns of previous thinking about the evolution of cities. These directions include the creation and reclamation of transportation corridors as urban fabrics, the genesis of new neighborhoods oriented to the pedestrian and to public transit in both urban and exurban contexts, a reconsideration of the idea and function of the master plan, and an increasing emphasis on public participation in the planning and design process.

Responding to this thematic framework, URBAN REVISIONS presents a selection of current and recent projects for a variety of primarily North American cities and contexts including Boston, New Haven, New York, Montreal, Raleigh, Des Moines, St. Louis, Portland, Oregon, and Los Angeles. Representing a broad spectrum of theoretical viewpoints, practical applications, and working methodologies, these projects manifest a strong desire to re-think accepted strategies of urban form-giving. Their embodiment of a diverse array of social, cultural, economic, political, technological, and ecological concerns has even in some instances generated a high degree of controversy within the design community and among the general public. Rather than attempting to define a movement, or endorsing one formal or ideological position, URBAN REVISIONS explores a wide range of fresh, responsive, and provocative approaches to the revisioning of cities by some of today's most creative and engaged architects, urban planners, and citizens.

Our water comes out of the ground @ 158 degrees.

We not only have our spa filled with the stuff, but also the swimming pool!

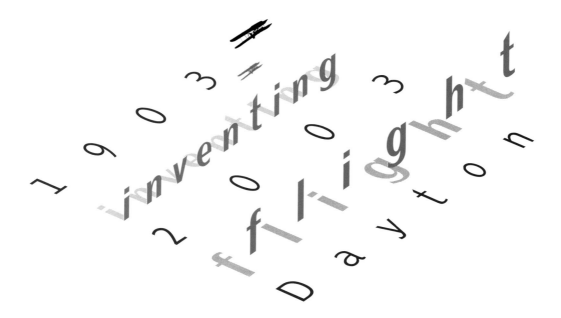

CLOCKWISE FROM TOP LEFT: Lobby theme panel, "Urban Revisions: Current Projects for the Public Realm," exhibition at the Museum of Contemporary Art, Los Angeles. Environmental graphics and catalogue design in collaboration with RoTo Architects (1994). Miracle Manor Retreat Website (miraclemanor.com). *Photo:* Benny Chan. Promotional materials for Miracle Manor Retreat (1997). *Photo:* April Greiman. Logo for "Inventing Flight," a centennial celebration of flight that will coincide with the Ohio Bicentennial.

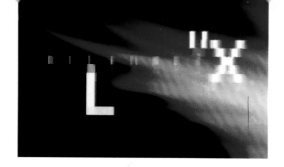

and exploration in the development of non-commercial images and projects. Regardless of client, the lab works in a variety of media ranging from traditional photography to new tools and technologies.

One of the original Flying Greimans speaks with great enthusiasm of her newest large-scale project, "Inventing Flight," originally titled "A Century of Flight." Greiman worked with a team of experts to develop an active approach to the concept instead of fixing the notion of flight in the past. For the event — a celebration of 100 years of flying to take place in Dayton, Ohio, in 2003 — Greiman and her team are developing a total identity — motion graphics, website, collateral materials, exhibitions, and an interactive installation. Greiman has taken her passion for science and technology and immersed herself in every detail of the history of flight. The celebratory event is particularly significant to her because it addresses the early stages of bringing information into space and the information revolution. "I love it when things come full circle like this," she says. "Everything is related, and makes this wonderful loop of interconnection."

Further expanding the very broad scope of her work, Greiman often collaborates with architects on spaces and environments, with most of her contribution in the areas of color, finishes, and materials. She sees these three- and four-dimensional collaborations as yet another aspect of hybridizing, in which she considers ideas of integration of building and landscape, interior and exterior, inner and outer selves. Miracle Manor, a business and creative collaboration with architect Michael Rotondi, is an ideal forum for such explorations.

Greiman sees the site as an opportunity to explore her own personal interests in color, myth, symbolism, and space in real time. "The entire place is sort of a laboratory," she notes, and one begins to realize that for Greiman, everything is a laboratory. From her investigations at the leading edge of the California New Wave to her pioneering work in digital media and hybrid processes, Greiman sets an example for future generations of designers to be willing to ask the questions that need to be asked.

CLOCKWISE FROM TOP LEFT: Push animation for Lux Pictures website (1996). "New Neighborhoods" exhibition theme panel for Urban Revisions, Current Projects for the Public Realm, MOCA, Los Angeles (1994). *Photo:* Paula Goldman. Color palette for Warehouse C, Nagasaki, Japan, in collaboration with RoTo Architects (1997).

Champion International Corporation

Capitalizing on Excellence

By Ellen Shapiro

For the AIGA 1997 national design conference in New Orleans, Champion wanted to do something responsible, reusable. So they got a 1965 Rambler convertible and had Stephen Doyle hand-paint geometric shapes on it in Champion Benefit colors: celery, chalk, ochre, squash, cactus, cloud. Tony McDowell, Champion's director of creative services, parked it in the valet parking area. "People knew immediately it was a Benefit car," he says. "No sign. That's how strong the branding is. I drove it into the exhibit area and opened the trunk, which was full of promotional giveaways. That was our booth. We had a palm reader in the back seat. The line was endless throughout the entire show, designers wanting to get their palms read. We raffled off the car to a lucky designer from Pennsylvania."

That's how Champion International Corporation does things.

Champion acts like the Fortune 500 it is — yet speaks with a distinctive, idiosyncratic voice. Controlling over five million acres of timberland, with 1997 sales of $5.7 billion, Champion makes "everything from the tree": lumber and plywood, laser and photocopy papers, catalogue and magazine papers. Its commitment to design excellence began in the early 1960s with designer-targeted promotions for premium printing papers, a segment that now accounts for less than ten percent of its business. However, that commitment — and, with it, the methodology that emanated from devising unprecedented ways to demonstrate what can be done with a cast-coated cover sheet or with colored kraft paper — has penetrated every niche of the company.

"A lot of companies do great marketing materials. For us it's across the board," explains McDowell. "Design is just as important when we talk to our employees, shareholders, and the community. Top designers

OPPOSITE PAGE: The Champion Benefit car (1997). THIS PAGE, ABOVE: additional objects from the Champion Benefit promotional campaign (1993). *Series design:* Doyle Partners.

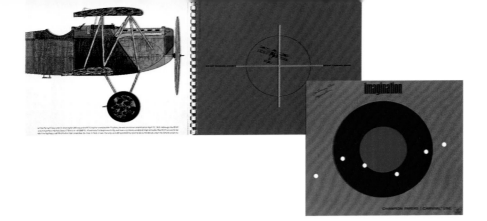

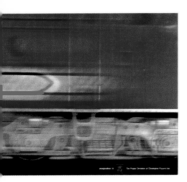

work on our recruiting materials, environmental pieces, safety posters, packaging, sports marketing programs."

Indeed, put on a blindfold, randomly spin around Champion's archives, and you're fairly certain to end up pointing at a piece that, if not representing a seminal moment in graphic design history, was a major source of inspiration to a generation of designers. If you came of age in the '60s you might have treasured *The Printing Salesman's Herald;* an issue, say, that took the mysteries out of web printing in a visually arresting way. In the '70s, it was likely that the *Imagination* series electrified you. For example, "Brazil," number XVI: with photography and design by James Miho, concept and creative direction by Edward Russell, Jr., and copy by David R. Brown. It's a visual and tactile bossa nova of masterfully engineered die-cuts and overlays, folk art and churches, doors and windows, food and drink, sports images. The pineapple! The papaya! Those blue and yellow tiles! No need to stop at Brazil. Your favorite *Imagination*

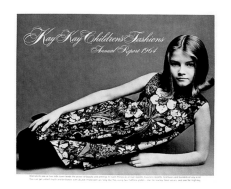

OPPOSITE PAGE, CLOCKWISE FROM CENTER: *Imagination* #10 (1967). *Creative direction:* Needham, Harper & Steers, Inc. *Design:* George Tscherny. *Photography:* Sam Zarember. *Imagination* #2 (1963). *Illustration:* Gordon Brusstar. *Imagination* "Fun and Games" Silver Anniversary issue (1985). THIS PAGE, CLOCKWISE FROM TOP LEFT: *Imagination* #3 (1964). *Creative direction:* Needham, Louis and Brorby, Inc. *Design:* Push Pin Studios. *Illustration:* Gordon Brusstar. *Imagination* #15 (1971). *Creative direction:* Needham, Harper & Steers, Inc. *Design:* James Miho. *Photography:* Nils Nilsson. *Imagination* #12 (1968). *Creative direction:* Needham, Harper & Steers, Inc. *Design:* James Miho. *Photography:* Ernest Braun. *Imagination* #19 (1975). *Creative direction:* Edward Russell, Jr. *Design and photography:* James Miho. *Illustration:* Mruta.

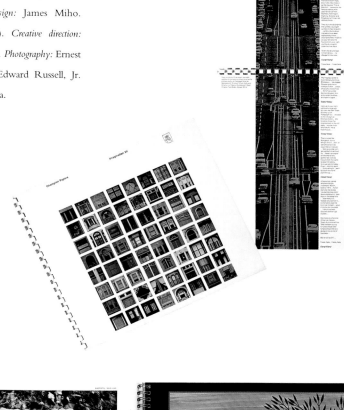

By Mary Domowicz

Over the past thirty-five years in particular, Champion has demo
strated its commitment to the arts through its advertising, promotio
employee communications, and architecture. Following are sor
examples of the seminal projects in Champion's history.

1962

Champion's first promotional
series, *Imagination*, jolts the inc
try with its innovative combina
tions of flat colors, unusual die
cuts, and stepped pages. This fi
issue showcases the versatility
business papers. Each issue ove
the next twenty-six years is dev
ed to a single theme. *Design:*
Carl Regehr.

1963

The Printing Salesman's Herald
is distributed to Champion's sales
force. The small magazine has
about six articles per issue, such as
"My Ten Golden Rules of Selling,"
and "Paper Tigers I Have Known."
This issue, designed by Louis
Danziger, 1966, portrays the
Herald's symbol as a multifaceted
element on the cover. Publication
continues until 1984.

might have been "Australia," "Hong Kong," "Scandinavia," "Rivers,"
or "Main Streets." There were twenty-six in all. When asked to
contribute one artifact to the AIGA virtual museum of design icons
featured in *Graphic Design USA 16* (1995), San Francisco designer
Jennifer Morla nominated the entire series: "I was a college freshman,"
she wrote. "*Imagination* awakened me to the possibilities of design…
it epitomized the power of great design by seducing, enchanting,
informing, stimulating the viewer." David Brown credits *Imagination*
for his transformation from freelance copywriter to visual/verbal
communicator. "Seeing 'Scandinavia' presented at the Institute for
International Education across from the United Nations, I was simply
stunned," says the former Champion vice president of creative
services, AIGA president from 1981 to 1984, and now president of
Art Center College of Design. "It wasn't just its beauty and inventive-
ness, it was the apparent generosity of motive. Why would a company want to bring another part of the world to life for thousands
of people who would never go there?" he asks, somewhat rhetorically.
"It seemed to me that above the obvious demonstrations of printing,
paper, and production, Champion was revealing its character as an
enterprise: education takes precedence over promotion; earning delight

ABOVE: *The Printing Salesman's Herald* (1971). *Design:* Dietmar Winkler.
Photography: Gertrude Marbach-Rau. BELOW: *The Printing Salesman's
Herald* (1969). *Design:* Chuck Ax.

CHAMPION PAPERS/THE PRINTING SALESMANS HERALD

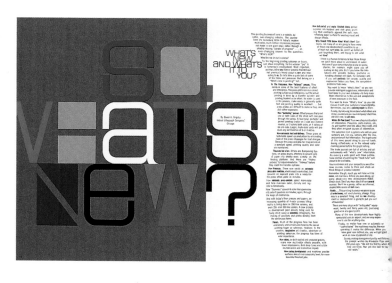

M

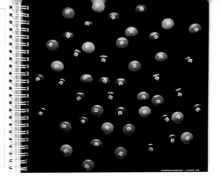

KROMEKOTE FROM A TO Z

CONTENTS
ABSORPTION
BRONZING/BINDING
COLORCAST
DIE CUT/DEBOSSING/DUOTONE
EMBOSSING
FLUORESCENTS/FOLDING BOARD/FLATNESS/FLEXOGRAPHY
GRAVURE/GLOSS
HALFTONE/MOAT
INK
JUST THE RIGHT SHEET
KROMEKOTE WEIGHTS AND SIZES
LITHOGRAPHY/LAMINATING/LINE
MATTE
NOTHING CAN IMPROVE ON A BLANK SHEET OF KROMEKOTE
OFFSET SPRAY
PROCESS COLOR
QUALITY CONTROL
REVERSE SIDE
SCORE AND FOLD
TRIMMING
ULTRAGLOSS STAMPING
VARNISH
WEB OFFSET
X-TRA SPECIAL JOBS
YOUR CHAMPION PAPERS REPRESENTATIVES
ZINC

CHAMPION PAPERS

from the discerning is more important than hammering home a sales message." Brown says he wanted to be part of that company and figured out how to get himself hired as copywriter on the project. If you own an *Imagination*, treasure it. According to Tony McDowell, they're selling for more than $150 in rare-book stores.

The mid-'70s brought elegant Dick Hess-designed and -illustrated annual reports with exquisite paintings of trees, classic examples of the annual-report-as-educational-tool genre. In 1978, Hess's lavishly art directed, beautifully detailed *Champion Magazine* broke new ground in editorial design. For other designers, a seminal moment might have been "White on White," by Janet Odgis (1988) a pristine, die-cut, recessed box that heralded the launch of Kromekote 2000 and defined the opposite end of the design spectrum. Today, copies of *Subjective Reasoning* might fill your shelves — perhaps the issue that tackled the Bosnia situation or the one that explored whether Jeff Koons's sculpture infringed the photographer's copyright to that image of the litter of puppies. Or you might be hoarding a little collection of Benefit notecards or bookplates, matches, tote bags, soaps, or pencil, recyclable

CLOCKWISE FROM TOP LEFT: *Kromekote A to Z* (1980). *Design:* Rene Vidmer. *Photography:* George Erlich. Cover and spreads from brochure on Champion's corporate headquarters in Stamford, Connecticut. *Design:* Danne and Blackburn.

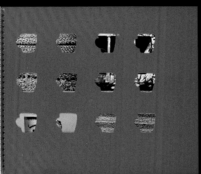

1972

The *Imagination* series changes direction, going on the road to exotic locales. Designer James Miho, working in close collaboration with creative director Edward Russell, Jr., experiments freely with production techniques.

1978

Champion Magazine, published until 1985, demonstrates Champion's commitment to design integration for internal as well as external audiences. *Design:* Richard Hess. *Photography:* Joe Baraban.

1980

For several years, Richard Hess designs Champion's annual reports. The design approach is extended to posters, brochures, and advertising. *Illustration:* Mark Hess.

1987

The Wire is an employee newsletter still in publication today. *Design direction:* Walter Bernard and Milton Glaser. *Art direction:* Colleen McCudden. *Photography:* Rudy Janu.

1988

Designframe creates a series of six *American Visions* promotions. Each offers unusual perspectives of the American landscape and its people. Photography: Jack Parsons.

Richard Hess develops a series of six promotions, *The Elders*, exploring the story of the passage America has traveled in the past century. Rich with vintage illustrations and photography, the series features commentary from American centenarians. Photography: Dmitri Kasterine.

1989

By sponsoring canoe and kayaking teams, Champion continues a long tradition of civic responsibility. Bart Crosby's sports sponsorship materials, unlike most, are compiled like a corporate identity manual. Subsequently, this method sets a new standard. Creative direction: John Hildenbiddle.

The **Champion Spirit**!

objects that have come to symbolize the recycled sheet that comes
in totally cool colors.

Champion kept reshaping the idea of paper promotion,
spawning innovation. When its competitors began spending big dollars
on promotions, Champion moved on to new ideas. Merely demonstrating six-color printing, embossing, and die-cutting has become
commonplace, hackneyed, says vice president of creative services John
Hildenbiddle. Now the purpose of a promotion is to establish a brand:
Kromekote, Pageantry, Benefit. In doing so, risk-taking was — and
is — encouraged. "Like launching Benefit with a little deck of color
chips with no identification," explains McDowell. "Designers could
play with the chips, just have fun. They didn't get a clue what it was
about until two weeks later. The idea was Stephen Doyle's," he says.
"We give designers freedom to think. After all, when our product
is sold, it's blank." Many paper companies prepare elaborate design
briefs that detail exactly what a promotion is supposed to demonstrate;
Champion, however, prides itself on finding out what it is that stimu-
lates designers' thinking. The freedom to suggest content ("If I love
this, so will other designers") has fostered some of the best work. For

ABOVE AND CENTER: Spread and cover of *Subjective Reasoning #6*
(1993). *Creative direction:* William Drenttel, Paula Scher, and Willem
Kars. *Design:* Gerard Hadders and Allen Hori. BELOW: *Subjective
Reasoning #2* (1993). *Creative direction:* William Drenttel, Paula Scher.
Design: Paula Scher.

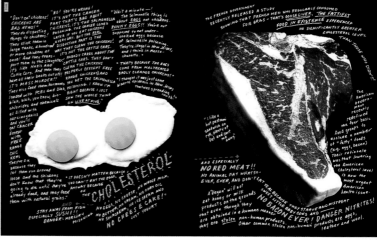

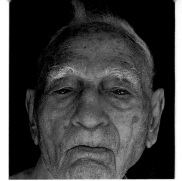

Samuel Leroy Mendel
Born June 23, 1884
Fort Worth, Texas
Vaudevillian, Shortstop, Lumberjack

example, Paula Scher's collection of antique dingbats and typefaces
grew into the company's most requested promotion, *Beautiful Faces
for Carnival.*

There was never a Champion house style, but there was
always smart strategic thinking and impeccable quality. "The communications program," wrote Dick Hess in *Graphis* magazine (no. 246,
November–December 1986), "rather than a clearly followed plan, was
more of an attitude — a string of opportunities recognized and capital-
ized upon and of dangers averted. This is a more tortuous path than
would be supposed. It is a pattern composed of small details and decisions, which only works because it is worked at every day. It is an art."

CLOCKWISE FROM TOP LEFT: *The Elders* #6 (1989). *Design:* Richard
Hess. *Photography:* Dmitri Kasterine. *The Elders* #4 (1989). *Design:*
Richard Hess. *Illustration:* Thomas Hart Benton. *Photography:* Dmitri
Kasterine and Birmingham Public Library Archives. *American Visions*
(1989). *Design:* Designframe. *Photography:* Peter Warchol. *American
Visions* (1990). *Design:* Designframe. *Photography:* William Garnett.

OF COMMUNISM IS A MESSAGE TO THE HUMAN RACE.

THE END

1992

A three-year series, each of the ten issues of *Subjective Reasoning* features issues and ideas that "characterize the quickly and dramatically changing world around us... through word and image." *Design:* Drenttel Doyle Partners. *Handlettering:* Stephen Doyle.

1996

Champion launches its first website, featuring "Bits of Words on Paper," an encyclopedia of paper and printing terms. *Design:* William Drenttel, Jessica Helfand, and Jeff Tyson.

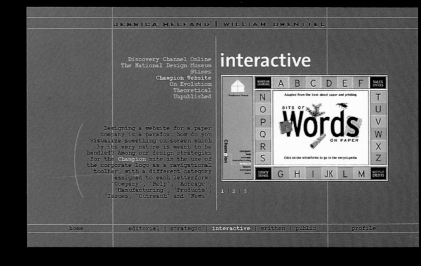

1997

Unlike any other promotion in Champion's history, Doyle Partner's campaign for Benefit focuses on the recycled paper's color palette. Instead of the customary swatch books, designers are sent objects, from pencils to candles to a clock.

47

Great Coats

In Which We Demonstrate How Carved Papers From Champion Capture the Imagination

It is also a matter of corporate policy. To Champion, corporate identity was never about the uniform application of symbol and typography. It is an attitude, a set of values, a significant investment. David Brown recalls, "In the early eighties we had some two hundred and twenty locations around the country: pulp and paper mills, corrugated plants, plywood and sawmills, timber yards, warehouses, sales offices. To document signage needs, Don Meecker of Danne & Blackburn hit the road one spring and visited over half of them. He found a cacophony of visual identification and some plants and facilities that were a visual public relations disaster. The presentation included recommendations that would cost many millions of dollars to implement. The response: 'Do it.'" "We learned to appreciate the contributions designers can make," explains John Hiddenbiddle. "Our department has internal credibility. But we've got to give the credit to our chairman, Richard Olson, who believes in commitment to quality no matter what happens, and to Carl Bendetsen and Andrew Sigler before him. Even in a down year, quantity may be reduced, but never quality. We won't do the product rather than cheapen it down. In lean years we'll go for higher impact." David Brown reminisces: "In 1974 Sigler had a meeting about the annual report with all the top executives. He said, 'You guys are not going to have a vote and you are not going to nitpick.' That didn't make us popular with the executive corps, but it did allow us to do something quite special."

Over the last ten years, Champion assembled a core group of design consultants that includes Doyle, Drenttel, and Scher as well as Bart Crosby, Tom Kluepfel, Woody Pirtle, Tony Russell, Jim Sebastian, and Lucille Tenazas. The task: to collaborate on projects. "They hated it at first," admits Tony McDowell. "But then they started building on each other's ideas. They'd talk without us. They even had *Subjective Reasoning* done by designers other than themselves, designers who were younger or weren't so well known at the time: Dana Arnett, William Bevington, Alan Hori, Chip Kidd."

Recalls Bill Drenttel, "At first the consultant group was quirky. Designers who had been pitching the Kromekote business had to work

OPPOSITE PAGE, CLOCKWISE FROM TOP LEFT: *Specification Frame* (1976). *Design:* Designframe. *Photography:* Max Waldman. *Dingbats* (1989). *Design:* Paula Scher. *Beautiful Faces* promotion. *Design:* Paula Scher. THIS PAGE: *Great Coats* (1982). *Design:* James Miho. *Illustration:* Koren.

CLOCKWISE FROM TOP: *The Enveloping Herbs* (1983). *Design:* Peter Good. *Illustration:* Peter Good and Janet Good. Carnival swatchbooks (1993). Press kit for Champion International Whitewater Series (1994). *Design:* Bart Crosby. *Champion Careers* (1988). *Design:* Woody Pirtle. *The Shakers* (1991), promotional line for Influence paper.

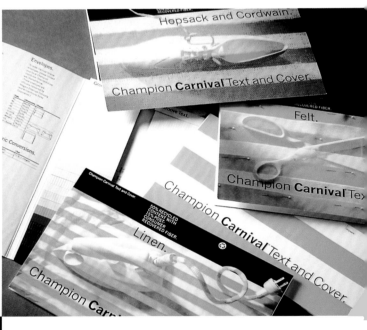

together. But in that room we stopped being competitive and focused on strategy, on larger marketing issues." This was a new twist on the idea behind the roll call of talent employed in earlier years: Ivan Chermayeff, Milton Glaser, Jay Maisel, Henry Wolf, George Tscherny, to name a few. Using top talent was the brainchild of legendary now-retired vice president of marketing services Edward Russell, Jr., who realized promotions would have more impact if they were designed by the kinds of people he wanted to become Champion's customers, such as Jim Miho and Dick Hess, both of whom he hired.

"A lot of stuff gets done that designers may never see," adds Hildenbiddle. Employee communications. Product packaging. Customer newsletters. Community advertising. Trade ads. District support programs for salespeople. Sports sponsorship. Using what is described as a "total event experience look," Champion sponsors the U.S. Rowing Team and the Canoe and Kayak Team. Bart Crosby designed everything for it — from team T-shirts and banners to signage, advertising, uniforms, even identity manuals. "Programs like this help employees feel proud of the company they work for," Hildenbiddle explains. The company is also making a difference with GAME ("Getting Ahead Means Education"), a sports-centered English, math, science, and social studies curriculum for middle schools in communities near its mills and plants.

Perhaps the company's commitment to excellence and the arts is best summed up in a Danne & Blackburn–designed, Alan-Orling–photographed brochure that commemorates the 1981 dedication of the company's aluminum-skinned headquarters in Stamford, Connecticut. The introductory copy reads: *"For Stamford, One Champion Plaza represents a distinguished architectural addition to the urban landscape. The main feature of the lobby floor is the permanent exhibition area of the Fairfield County branch of the Whitney Museum of American Art — a unique and first-ever collaboration between business and the arts."* The Whitney, funded by Champion, mounts five exhibitions a year and is open to the public five days a week, free of charge.

It's not easy being unique and first-ever all the time. Champion has been doing it for more than thirty-five years.

Is there a better way to do it?

Deferiet's Luke Galloway thinks so. He authored a briefing book for the mill's foremen and first line supervisors called Communicating Honestly About Mill Performance (CHAMP). The book covers a range of mill subjects concerning production, cost data, and other information supervisors need to keep their people informed. There *is* a better way to do it — just ask the people who do it. It's the Champion Way at work. ⚙ **Champion**

Think Cost, Quality and Service!

ABOVE: *Special Places in the Forest* (1993). *Design:* Anthony Russell.
BELOW: Motivational/safety posters for Champion mills (1987). *Design:* Peter Good.

The 1998 Brand Design Association Gold Awards

The Brand Design Association (formerly the Package Design Council) formed an alliance with the American Institute of Graphic Arts in 1998 as part of its effort to become a key force in promoting greater under-standing of the value of effective design to a branding strategy. *Design to Relevance*, the exhibition of the works selected from the Brand Design Association's Gold Awards competition, celebrates the designs of the past year that embody excellence and relevance in the field. The exhibition was on view at the Strathmore Gallery at the AIGA from June 2–12, 1998.

The Gold Awards

The Gold Awards competition has been the world's premier brand and package design competition for the past four decades. This international award program is peer reviewed and peer judged on the basis of the following criteria:

Excellence in aesthetics

Is the entry visually appealing and emotionally compelling?

Excellence in innovation

Is the entry a breakthrough for this product category and therefore likely to inspire and influence future package designers?

Excellence in effectiveness

Is the package well produced and an effective marketing tool, as evaluated against marketing objectives submitted by the entrant?

In addition to the awards presented in each category, the following Gold Awards are bestowed: Best in Aesthetics, Best in Innovation, Best in Redesign, Best in Effectiveness, and the Best in Show.

Michael Livolsi, *Chair*

The Americas

Sam J. Ciulla, Lipson-Alport-Glass & Associates

Karen Corell, The Coleman Group, Inc.

Laura Fang, The Coleman Group, Inc.

Flavio Gomez, SBG Enterprise

Ron Jesiolowski, SmithKline Beecham Corporation

Keith Steimel, Cornerstone Design

Asia

Fumihito Sasada, Bravis International Limited, *Lead Judge*

Kikugoro Mori, Create Five

Yoshitomo Ohama, Avon Products Co.

Hiroko Yamada, Kose Cosmoport

Europe

Rob van den Berg, Mountain Design, *Lead Judge*

Jonathon Ford, Pearlfischer International Design Partnership

Bridget Heming, Pineapple Design

Rowland Heming, Pineapple Design

Soren Salling-Peterson, Inter Profil

Best in Innovation

Antiquities Box

Client Firm Timex Corp.

Design Firm Leslie Evans Design Associates

Art Director Leslie Evans

Chief Designer Leslie Evans

Graphic Designers Tom Hubbard and Frank Nichols

Structural Designers FN Burt and Leslie Evans Design

The designers created a tomblike box with a unique opening that creates interest at point-of-sale. The historical and archaeological elements of the package design align it with the watch designs.

GOLD AWARD

Gatao Vinho Verde

Client Firm Sociedade Dos Vinhos Borges SA

Design Firm Blackburn's Ltd.

Creative Director John Blackburn

Chief Designer Belinda Duggan

The challenge the designer faced in redesigning Gatao Vinho
Verde was that, although consumers have an affection for
the brand and recognize it as a symbol of popular culture, it
had become rustic, gauche, and tacky. In the new design,
the cat is the hero, becoming an aristocrat rather than a pan-
tomime figure. The bottle has been made more contemporary
and sophisticated, while the brand's existing distinctive,
valued identity and Portuguese heritage have been updated.

Best in Aesthetics

Gardeners

Client Firm Crabtree & Evelyn

Design Firm Peter Windett & Associates

Art Director Peter Windett

Chief Designer Peter Windett

Graphic Designers Pene Parker and Peter Windett

The package design appeals to the serious gardener
as well as the regular Crabtree & Evelyn customer.

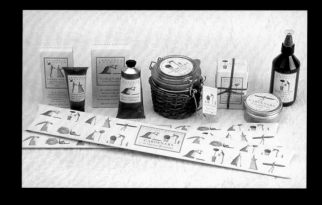

G O L D   A W A R D

R i t z   C r a c k e r   R e d e s i g n

Client Firm Nabisco Biscuit Company

Design Firm Scott W. Baker Associates, Inc.

Creative Directors Scott Baker and Todd Dalebroux

Chief Designer Todd Dalebroux

Graphic Designer Mike Tophen

The objective of this redesign was to reposition the product
to a younger audience while maintaining mature audiences
(age 25 to 54), particularly young mothers. The designers made
a cultural icon more contemporary by freshening and building
on the brand's equities — the Ritz orb and necklace of crackers.

GOLD AWARD

Alta Water Bottle

Client Firm Alta Beverage Company

Design Firm Hornall Anderson Design Works

Art Director Jack Anderson

Graphic Designers Jack Anderson, Larry Anderson, and Julie Keenan

The rippled bottle, reflecting a water motif, was designed from a positioning strategy to stand out from competing bottles in the marketplace. The cold winds that chill the snow in the high Canadian mountains was the basic theme for the final look. The design conveys a strong sense of the water's source of origin and the pure, natural qualities inherent in the spring water. The mark developed a strong, classic feel with a spontaneous twist. The brushlike stroke was designed to evoke snow-capped mountains, while the ice-blue glow around the mark, also reminiscent of wind and snow, gives Alta a fresh, outdoorsy appearance.

1998 Gold Award "Design to Relevance" Selected Entries

Gold Awards

Ortho Home & Garden

Fire Ant Killer Redesign

Design Firm *Addis Group*

Art Director *Joanne Hom*

Chief Designer *David Leong*

Score Soda

Design Firm *Antista Fairclough Design*

Art Directors *Thomas Fairclough and Tom Antista*

El Picu

Design Firm *BrandNew Design*

Creative Director *Willem Kroon*

NEC Computer Supportive Products

Design Firm *Bravis International Ltd.*

Creative Director *Fumi Sasada*

Chief Designer *Tatsuo Takamura*

Viansa Frescolina

Design Firm *Britton Design*

Creative Director *Patti Britton*

Commotion

Design Firm *Cabra Diseño*

Art Director *Raul Cabra*

Remington Men's Shavers Redesign

Design Firm *Coley Porter Bell*

Art Director *Allison Miguel*

Kenzo Jungle For Men

Design Firm *Desgrippes Gobé & Associates*

Creative Director *Joel Desgrippes*

Chief Designers *Sophie Farhi and Corine Restrepo*

Pepe Lopez Tequila Redesign

Design Firm *Desgrippes Gobé & Associates*

Creative Director *Joanna Feldheim*

Versace Make-up

Client Firm *Versace*

Design Firm *Desgrippes Gobé & Associates*

Creative Director *Joel Desgrippes*

Chief Designer *Sophie Farhi*

Winter Sampler Pack

Design Firm *Deutsch Design Works*

Creative Director *Barry Deutsch*

Chief Designer *Lori Wynn*

Speakeasy Mints

Design Firm *Hornall Anderson Design Works*

Art Director *Jack Anderson*

Taco Bell Packaging

Design Firm *Landor Associates*

Creative Director *Nicolas Aparicio*

Five Brothers Pasta Sauce Redesign

Design Firm *Lipton Creative Resources*

Creative Director *Jeff Brall*

Chief Designer *Bart Goodell*

Illustrator *Brent Watkinson*

P. C. Semifreddo

Design Firm *Loblaw Brands, Ltd.*

Creative Director *Russell Rudd*

Murad 365 Vitamin Line

Design Firm *Maddocks & Company*

Creative Director *Mary Scott*

Chief Designer *Paul Farris*

Perfumes Isabell Fragrances

Design Firm *Matsumoto Incorporated*

Art Director *Takaaki Matsumoto*

Albert Heijn Cold Prepacked

Meat Products Redesign

Design Firm *Millford-Van den Berg Design*

Art Director *Ype Jorna*

Chief Designer *Ype Jorna*

Campbell's 100th Anniversary Soup

Design Firm *Plewes Bertouche Design Group*

Creative Director *Chris Plewes*

S&W Growers' Reserve Peaches

Design Firm *Primo Angeli Inc.*

Creative Director *Carlo Pagoda*

Art Director *Marcelo DeFreitas*

Chief Designer *Jan Layman*

Mad Mex Tortilla Chip Packaging

Design Firm *Wall-to-Wall Studios*

Creative Directors *James Nesbitt and Bernard Uy*

Silver Awards

Citra Soda

Design Firm *Antista Fairclough Design*

Art Directors *Thomas Fairclough and Tom Antista*

Le Cirque

Design Firm *Avon Products, Inc.*

Creative Director *Ellen Caruso*

The Scent

Design Firm *Bérard Associates*

Creative Director *Jerome Bérard*

Albert Heijn Color Film Rolls

Design Firm *BrandNew Design*

Creative Director *Willem Kroon*

Buehler Vineyards Reserve Packaging

Design Firm *Britton Design*

Creative Director *Patti Britton*

Devil Mountain Redesign

Design Firm *Cornerstone Design Associates*

Art Director *Keith Steimel*

Chief Designers *Paul McDowell and Juno Hinchliffe*

Golden Pilsner

Design Firm *Deutsch Design Works*

Creative Director *Barry Deutsch*

Chief Designer *Lori Wynn*

UPS OnLine International Tracking

Design Firm *EM2 Design*

Creative Director *Maxey Andress*

Anna Kannenberg Packaging

Design Firm *Hallmark Cards, Inc.*

Art Director *Lisa Mayer*

Maptitude

Design Firm *Hornall Anderson Design Works*

Art Director *Jack Anderson*

Seattle Chocolates Truffle Bars

Design Firm *Hornall Anderson Design Works*

Art Director *Jack Anderson*

TileLab Redesign

Design Firm *Hornall Anderson Design Works*

Art Director *Jack Anderson*

Boaters Flavoured Coffees

Design Firm *The Ian Logan Design Co.*

Art Director *Alan Colville*

GM Parts Redesign

Design Firm *Interbrand Gerstman+Meyers Inc.*

Creative Director *Juan Concepcion*

Chief Designer *Annie Baker*

Zest Deodorant Bar Redesign

Design Firm *Interbrand Gerstman+Meyers Inc.*

Creative Director *Juan Concepcion*

Chief Designer *Chris Sanders*

PAM Cooking Spray Redesign

Design Firm *I.Q. Design Group, Inc.*

Creative Director *Leslie Tucker*

Nordstrom Business Softwear

Design Firm *The Leonhardt Group*

Art Director *Greg Morgan*

Loriva Oil Redesign

Design Firm *Lipson-Alport-Glass & Associates*

Creative Director *Sam J. Ciulla*

Chief Designer *Lynn Mueller*

StarTAC Cellular Phone

Design Firm *Lipson-Alport-Glass & Associates*

Creative Director *Sam J. Ciulla*

Chief Designers *Keith Shupe and*
Katherine Holderied

Warner Bros. Boys' Bath Line/ Body Line

Design Firm *Maddocks & Company*

Creative Director *Julia Precht*

Chief Designer *Amy Hershman*

Warner Bros. Taz Men's Fragrance Line

Design Firm *Maddocks & Company*

Creative Director *Julia Precht*

Chief Designer *Catherine Cedillo*

Cleverline-Cable Turtle

Design Firm *Millford-Van den Berg Design*

Art Director *Oscar van Geesbergen*

Albert Heijn-Meat in Sauce Redesign

Design Firm *Millford-Van den Berg Design*

Art Director *Erik de Graaf*

Hero-Izi

Design Firm *Millford-Van den Berg Design*

Art Director *Ype Jorna*

Lunch Mates

Design Firm *Plewes Bertouche Design Group*

Creative Director *Chris Plewes*

Hausbrandt Redesign

Design Firm *Robilant & Associates*

Creative Director *Maurizio di Robilant*

Sun Spuds

Design Firm *Russell Incorporated*

Art Director *Bob Russell*

Wiser's Redesign

Design Firm *Russell Incorporated*

Art Director *Bob Russell*

Adaptec SCSI Card Redesign

Design Firm *SBG Enterprise*

Creative Director *Mark Bergman*

Diet Coke Redesign

Design Firm *SBG Enterprise*

Creative Director *Mark Bergman*

Alka Seltzer Redesign

Design Firm *Sterling Group*

Creative Director *Marcus Hewitt*

Chief Designer *Sharon Reiter Lindberg*

InSync

Design Firm *Tim Girvin Design, Inc.*

Chief Designer *Kathy Saito*

Pods of Pleasure

Design Firm *The Wyant Simboli Group, Inc.*

Creative Director *Julia Wyant*

For eighty years, the AIGA has held juried competitions to identify and recognize examples of the very best in American graphic design. Most people aware of these competitions assume that the standards of design excellence are principally aesthetic. Yet many designers today believe that the most important measure for their work is effectiveness — effectiveness in meeting the communications brief developed for them by their clients.

This is not new. Early in the AIGA's history, the predecessor of *Communication Graphics* was the *Printing for Commerce* competition, back when the AIGA was composed of book designers, typographers, and printers. In recent years, the AIGA has been encouraged by many members to create a *Design for Commerce* competition. Some very successful designers have felt that the *Communication Graphics* juries were more likely to select precious designs done for vanity projects than solid design that fully meets the narrow objectives of clients.

In an attempt to bridge the distance, this year the AIGA has modified the criteria for the *CG* competition in order to evaluate projects in terms of their objectives — branding, promoting, informing, entertaining — rather than their formats — annual reports, books, posters, and so on. And in future years, we will be more emphatic in requiring clear objective statements and comments on effectiveness from each entrant. The juries will need to evaluate each entry against both aesthetic and effectiveness criteria.

This evolution reflects the increasing focus of the AIGA on the role of communicating to business and the public the value of design and improving understanding of design as a problem-solving process. We hope that in explaining the challenge each designer faces in executing a design, others will understand the profession better. We want the competition and the annual to be learning experiences for young designers and others, so that the amount of editorial text will increase. At the same time, the standard for selection has been raised, with the number of winning entries only one-third the number chosen in recent years.

The reformatting of the annual is also part of this reorientation. Our distributors made clear that we needed to make a more accessible book if we were seeking a wider audience outside the membership. Accordingly, we have chosen a more dynamic trim size and are offering the book at a 25 percent lower retail price than in previous years.

We hope these changes will increase the relevance of the competition and its value as part of the broader mission of supporting designers in their pursuit of excellence and professional success.

— RICHARD GREFÉ
Executive Director, AIGA

Branding. Promoting. Informing. Entertaining. Evaluating design has never been so complicated! In its call for entries this year, the AIGA asked us to consider the value of our work in new ways. Instead of asking "Is it a well designed brochure?," they asked, "What does it do?" and "How well does it do it?" Many of us were caught off guard by the unfamiliar questions.

As designers we are increasingly faced with new pressures and asked to justify our work using new vocabularies and strategies we weren't taught in design school. Many of us are struggling to redefine our roles, to see ourselves as problem solvers and business strategists rather than decorators and image makers. We are asking our clients to value us for our ability to think in addition to our ability to make things.

As an industry, we have a long history of talking to ourselves. This show is a first step toward a new goal of being judged on the success of our work in a broader context. Our work is finally being evaluated in terms of function, strategy, and communication, not just aesthetics. These new criteria made the judging process more difficult, but the result is a small collection of very powerful work.

As judges reviewing each entry we asked: "What is this piece trying to do? What is its intent? Is it doing it clearly? Is the way it looks helping this intention or hindering it?" We are still missing several important pieces of the puzzle. We don't know whether the redesign of a package actually increased sales. We can't tell if a piece of branding really improved brand recognition in a particular market. In respect to their functional as business tools, our attempts to judge the success of the entries had to fail. But it's a failure that points a way for the future. If we want to be taken seriously as communicators and strategic thinkers, we must begin to evaluate our work from the client's perspective as well as our own. We must begin to talk to a wider audience and eventually be judged by it as well.

— MARGO CHASE

Chair, *Communication Graphics 19*

Communication Graphics 19

Margo Chase

is the owner/principal of Margo Chase Design, a Los Angeles–based graphic design studio specializing in print, Web, and film design. In June 1997, Margo Chase Design's motion graphics earned both gold and silver awards at the Promax/BDA Conference in Chicago. Margo's love of letterforms, Gothic architecture, and medieval manuscripts may explain the organic and often unusual nature of her work. Her studio's dynamic, award-winning style can be seen in motion graphics for ESPN, Adobe Systems, the Billboard Live nightclub on L.A.'s Sunset Strip, and on websites for the Hard Rock Hotel, Microsoft Network, and the Energizer Bunny. Over the past eleven years, Margo Chase Design's landmark CD cover art (for Madonna, Prince, and Bonnie Raitt) and movie posters (including Francis Ford Coppola's *Dracula*) have gained international recognition. Margo Chase Design has been named to the 1997 *I.D.* 40 and was featured in the January/February 1997 issue of *Graphis*. Her current video and Web projects, along with her new digital font foundry, Gravy Fonts, keep her on the cutting edge of technology and style.

Title *Oklahoma Poster*
Design Firm *Margo Chase Design, Los Angeles, CA*
Art Director/Graphic Designer *Margo Chase*
Illustrator *Margo Chase*
Photographer *Merlin Rosenberg*
Typeface *Pterra, Custom Typeface for Poster*
Clients *Margo Chase Design and AIGA/Oklahoma*

The Oklahoma poster was developed as an invitation/announcement of Margo's lecture for AIGA/Oklahoma. Reflective of an MCD promotional campaign that was in progress at the time of this lecture, the poster features elements from various cultures, printer's makeready sheets, photography, and custom typography, all layered under the title of the lecture, *Digital Organic.*

Title *Apollo Logo*
Design Firm *Margo Chase Design, Los Angeles, CA*
Creative Director *Margo Chase*
Graphic Designer *Brian Hunt*
Typefaces *Box Gothic, Custom Letterforms*
Client *Apollo Interactive*

Apollo Interactive is an Internet development company. Margo Chase Design created a futuristic hip, techno identity for Apollo that reflects their industry.

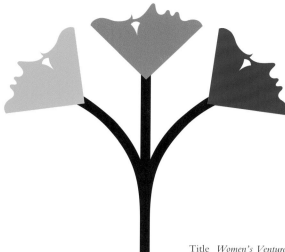

Title *Buick Signia*
Design Firm *Margo Chase Design,*
Los Angeles, CA
Art Directors *Julio Desir, Margo*
Chase, and Brian Hunt
Graphic Designer *Brian Hunt*
Copywriter *Mark Lowenstein*
Typefaces *Scarab, Base,*
Engravers Roman
Client *General Motors / Buick*

Buick Signia is a promotional
CD-ROM developed to help position Buick as a high-tech, futuristic
car manufacturer. Signia was Buick's
concept car, featured at auto shows
throughout the country. This package, which contains a Web browser
to launch www.buick.com, was
distributed at auto shows.

Michael Gericke

Michael Gericke, a partner in
Pentagram's New York office,
joined the firm in 1986. He has
developed identity systems, environmental graphics, and communications
programs that have repositioned
such corporations and institutions as
the American Institute of Architects,
JP Morgan, Liz Claiborne, Public
Radio International, and UPS.

Michael has also produced comprehensive identities for the Hotel
Hankyu International, a luxury hotel
in Osaka, Japan; CBS's television
coverage of the 1992, 1994, and 1998
Winter Olympic Games; and the
1994 FIFA World Cup soccer. He
is the design consultant to Hammond
Incorporated, and led the team that
created their acclaimed *Atlas of*
the World series. Michael has received
many accolades from design associations and museums, including
the Beacon award. His identity,
promotional, and poster work appears
regularly in international design
exhibitions and can be found in the
permanent collections of the Paris
Musee de la Poste, the Warsaw
Poster Museum at Wilanow, the
Hamburg Museum of Arts and Crafts,
and the Neue Sammlung Museum in
Munich. He lectures frequently at
universities and professional organizations and has taught identity design
at the Cooper Union for the
Advancement of Science and Art.

Title *Women's Venture Fund Symbol*
Design Firm *Pentagram Design,*
New York, NY
Art Director/Graphic Designer
Michael Gericke
Client *Women's Venture Fund*

The Women's Venture Fund is
an organization that provides under-
privileged women with funds
tostart and develop new businesses.
The logo expresses hope, growth,
and optimism.

Title *Building the Empire State*
Building Poster
Design Firm *Pentagram Design,*
New York, NY
Art Director/Graphic Designer
Michael Gericke
Client *The Skyscraper Museum*

The Skyscraper Museum in New
York mounted an exhibition on the
design and construction of the Empire
State Building. The poster conveys
the speed of construction, rising more
than a story a day.

Title *Coaches' Choice College
Football Player of the Year Award*
Design Firm *Visual Dialogue,
Boston, MA*
Art Directors/Sculptors
Fritz Klaetke and Paul Montie
Fabricator *Scott Metals, Indianapolis*
Client *Domino's Pizza, Inc.*

This sculpture was approached as
a design problem: the objective was
to create a trophy that was dynamic,
powerful, distinctive, and unlike any
existing award in the field of sports.
The coaches' choice trophy, awarded
to the top player in each of the four
collegiate divisions, abstracts football
pads and musculature into an angular
cast stainless-steel figure. This figure
forms a wedge bursting forth from
the broken black granite base. The
result is a symbolic athlete representing the essence of football — not
a specific position or only one race.

Fritz Klaetke

The offspring of an architect and
a painter, Fritz Klaetke was destined
to be a graphic designer. His Boston-
based studio, Visual Dialogue, special-
izes in whatever sounds interesting
at the time — CD covers, identity
systems, books, websites, magazines,
video, posters, and sculpture. This
work, often created in solitude, has
been shared with the world by the
AIGA, ACD, ADC, TDC, I.D., CA,
and the CHNDMSI (aka the Cooper-
Hewitt, National Design Museum,
Smithsonian Institution). Klaetke is
known for being highly opinionated
as well as color blind, and was therefore selected to be a juror for this
competition.

Title
Mind/Brain/Behavior Initiative Identity
Design Firm *Visual Dialogue,
Boston, MA*
Art Director *Fritz Klaetke*
Graphic Designers
Fritz Klaetke and David Kraljic
Photographer *PhotoDisc*
Typefaces *Adobe Garamond,
News Gothic*
Printer *Color Express*
Paper *Strathmore Elements*
Client *Harvard University*

The Mind/Brain/Behavior inter-
faculty initiative is a new program at
Harvard University that brings together specialists from diverse fields to
study complexities of the mind and
human behavior. These different areas
(ranging from law to religion, business
to neurobiology) are represented by
the various images that come together
in a random pattern around a set
typographic structure to create the
ever-changing logo of the initiative.

Title *Dance Month Poster Series
(1994–1998)*
Design Firm *Visual Dialogue,
Boston, MA*
Art Director/Graphic Designer
Fritz Klaetke
Photographers *William Huber (1994),
Charles Barclay Reeves (1995), Russ
Quakenbush (1996), Joshua Weinfeld
(1997), and Liz Linder (1998)*
Typeface *Interstate*
Printer *Pride Printers*
Paper *Champion Carnival*
Client *Dance Complex*

These posters announcing Dance
Month, an annual celebration
of dance in the city of Cambridge,
Massachusetts, attempt to convey
dance and movement in a new way.
Each year a different photographer
applies his or her particular vision
to create an image that will capture
the attention of passers-by amid the
visual clutter of the street.

Michael Mabry

Michael Mabry heads Michael Mabry
Design, a San Francisco–based graphic
design firm providing services in retail
identity, collateral, packaging, and
illustration. Michael received his BFA
in graphic design from the University
of Utah and worked for SBG Partners
as a senior designer before starting his
own firm in 1981. He has served on
the faculty at the California College of
Arts and Crafts and lectured at various
design organizations throughout the
country.

His work has received many awards,
is well documented in design and
illustration annuals, and is included
in the permanent collections of
the Library of Congress and the San
Francisco Museum of Modern Art.
Michael's work was featured in a solo
exhibition in Osaka, Japan, as well
as a group exhibition on California
design at the Museo Fortuny in
Venice. He has served as president
of AIGA/San Francisco and is a past
member of the AIGA's national
board of directors.

Title *Ella and Louis*
Design Firm *Michael Mabry Design,
San Francisco, CA*
Art Director *Kero Matsui*
Illustrator *Michael Mabry*
Writer *Michael Mabry*
Typeface *Hand Drawn*
Client *DDD Gallery, Osaka, Japan*

These two posters were created for
a commemorative exhibition for the
DDD Gallery in Osaka, Japan. The
assignment was to create two images
that have some kind of relationship
to one another. The exhibition was
represented by a group of international designers, so I felt that my two
submissions should represent my
country, the United States, as well as
relate symbiotically to each other.

My search for the appropriate subject
led me to choose the true American
art form of jazz. It is a form of music
that cross-pollinated Spanish, French,
and Protestant revivalist music with
African slave hymns, and was bred in
the steamy honky tonks of New
Orleans. The mixture of cultures and
emotions makes jazz very American,
as it evolved from within the melting
pot that is at the root of America's
diversity. Jazz became an international
sensation symbolizing American
originality.

The materials I used were old
shipping box cardboard, gouache
paints, colored pencils, colored paper,
and magazine clippings. The modest
materials are symbolic of Ella and
Louis's simple origins. The lyrics of
George and Ira Gershwin's sentimental song "Our Love Is Here to Stay,"
written in the top portion of each
image, is characteristic of the kind of
songs Ella and Louis sang together,
while the words in the body of each
portrait chronicle their lives.

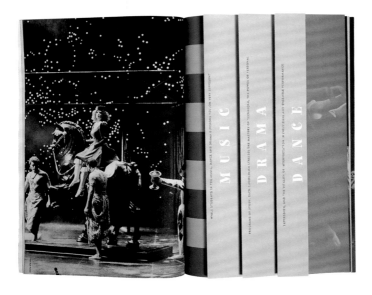

Title *Ethan Allen Clockworks Logo*
Design Firm *Salsgiver Coveney Associates Inc., Westport, CT*
Graphic Designer *Karen Salsgiver*
Client *Ethan Allen, Inc.*

Clockworks is a line of clocks designed and sold by Ethan Allen, including one particularly distinctive triangular piece. This solution is one in a series of logos designed to reflect the changing nature of this furniture manufacturer.

Karen Salsgiver

For Karen Salsgiver, principal designer of Salsgiver Coveney Associates Inc. in Westport, CT, the creative process is a distilling of complex meaning and messages, creating graphically simple work that is functional yet playful. This way of thinking has earned Salsgiver Coveney over thirty national awards from distinguished professional organizations and a devoted clientele in the arts, publishing, finance, home furnishings, fashion, and paper industries. Key clients include the Carnegie Museum of Art, Champion International Corporation, Condé Nast Books, Ethan Allen, the Julliard School, Harvard Business School Press, Lincoln Center for the Performing Arts, MasterCard, the New York Public Library, and Random House Inc. Karen's work has also been published in *Print, I.D. Magazine, International Design, Graphic Design USA,* and the New York Art Directors Club annual.

Title *The Julliard School Annual Report*
Design Firm *Salsgiver Coveney Associates Inc., Westport, CT*
Graphic Designers *Karen Salsgiver and Cathleen Mitchell*
Paper *Champion Benefit*
Printer *Berger McGill*
Client *The Julliard School*

This is the third in a series of four annual report designs that are variations on a theme, using progressively changing formats and rhythms as a metaphor for the discipline, constant growth, and evolution of Julliard's educational process. The annual reports recap the academic year for a visually sophisticated audience of faculty, board members, donors, and prospective students.

Title *Champion Hopsack*
Design Firm *Salsgiver Coveney Associates Inc., Westport, CT*
Art Director/Graphic Designer *Karen Salsgiver*
Typefaces *Gill Sans, Garamond Three*
Paper *Champion Hopsack*
Printer *API*
Client *Champion International Corporation*

This piece was intended to demonstrate the characteristics of a paper inspired by a fabric, to an audience of designers and paper specifiers. Research into the source of the paper's name led to a rich history of the hops plant and the brewing of beer, going back to ancient Egypt and the fabric's role in sports, economics, and fashion. The solution is a series of profiles packages into a "hops sack." The value of the piece comes from its distillation of many aspects of the subject into something that engages, entertains, enlightens, and informs the user on many levels.

Sharon Werner

Sharon Werner is principal and designer of Werner Design Werks Inc. in Minneapolis. After starting her career fresh out of college at Duffy Design Group, Sharon opened WDW in 1991 with no clients and no prospects, keeping her fingers crossed.

Visual language accompanied by sound design solutions soon attracted clients that include Chronicle Books, Nick at Nite, VH-1 Networks, Foote, Cone & Belding, Minnesota Public Radio, Amazon.com, Comedy Central, fX Cable Station, Urban Outfitters, MTV Latino, and Nike. Werner Design Werks has been recognized with national and international awards and honors. Their work is included in the 100 World's Best Posters and is part of the permanent collection of the Library of Congress, the Paris Musee de la Poste, the Victoria and Albert Museum in London, and the Cooper-Hewitt, National Design Museum in New York.

Title *Mohawk 50/10 Plus*
Authors *Jeff Mueller and Laura Shore*
Design Firm *Werner Design Werks, Minneapolis, MN*
Creative Director *Laura Shore*
Art Director *Sharon Werner*
Graphic Designers *Sharon Werner and Sarah Nelson*
Photographer *Darrell Eager*
Typeface *Futura*
Printer *Heartland Graphics*
Paper *Mohawk 50/10 Plus*

Title *Cheetah Valley Wine*
Design Firm *Werner Design Werks, Minneapolis, MN*
Art Director *Sharon Werner*
Graphic Designers *Sharon Werner and Sarah Nelson*
Photographer *Rip Saw Photography*
Typeface *Hand Lettered / Elvis Swift*
Printer *Ace Label, Creative Carton*
Paper *Label Stock*

Heartport 1996 Annual Report

Design Firm • *Bill Cahan & Associates,*
San Francisco, CA
Creative Director • *Bill Cahan*
Graphic Designer • *Craig Bailey*
Photographers • *Ken Schles, Tony Stromberg,*
and William Mercer McLeod
Copywriter • *Jim Weiss*
Typefaces • *Trade Gothic Condensed and*
Trade Gothic Condensed Bold
Printer • *Alan Lithograph, Inc.*
Paper • *Cougar 80# White*
Client • *Heartport, Inc.*

Project Statement
Heartport is advancing the frontiers of cardiac surgery
by developing systems that enable minimally invasive
approaches to major heart surgery. The company's port
access systems allow surgeons to operate on the heart
without needing to crack open the chest, as required in
conventional heart surgery. The die-cut holes in the annual
report are the exact size and approximate location of the
company's port access holes. The annual was designed to
be a compelling snapshot of the advantages of port access
over conventional heart surgery.

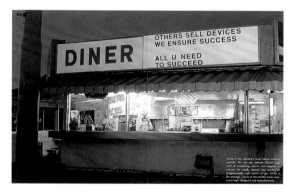

Xilinx 1997 Annual Report

Design Firm • *Bill Cahan & Associates,*
San Francisco, CA
Creative Director • *Bill Cahan*
Graphic Designer • *Kevin Roberson*
Photographer • *William Mercer McLeod*
Copywriter • *Thom Elkjer*
Typefaces • *Caslon, Found Letters*
Printer • *Alan Lithograph*
Paper • *Springhill Inventive, Mead Richgloss*
Client • *Xilinx*

Project Statement

The reduced size and densely packed cover symbolize
a Xilinx semi-conductor chip, demonstrating a focus on
increased density while reducing size. The attached magni-
fying lens allows the reader to zoom in on the text and
detailed charts. Inside, photos reveal a series of attractions
along the "Technological Highway" with the signage
changed to reveal Xilinx's key messages.

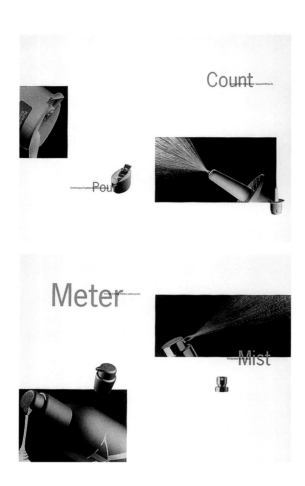

Aptar Group 1996 Annual Report

Design Firm • *SamataMason, Dundee, IL*
Art Directors • *Pat Samata and Greg Samata*
Graphic Designers • *Kevin Krueger, Erik Cox, and Jack Jacobi*
Photographer • *Sandro*
Writer • *Jerry Schwimmer and Ralph Poltermann*
Typeface • *Trade Gothic*
Printer • *Bruce Offset*
Paper • *Monadnock Astrolite Vellum 80# Cover and 100# Text, Champion Carnival Vellum Moss 70# Text*
Client • *Aptar Group*

Project Statement
Aptar Group is a international supplier of convenience dispensing products for the fragrance/cosmetics, personal care, pharmaceutical, household, and food markets. Through the use of type and photography, we displayed the broad range of these products, which are part of every consumer's daily life.

Design Firm • *Bill Cahan & Associates,*
San Francisco, CA
Creative Director • *Bill Cahan*
Graphic Designer/Illustrator •
Kevin Roberson
Photographers • *Keith Bardin, John Kolesa,*
and Tony Stromberg
Copywriters • *Marc Bernstein and*
Alicia Cimbora
Typefaces • *Trade Gothic, Courier, and Orator*
Printer • *Lithographix*
Paper • *Cougar White Vellum, French*
Dur-O-Tone Gold Primer, Strathmore Elements
Grid, Railroad Board, Mylar, and Manila
Envelope
Client • *COR Therapeutics, Inc.*

Project Statement
Each year, COR includes an educational section in their annual report that gives readers background and insight into the world of cardiovascular care. This year, we looked at the cases of three patients diagnosed with cardiovascular disease. A physician's docket contains many of the tests, reports, and documents that each patient must undergo. Included in the docket are an angiogram in a slipsleeve, EKG strips, a thallium scan, and a cath report.

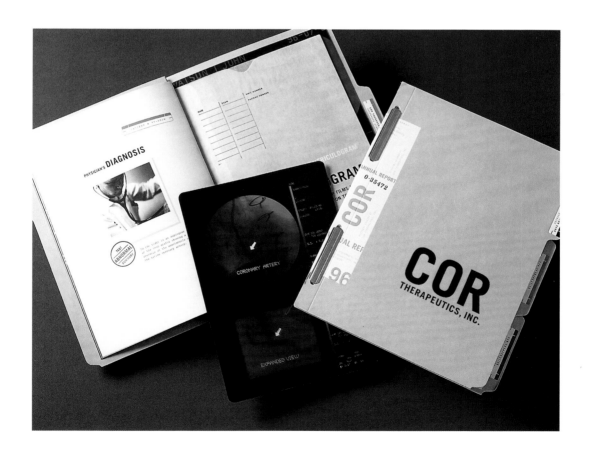

Design Firm • *Bill Cahan & Associates,*
San Francisco, CA
Creative Director • *Bill Cahan*
Graphic Designer • *Sharrie Brooks*
Photographers • *Various*
Copywriter • *Executive Communications*
Typefaces • *Univers 55, Adobe Caslon*
Printer • *George Rice & Sons*
Paper • *Cougar Opaque Vellum 80#,*
Starwhite Vicksburg Hitech
Client • *GaSonics International Corporation*

Project Statement
GaSonics International is the world leader in Integrated Clean Solutions, an expanding and increasingly important phase of semiconductor manufacturing. Currently, processes for cleaning wafer surfaces are becoming segmented as manufacturers introduce new materials — new cleaning processes must be developed to remove tougher residues from increasingly smaller areas. The annual report comes sealed in a Band Aid-like wrap that must be torn open to read the book inside, playing off the "clean is critical" theme. The diagrams inside illustrate the problems that face the industry and GaSonic's solution to these problems.

Performance Leader

20,000

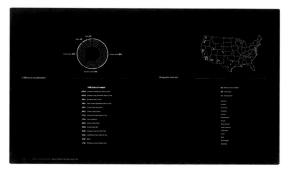

Reliance Steel & Aluminum Co. 1997 Annual Report

Design Firm • *Louey/RubinoDesign Group Inc.,*
Santa Monica, CA
Creative Director • *Robert Louey*
Graphic Designers • *Robert Louey and*
Tammy Kim
Photographer • *Eric Tucker*
Writer • *Kim Feazle*
Typeface • *Trade Gothic*
Printer • *Lithographix*
Paper • *Mead Signature Dull and*
Gilbert Gilclear Medium
Client • *Reliance Steel & Aluminum*

Project Statement

Following its third successful year as a public company,
Reliance Steel & Aluminum wanted to outline not only the
story of their excellence but also the reasons and the philosophy of their growth: customer service, product diversifi-
cation, and increased market share through acquisition.

Using transparent vellum sheets that involve the reader
in the story as they unfold, we told the story of management's approach to a hard-core manufacturing business with
a sophisticated attitude. The goal is quietly stated on the
vellum while the dramatic duotone photography shouts the
results in bold white type. The shape of the book, its
rounded corners and bolt binding, reflects the products that
the company produces.

Chicago Volunteer Legal Services 1997 Annual Report

Design Firm • *Froeter Design Co., Inc.,*
Chicago, IL
Creative Director/Graphic Designer •
Tim Bruce
Photographer • *Tony Armour*
Writers • *M. Lee Witte and Margaret C. Benson*
Printer • *H. MacDonald Printing*
Paper • *Canson Vellum 29# and Starwhite*
Vicksburg 80# Text
Client • *Chicago Volunteer Legal Services*

Project Statement
Chicago Volunteer Legal Services is the state's largest
general law firm serving the working poor, a fact often
misunderstood by the public. This year's annual report takes
a trip through five general practice areas of the organization, illustrating their law work through the eyes of their
beneficiaries. CVLS believes equal access to the law cannot
carry a price tag.

Design Firm • *Bill Cahan & Associates,*
San Francisco, CA
Creative Director • *Bill Cahan*
Graphic Designer • *Bob Dinetz*
Illustrators • *Lorraine Maschler and*
Bob Dinetz
Photographers • *Etta Clark,*
William Mercer McLeod, and Geron Corporation
Copywriter • *Carole Melis*
Typefaces • *Rosewood Fill and Trade Gothic*
Printer • *Alan Lithograph*
Paper • *Lexan Mylar, Endeavor Velvet Cover*
& Book, Champion Benefit Chalk Vellum
Client • *Geron Corporation*

Project Statement

Geron is working to discover drugs that will provide thera-
pies for age-related diseases such as cancer. Our approach
in designing the large-format book was to embrace the idea
that breakthroughs in science can lead to a healthier life.
The combination of microscope images of cells next to portraits of senior athletes conveys this idea. The importance
of the issue is highlighted in a section in which people
respond to the question, "What does getting old mean to
you?" Geron research programs are shown as informal
sketches meant to feel as if the scientists had drawn them
while talking to the reader.

   Intended to accompany the annual report or live on its
own, the pocket-size book also asks the question, "What
does getting old mean to you?" Photos of the respondents
and their answers are highlighted throughout the book.
Readers are given a chance to participate by answering on
a tear-out reply postcard.

Swiss Army Brands 1996 Annual Report

Design Firm • *SamataMason, Dundee, IL*
Art Director • *Dave Mason*
Graphic Designers • *Pamela Lee, Dave Mason*
Photographer • *Victor John Penner*
Writer • *Steven Zousmer*
Typeface • *Helvetica*
Printer • *H. MacDonald Printing*
Paper • *Potlatch Eloquence Silk 100# Cover
and 100# Text, Fox River Coronado SST
Modified Antique 80# Text*
Client • *Swiss Army Brands, Inc.*

Project Statement
This report was designed to demonstrate Swiss Army
Brand's approach to business. That form follows function
not only in the company's products but also in its
corporate structure and systems.

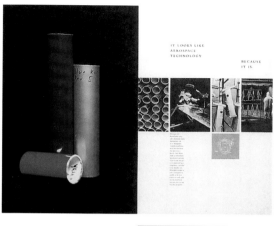

Klein Catalogue

Design Firm • *Bill Cahan & Associates,*
San Francisco, CA
Creative Director • *Bill Cahan*
Graphic Designer • *Bob Dinetz*
Illustrators • *Bob Dinetz and*
Trek Bicycle Corporation
Photographer • *Robert Schlatter*
Copywriter • *Lisa Jhung*
Typeface • *Bembo*
Printer • *Lithographix*
Paper • *Mead Signature*
Client • *Trek Bicycle Corporation*

Project Statement
Our intent was to create a catalogue that would stand out
from the competition in a noisy adrenaline-hungry industry,
tell the unique story of Klein, and justify the cost of their
bicycles. These goals were accomplished through a conservative, quiet design that focused on Gary Klein, an MIT
engineer, and featured elegant photographs of the technology that makes the bikes perform the way they do.

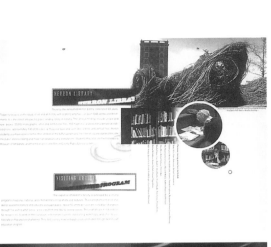
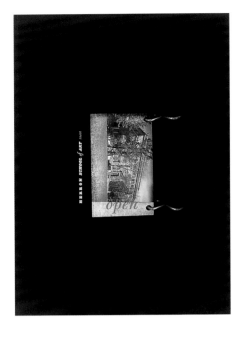

Herron School of Art Prospectus

Design Firm • *Loft 219, New York, NY*
Graphic Designers • *Elisabeth Charman
and Bradley Trost*
Photographers • *Elisabeth Charman,
Jenny Ganser, Joh Hines, and Jun Itoi*
Typefaces • *Bulmer, Ziggurat, and
Helvetica Neue*
Printer • *Mossberg and Company, Inc.*
Client • *Herron School of Art, IUPUI*

Project Statement
Herron School of Art's prospectus is used as a tool to
gain the attention of potential students. In considering
how to present the information, we separated each section
through materials and formal language. The portfolio section presents the students' artwork in more of a traditional
manner, in contrast to the front sections, which are given
to fits of fussiness. The success of the prospectus is simply
in its embodiment of the energy and spirit of Herron.

Design Firm • *Jennifer Sterling Design,*
San Francisco, CA
Art Director/Graphic Designer •
Jennifer Sterling
Illustrator • *Jennifer Sterling*
Copywriter • *Lisa Citron*
Typefaces • *Garamond, Futura*
Printer • *Active Graphics*
Paper • *Fox River Mystic Blue Cover,*
Howard Text
Client • *Blue Shield of California*

Bhoss Promo CD

Design Firm • *Jennifer Sterling Design,*
San Francisco, CA
Art Director/Graphic Designer •
Jennifer Sterling
Illustrator • *Jennifer Sterling*
Copywriter • *Deonne Kahler*
Typefaces • *Various*
Printer • *Rohner Letterpress*
Paper • *Crown Coaster Stock*
Client • *Bhoss*

Project Statement
The objective was to create an innovative packaging design for the band Bhoss. The packaging is metal die cut top and bottom and the lyrics are letterpressed (both sides) on coaster stock. Each coaster holds the lyrics to an individual song, and depicts the lyrics and musical style of that song.

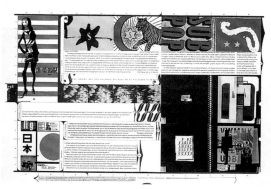

U&lc Magazine (Vol. XXIII, No. IV, Spring 1997)

Design Firm • *Johnson & Wolverton,
Portland, OR*
Art Directors • *Alicia Johnson and
Hal Wolverton*
Graphic Designers • *Hal Wolverton,
Heath Lowe, and Robin Muir*
Client • *U/lc, International Typeface
Corporation*

Project Statement
We were apprehensive about the prospect of designing
an issue of *U&lc*, since the body of ITC's typography is
not reflective of current developments in the world of type.
We were aware of the wit and lyricism of the *U&lc* that
Herb Lubalin created and subsequently of the way *Emigre*
and others have eclipsed the role that ITC and *U&lc* had
played. How the publisher could claim a position of relevance was unclear.

Since the issue focused on concurrent global trends in
graphic design, we showed the various articles concurrently
rather than sequentially. Harmonious layers reflect harmonious design. Dissonant layers reflect dissonant design
trends. The grid was based on the breaking down of the
ITC Bodoni Old Style family (6, 7, and 12) — a claim
ITC could make to relevance — and was influenced by
classic map and timeline metaphors and constructions. This
issue inspired empassioned letters to the publication, quite
mixed — another installment in the ongoing philosophic
debate in design between old and new.

Dicksons AIGA Promotion

Design Firm • *Design: M/W, New York, NY*
Creative Director • *J. Phillip Williams*
Graphic Designers • *Allison Muench-Williams,*
Mats Hakansson, Ariel Apte
Client/Printer • *Dicksons Inc.*

Project Statement
Dickson's commissioned this piece to showcase their abilities as a specialty printer and engraver to the designers attending the AIGA's National Design conference in New Orleans. They requested that the piece be a commemorative reminder of New Orleans. We chose to make the piece in scrapbook format, which naturally calls for many different kinds of materials to be combined, thereby making the large range of techniques that Dickson's wanted to show make sense in one piece. In addition, Dickson's positioned themselves as problem solvers who can realize unique techniques. The irreverent use of engraving and foil stamping, as well as the complexity of the piece, immediately conveys their willingness to experiment and competence at producing a quality result.

Design Firm • *Design: M/W, New York, NY*
Creative Directors • *Allison Muench-Williams
and J. Phillips Williams*
Graphic Designer • *Allison Muench-Williams*
Photographer • *Marie Robledo*
Copywriter • *Laura Silverman*
Typefaces • *Filosofia and ITC Bodoni 72*
Printer • *Hennegan*
Paper • *French Parchtone*
Client • *Takashimaya New York*

Project Statement
That Takashimaya is a breed apart from the traditional
retail store is immediately conveyed by the unconventional
"envelope" that houses their gift catalogue. The use of
various shades of red throughout the piece and the photographic sets serves to unite a disparate range of merchandise.
The piece reflects the store in several other ways: the
commingling of Eastern and Western aesthetics, the subtle
interplay of a multitude of textures, and the juxtaposition-
ing of simple utilitarian and highly decorative design
elements.

Elvis Swift Promo

Design Firm • *Werner Design Werks Inc.,*
Minneapolis, MN
Art Director • *Sharon Werner*
Graphic Designer • *Sharon Werner,*
Sarah Nelson
Illustrator • *Elvis Swift*
Printer • *Nomadic Press*
Client • *Joanie Bernstein: Art Rep*

Project Statement
When Elvis sends out his portfolio, it looks much like this.
He draws on any sort of paper scrap, often ripped, folded,
or stained, and it only adds to the beauty of work. The
challenge was to recreate this very personal quality and mass
produce it. This was done so by using a wide variety of
unusual papers and letterpress printing them for the maximum tactile experience.

New Work 2

Design Firm • *Tolleson Design,*
San Francisco, CA
Creative Director • *Steve Tolleson*
Art Director/ Graphic Designer •
Jean Orlebake
Photographers • *Neal Brown, Ann Elliott*
Cutting, Hugh Kretschmer, Jamey Stillings,
and Everard Williams, Jr.
Copywriter • *John Sharpe*
Typefaces • *Berthold Script, Brown*
(Tolleson Design font), Courier, Democratica,
Garamond, Keedy Sans, Madrone, OCRB,
Orator, Syntax, Trade Gothic, Trajan, Univers
Printer • *Prisma Graphic Corporation*
Paper • *Glassine, Starwhite Vicksburg*
110# Cover, Tiara White, Smooth Finish
Client • *Sharpe & Associates, Inc.*

Project Statement
New Work 2 is a direct-mail promotion piece targeted
to buyers of commercial photography. We wanted a mailer
that stood out in terms of scope, production values, overall
design, and uniqueness. Paper choices, type design, and
overall tone came from the artfulness of the imagery and
the desire to connote a gallery experience with the viewer.
Perforation was added to make the work seem more accessible and increase the piece's usability. The vellum envelope
is an attention-getting setup for the quiet elegance of the
contents.

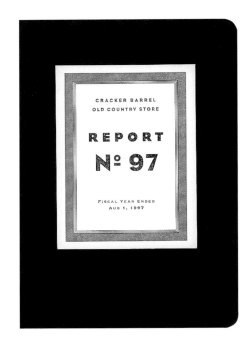

Cracker Barrel Old Country Store 1997 Annual Report

Design Firm • *Thomas Ryan Design,*
Nashville, TN
Art Director/Graphic Designer •
Thomas Ryan
Photographer • *Jim McGuire*
Copywriter • *John Baeder*
Typeface • *Modern*
Printer • *Lithographics*
Paper • *Fox River Leather, French Dur-O-Tone,*
French Construction
Client • *Cracker Barrel Old Country Store, Inc.*

Project Statement
Since Cracker Barrel restaurants feature rural American comfort foods in the setting of an old country store, the annual report's narrative uses fragments of nostalgia to invoke warm memories of the past.

The almanac-size book fits in the hand like a small black bible. French-folded full-bleed color divider sections using cropped pieces of rural advertising images of the '30s and '40s surround black-and-white letterpress text sections. Since the restaurant chain is expanding out of the South to a national presence, the narrative text describes anecdotes about favorite foods told by regional voices. Black and white quadrotones of food contrast the brightly colored dividers.

Design Firm • *Planet Design Co,*
Madison, WI
Creative Directors • *Kevin Wade and*
Lori O'Projects
Graphic Designers • *Martha Graettinger*
and Kevin Wade
Photographer • *Stock*
Writer • *Lori O'Projects*
Typeface • *Interstate Family*
Printer • *American Printing*
Fabricator • *Boom Design (Metal Binder)*
Paper • *Neenah Classic Crest*
Sound Editor • *Haggar Studios*
Client • *Miller Brewing Co.*

Design Firm • *Victore Design Works,*
New York, NY
Creative Director • *Gimma Gatti*
Graphic Designer • *James Victore*
Photographer • *Thomas Schierlitz*
Writer • *Sally Hogshead*
Typefaces • *Sabon, Univers*
Printer • *Graphic Press*
Client • *Portfolio Center*

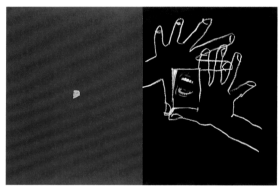

Russell Sage Viewbook

Design Firm • *Rutka Weadock Design,*
Baltimore, MD
Art Directors • *Anthony Rutka and*
Priscilla Henderer
Graphic Designer • *Priscilla Henderer*
Illustrator • *Steve Vance, Jonathan Carlson,*
and Marc Rosenthal
Photographers • *Mark Ferri, Bob Krist,*
and Bruce Weller
Writer • *Joan Weadock*
Typefaces • *Letter Gothic, Meta, and Biorst*
Printer • *Peake Printers, Inc.*
Paper • *Finch Fine Opaque*
Client • *Russell Sage College*

Project Statement

The viewbook is the primary admission recruiting publication sent out to high school students by Russell Sage College, a women's college in Troy, New York.

We wanted to develop a viewbook that gets down to the nitty gritty of higher education. We got rid of the slick production, pretty pictures, and superficial text common to most college publications and emphasized content. The folder/mailer contained a montage of 140 photos to show people and places around campus, so we were able to use visuals in the viewbook that really speak to the copy ideas.

The report helped raise $10 million in eight months. It won awards of gold, silver and other colors. It was in the AR100, a selection of the world's top 200 annual reports. The writing won a gold award, too. So the boys did more reports, for companies that made movies and corn chips and computer codes. One was in a list of the seven best reports of the year. Magazines asked Frank how he designed the reports, and he told them.

One day Frank said, "I know—why don't we get someone in a movie to hold up one of our brochures?"
"I'll bet that costs a lot of money," Doug said. "And they might not h—
willing to say our names out loud."
"Okay," Frank said. "Let's do an annual report instead."
So they did, for the the YMCA of Greater Toronto.

Let's Sell Ourselves!

A Frank & Doug Adventure

Let's Sell Ourselves

Design Firm • *Viva Dolan Communications*
& Design, Toronto, Ontario
Art Director/Graphic Designer • *Frank Viva*
Illustrator • *Frank Viva*
Photographer • *Hill Peppard*
Writer • *Doug Dolan*
Typeface • *Meta*
Printer • *C.J. Graphics*
Fabricator • *Ansley Bookbinding*
Client • *Viva Dolan*

Project Statement
We wanted to create a self-promotional piece that potential clients would notice and keep on their shelves. We were inpsired in part by one of our clients, Golden Books, whose classic story books were scattered around our studio. The format enabled us to show portfolio highlights without the predictability of a catalogue, but rather by weaving examples in among the playful illustrations and story line. Above all, the story book was an ideal way to explain our firm through words and pictures working together, in an ironic simplification of what we do for our clients.

Butterfield & Robinson Biking Catalogue

Design Firm • *Viva Dolan Communications &*
Design, Toronto, Ontario
Art Director/Graphic Designer • *Frank Viva*
Illustrator • *Malcolm Hill*
Photographer • *Ron Baxter Smith*
Writer • *Doug Dolan*
Typeface • *Mrs Eaves*
Printer • *Arthurs Jones Inc.*
Paper • *Evergreen Matte Natural Text,*
Carolina Cover
Client • *Butterfield & Robinson*

Project Statement
Butterfield & Robinson's annual catalogues are designed
to reinforce the company's position as the world leader in
biking and walking vacations for a sophisticated, upscale
North American clientele. For 1998, we sought to take the
best of our previous work in a new direction — most
notably in the introductory gallery of full-page photographs
with interplaying type. Also new was the continuous strip
of photo images that complements each spread, emphasizing
that these are biking trips. Finally, we commissioned an
illustrated cover that sets the tone — fun, urbane, culturally
sophisticated — for readers who see the catalogue as a
reflection of their own tastes.

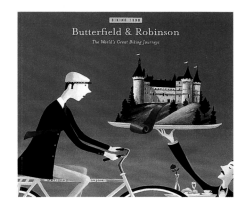

Tom Brochure

Design Firm • *Concrete Design*
Communications, Inc., Toronto, Ontario
Art Directors • *Diti Katona and*
John Pylypczak
Graphic Designer • *John Pylypczak*
Photographer • *Karen Levy*
Copywriter • *John Pylypczak*
Typeface • *Bell Centennial*
Printer • *Arthurs-Jones Inc.*
Paper • *Warren Lustro Dull*
Client • *Keilhauer Industries*

Project Statement
This brochure was used to introduce a new office chair —
called "Tom." Although the chair was fashioned with the
lastest technology, the brochure instead emphasizes its simplicity, beauty, functionality, and friendly appeal.

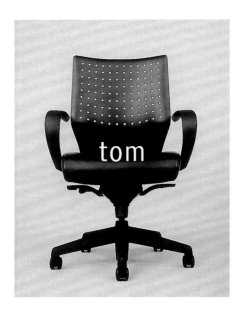

AIGA/Minnesota Design Camp '97 Brochure

Design Firm • *Haley Johnson Design Co.,*
Minneapolis, MN
Art Director • *Haley Johnson*
Graphic Designer/Illustrator •
Haley Johnson
Writer • *Jeff Mueller (Floating Head)*
Typefaces • *Trade Gothic and Clarendon*
Printer • *Challenge Printing*
Paper • *Utopia Premium Ivory Matte*
115# Text
Client • *AIGA/Minnesota*

Project Statement
Potential participants were tempted with fun, illustrative
characters enjoying a stress-free weekend at Design Camp,
where seriousness is left behind and we can remember
why we fell in love with graphic design in the first place.

AIGA Sound Off Competition Certificate of Excellence

Design Firm • *Spot Design, New York, NY*
Creative Designer • *Drew Hodges*
Graphic Designer • *Kevin Brainard*
Typefaces • *Champion, Rockwell Condensed,*
Leviathan, Trade Gothic
Printer • *Evatone*
Client • *AIGA*

Skate School Booklet

Design Firm • *Nike, Inc., Beaverton, OR*

Art Director • *Dan Richards*

Graphic Designers • *Dan Richards and James Parker*

Illustrators • *Dan Richards and James Parker*

Writer • *Neil Webster*

Typeface • *Franklin Gothic Modified*

Printer • *Irwin Hodson*

Paper • *French Butcher*

Client • *Nike Equipment*

Project Statement

The purpose of the Skate School booklet was to teach sales clerks the basic technical features of Nike inline skates. After studying the booklet, clerks were asked to take a test and could win prizes for high scores. The booklet's small size made it handy to use as a reference guide. The simple illustrations and retro look related to the corresponding skate school educational filmstrip.

Cadence 1996 Annual Report

Design Firm • *Bill Cahan & Associates,*
San Francisco, CA
Creative Director • *Bill Cahan*
Graphic Designer • *Bob Dinetz*
Illustrators • *Mark Todd, Riccardo Vecchio,*
Jason Holley, and Bob Dinetz
Photographers • *Tony Stromberg and*
Amy Guip
Copywriter • *John Mannion*
Typefaces • *Trade Gothic and Bembo*
Printer • *Lithographix*
Paper • *Kashmir and Cougar*
Client • *Cadence Design Systems, Inc.*

Project Statement
Cadence benefits from technology getting too complicated. As electronics become smaller and more difficult to design, Cadence's business grows. The irony of this situation is captured on the cover and opening pages of this report. A great year for Cadence is when the process gets too complicated for customers to handle on their own. Several different styles of illustration and photography are placed next to each other to suggest the wide range of products that use Cadence technology.

IT'S BEEN
A GREAT YEAR.

**FEELS DIFFERENT,
DOESN'T IT?**

CADENCE 1996 ANNUAL REPORT

Matre Productions Promotion

Design Firm • *Haley Johnson Design Co.,*
Minneapolis, MN
Art Director • *Haley Johnson*
Graphic Designer • *Richard Boynton*
Illustrator • *Haley Johnson*
Writer • *Richard Boynton*
Typefaces • *Trade Gothic and Garamond*
Printer • *Gopher State Litho*
Paper • *Utopia Premium 100# Cover,*
Blue White Silk
Client • *Matre Productions*

Project Statement
Potential clients were reached with this accordion-fold
promotion in the shape of a Polaroid print. It literally draws
a connection between Matre's print and film work. Matre's
print work is used as the foundation for the illustrations,
which reinforce the film aspects of Matre's business.

Channel One Teen Fact Book

Design Firm • *Lee Hunt Associates,*
New York, NY
Creative Director • *Cheri Dorr*
Graphic Designer • *David J. High*
Illustrator • *David J. High*
Writer • *Sharon Glassman*
Typefaces • *Franklin Gothic, Platelet,*
Trade Gothic, and Zapf Dingbats
Printer • *Manhattan Color*
Client • *Channel One Network*

Project Statement
The *Teen Fact Book* is a research tool developed by
Channel One Network targeting the marketing and advertising community. There were two main objectives in the
creation of this book. The first was to position Channel
One Network as an expert among the teen demographic.
The other objective was to create a hip reference guide
that reflected the brand and lifestyle preferences of the ever-
elusive teen. Production note: because of a limited budget,
the interior of the book was created as a two-color job and
the exterior as a one-color foil stamp.

Anni Kuan Stationery

Design Firm • *Sagmeister Inc.,*
New York, NY
Art Director • *Stefan Sagmeister*
Graphic Designers • *Stefan Sagmeister and*
Hjalti Karlsson
Typeface • *Franklin Gothic*
Printer • *Dependable Printing*
Fabricator • *Lasercraft*
Paper • *Strathmore Writing*
Client • *Anni Kuan*

Project Statement
The business card for this New York fashion designer
consists of two abstract, somehow Asian-looking patterns.
The logo appears (and becomes readable) only when
you fold the card over. The same is true for the stationery,
where the logo is completed only when the letterhead is
inside the transparent envelope.

Blink Stationery

Design Firm • *Concrete Design*
Communications, Inc., Toronto, Ontario
Art Directors • *Diti Katona and John Pylypczak*
Graphic Designer • *Dana Samuel*
Illustrator • *Christian Northeast*
Typeface • *Grotesque*
Printer • *Wood Printing and Graphics Inc.*
Paper • *French Speckletone*
Client • *Blink Pictures*

Project Statement
Blink Pictures represents film directors for the advertising industry. We commissioned Christian Northeast to provide an illustration as an identifying visual for the various promotional materials. In addition, the word "blink" wraps around the other side of the letterhead, business card, etc., as a visual pun on the company name.

Matre Productions Stationery

Design Firm • *Haley Johnson Design Co.,*
Minneapolis, MN
Art Director • *Haley Johnson*
Graphic Designer • *Richard Boynton*
Typefaces • *Trade Gothic and Garamond*
Printer • *Flair Print Communications*
Paper • *Mohawk Superfine 70# Text,*
Ultrawhite Smooth
Client • *Matre Productions*

Project Statement
This stationery system was inspired by the dual capabilities
offered by Matre, film and print. A screen test pattern was
the inspiration for the logo. The use of red, green, and
blue on alternate items of the stationery system relates to
the three colors used on the TV screen, from which all
other colors are made. The technical drawing of projection,
and the use of metallic silver, refer to the print side of
Matre's business.

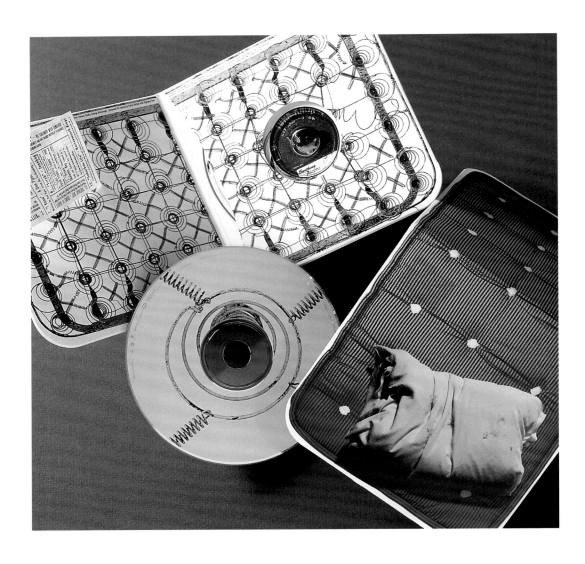

Strange Bedfellows CD

Design Firm • *Capitol Records,*
Hollywood, CA
Art Directors/Graphic Designers •
Tommy Steele and George Mimnaugh
Photographer • *Larry Dupont*
Typeface • *Futura Condensed*
Printer • *AGI, Inc.*
Paper • *10pt. C1S Board*
Client • *Capitol Records*

Project Statement
Periodically, we are asked to provide a sampler of our
upcoming releases for our marketing department. In this
case, the South X Southwest music convention in Austin,
Texas, provided the incentive. We're always looking for
ways to get noticed and to actually have our music listened
to; a good conceptual package could help that cause. We
heard that our marketing team wanted to rent an old rusty
bed and roll it down the main street of Austin and give
away these promotional compact disks. We're not sure if
that happened, but flattered that we inspire such pranks.

Pat Metheny Group "Imaginary Day" CD

Design Firm • *Sagmeister Inc., New York, NY*
Art Director • *Stefan Sagmeister*
Graphic Designer • *Hjalti Karlsson*
Photographer • *Tom Schierlitz, Stock*
Copywriter • *Pat Metheny Group*
Typeface • *Trade Gothic*
Printer • *Warner Media Services, Ivy Hill*
Fabricator • *WEA*
Paper • *80# Coated Gloss*
Client/Publisher • *Warner Bros. Records, Inc.*

Project Statement
All type on the "Imaginary Day" cover for the Pat
Metheny Group has been replaced by code. The images
connect to the songs and mood of the album and can be
decoded by using the diagram printed on the CD itself.
A twelve-page booklet with more coded type/imagery
is also included.

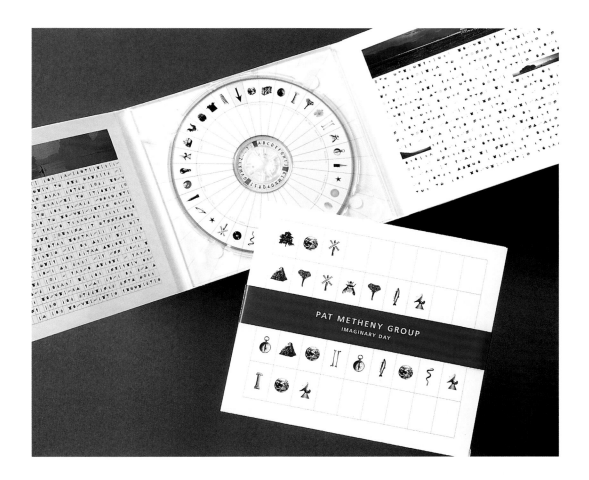

David Byrne "Feelings" CD

Design Firm • *Sagmeister Inc.,*
New York, NY
Art Director • *Stefan Sagmeister*
Graphic Designer • *Hjalti Karlsson*
Model Maker • *Yuji Koshimoto*
Photographer • *Tom Schierlitz*
Copywriter • *David Byrne*
Typefaces • *Trade Gothic, Frutiger, and*
Franklin Gothic
Printer • *Warner Media Services/Ivy Hill*
Fabricator • *WEA*
Paper • *80# Coated Gloss*
Client/Publisher • *Warner Bros. Records, Inc.*

Project Statement
This round-cornered "Feelings" CD packaging features happy, angry, sad, and content David Byrne dolls. The packaging includes a sophisticated color-coded David Byrne Mood Computer (printed on and under the disk) that lets you determine your current feelings. The type was made as a model and then photographed.

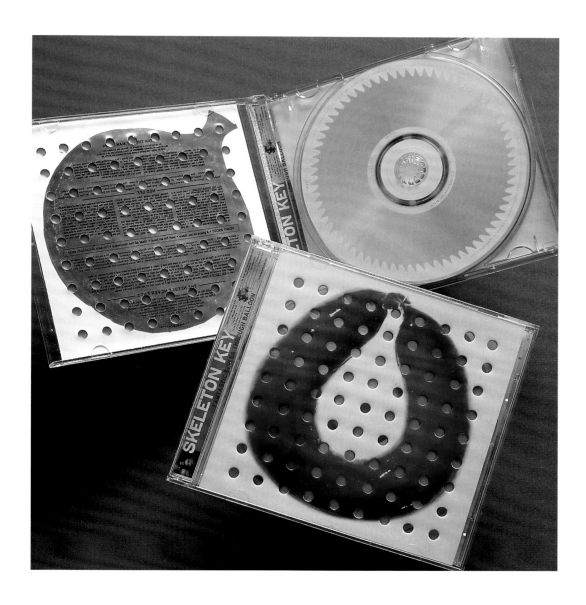

Skeleton Key "Fantastic Spikes Through Balloon" CD

Design Firm • *Sagmeister Inc., New York, NY*
Art Director • *Stefan Sagmeister*
Graphic Designer • *Hjalti Karlsson*
Photographer • *Tom Schierlitz*
Copywriter • *Skeleton Key*
Typefaces • *News Gothic, Hand Type*
Paper • *80# Coated Gloss*
Client • *Capitol Records*

Project Statement
True to the album title "Fantastic Spikes Through
Balloon," we photographed all the balloon-like objects
we could think of (sausage, whoopee cushion, blowfish,
etc.) and punched a lot of holes through them. Since
the band did not want their audience to read the lyrics
while listening to the music ("This is not a poetry affair"),
the words to the songs are printed flipped so they are only
readable when seen reflected in the mirror of the CD.

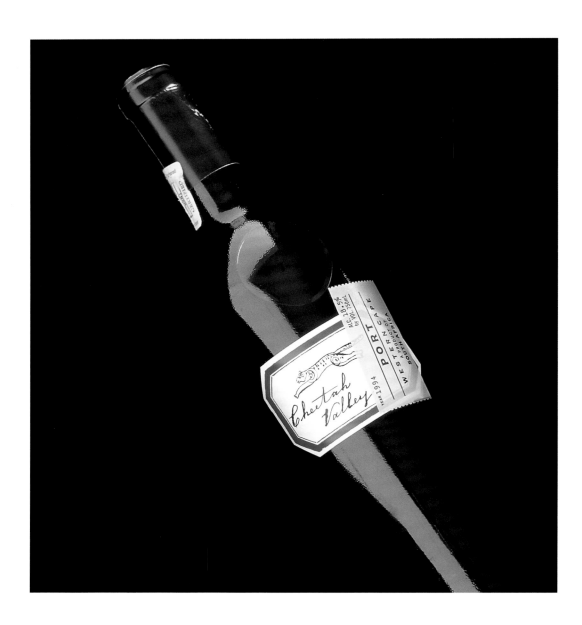

Cheetah Valley Port Label

Design Firm • *Werner Design Werks Inc.,*
Minneapolis, MN
Art Director • *Sharon Werner*
Graphic Designer • *Sharon Werner,*
Sarah Nelson
Illustrator • *Elvis Swift*
Printer • *Ace Label*
Client • *Rafiki Wine Co.*

Project Statement
This South African port label looks like a hand-labeled
bottle from a vintner's personal stock, a special gift from a
limited vintage, personally selected. The script is reminiscent of a classic French wine label, but goes back to a time
when the script was not typeset, but rendered by a calligra-
pher. Because the labels had to be on a roll for application
purposes, one of the greatest challenges was reproducing the
aged quality with flexographic printing.

Briggs & Riley Accessories Packaging

Design Firm • *Gensler Studio,*
San Francisco, CA
Art Director • *Beth Novitsky*
Graphic Designer • *Cathy Noe*
Photographer • *Wendi Nordeck*
Typeface • *Avenir*
Printer • *Klearfold, RLV*
Client • *Briggs & Riley*

Project Statement
Based in Half Moon Bay, California, Briggs & Riley
manufactures and sells high-quality, mid-priced luggage.
As part of a comprehensive branding package, Gensler
Studio 585 developed accessories packaging that character-
izes their new identity: the "Par Avion" blue logo is reinforced by a time zone motif and the orange color refers to
Half Moon Bay's famous pumpkin festival. The packaging,
previously consisting of polybags, now better represents
the products' quality and price point. Cardboard sleeves
provide critical information about small-scale luggage items
while maintaining product visibility. To economize on
printing costs, pre-printed translucent plastic envelopes are
customized with clear product-specific stickers.

Superdrug Specialist Vitamin Supplements Packaging

Design Firm • *Turner Duckworth,*
San Francisco, CA
Creative Directors • *Bruce Duckworth,*
David Turner
Graphic Designer • *Bruce Duckworth*
Illustrator • *Justin De Lavinson*
Product Designer •
Graph Thompson/Product First
Client • *Superdrug*

Project Statement

The existing Superdrug vitamin range was confusing and inconsistent with the desired Superdrug personality, i.e., quality combined with fun and approachability. Given the complexity within the range, the design task was to create a simple system that could accommodate a vast product range — single vitamins, multi-vitamins, with added vitamins, children's vitamins, plus a more premium range commanding a higher price.

The solution was to create a design system made up of simple vitamin shapes (tablets or capsules). The shapes are superimposed on a super-vibrant color signposting system that used a new print technology. The communication hierarchy was then simplified and made consistent across the range. The end result is a range that is easier to select, easier to understand, and sings on the shelf.

In addition to the original carton shape, a new bottle shape was designed with a unique cap closure. The cap is helpful to the older generation, particularly arthritics, who can use a pen or similar item to open it. It can also be used as a hanging device.

Superdrug Bathroom Accessories

Design Firm • *Turner Duckworth,*
San Francisco, CA
Creative Directors • *Bruce Duckworth,*
David Turner
Art Director • *Janice Davison*
Graphic Designer • *Ruper Rawlinson*
Illustrator • *Anton Morris*
Client • *Superdrug*

Project Statement

The brief was to create an icon to brand a diverse range of mainstream family bathroom accessories. The solution was a fluffy yellow plastic duck — a classic, nostalgic bathtime icon that works as a simple, consistent branding device across the range and communicates the fun and playfulness associated with family bathtime.

"Bravo Towell" Bravo Photo Masters Brochure

Design Firm • *Emerson Wajdowicz Studios, Inc.,*
New York, NY
Art Director • *Jurek Wajdowicz*
Graphic Designers • *Lisa La Rochelle*
and Jurek Wajdowicz
Photographer/Writer • *Larry Towell*
Printer • *Active Graphics, Inc.*
Paper • *Bravo Dull 100# Text and Cover*
Client • *E.B. Eddy Paper/Island Paper Mills*
Division

Project Statement
"Bravo Towell" is the third brochure in the Bravo Photo
Masters Series published by E.B. Eddy Paper, which presents a sampling of the best photojournalism in the world.
This brochure, produced on Bravo Dull stock, offers poetry
and drama of ordinary events. Beautiful photographs (using
a variety of duotones, tritones, and quadrotones) by Larry
Towell, rich in human contexts, are thoughtfully merged in
an understated design and typography into one expressive
and long-lasting new form.

"Eagle's Eye — A New Perspective" Catalogue

Design Firm • *Socio X, New York, NY*
Creative Director • *Bridget de Socio*
Graphic Designer • *Albert Lin*
Digital Imager • *Ninja van Oertzen*
Photographer • *Ivven Afanador*
Typeface • *Futura*
Printer • *Diversified Graphics*
Paper • *Gilbert Gilclear Translucent 90#,*
Mead Signature Dull 80# Cover
Client • *Eagle's Eye*

Project Statement
The Eagle's Eye catalogue of sweaters titled "A New Perspective" was produced and designed to reposition this conservative sweater maker. Its audience is composed of buyers of women's and children's apparel. We approached this new view of the classic sweater through the lens of a kaleidoscope. The classic sweater often shares its place with many more of the same, unlike the unusual couture piece or the special-occasion fashion statement. Using multiples and a new way of seeing something ordinary was an effective way to engage the existing buyers and renew interest in this conservative company.

Art Directors • *Eva Roberts and
Stanton Blakeslee*
Graphic Designers • *Stanton Blakeslee,
Dana Gay, and Eva Roberts*
Cover Illustrator • *Hayes Henderson*
Typefaces • *Adobe Stone Serif and Stone Sans*
Printer • *Carter Printing*
Paper • *Cross Pointe Torchglow Opaque*
(Archival Quality)

Project Statement
Based in the English department at East Carolina
University, the *North Carolina Literary Review* seeks to combine the best attributes of an academic journal with those of
a contemporary publication for serious readers. Nonfiction,
fiction, and poetry are linked thematically in an eclectic
manner with footnotes, etc., that follow Modern Language
Association guidelines. The design is structured around a
grid, consistent type families, and graphic elements. Though
interpretive and sometimes challenging, the typography is
designed with readability in mind. Our greatest asset is the
dedicated individuals (faculty, students, artists, volunteers)
who contribute to each issue. All are enthusiastic about language — visual and verbal — and where the two meet.

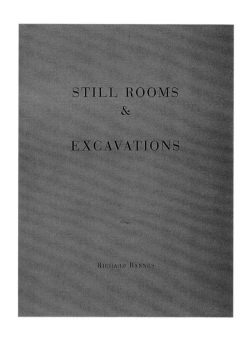

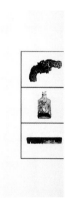

"Still Rooms and Excavations" Exhibition Catalogue

Design Firm • *Tenazas Design,*
San Francisco, CA
Art Director • *Lucille Tenazas*
Graphic Designers • *Lucille Tenazas and*
Kelly Tokerud
Photographer • *Richard Barnes*
Writer • *Richard Barnes and Doug Nickel*
Typeface • *Bodoni*
Printer • *The Studley Press*
Paper • *Mohawk Superfine,*
Warren Lustro Dull Enamel
Client • *Richard Barnes*

Project Statement
Still Rooms and Excavations was a collaborative effort with
my husband, Richard Barnes. This catalogue (and the
traveling exhibition it accompanies) documents the seismic
excavation of the DeYoung Museum in San Francisco
and the ensuing discovery of a potter's field. In designing
Still Rooms, my desire was to highlight the photographs
in a way both provocative and understated, allowing the
images to speak for themselves. My own intervention was
minimal out of respect for both Richard's work and for
those buried beneath the DeYoung. The size of *Still Rooms*
and Excavations reflects the enormity of the project itself,
a project that literally delved beneath the surface. Like the
site it documents, this piece has tactility and an emotional
draw that is palpable. The pacing of *Still Rooms* is as quiet
as the title suggests: hushed and measured, almost to the
point of stillness.

JOHN DEERE CREDIT HORIZONS ANNUAL REPORT 1997

John Deere Credit 1997 Annual Report

Design Firm • *SamataMason Inc., Dundee, IL*
Art Director • *Greg Samata*
Graphic Designers • *Joe Baran and Greg Samata*
Illustrator • *Nanette Biers*
Photographer • *Sandro*
Writer • *David Brija-Towery*
Typeface • *Garamond 3*
Printer • *Active Graphics*
Paper • *Neenah Havana Tobacco 111# Cover,*
Potlatch Karma 80# Text, Fox River Starwhite
Vicksburg Natural Vellum 70# Text
Client • *John Deere Credit*

Project Statement
From farm and construction equipment to boats and
recreational vehicles, John Deere Credit is in the business
of financing vehicles that are used in a variety of landscapes.
This annual report illustrates their horizons by showing
the various markets they serve. The goal was to show these
markets individually and together as a whole by placing
each next to another.

Design Firm • *Shanosky & Associates,*
Baltimore, MD
Art Director/Graphic Designer •
Adam Shanosky
Photographer • *Lise Metzger*
Copywriter • *Adam Shanosky*
Typeface • *ITC New Baskerville*
Printer • *Schneiderieth & Sons*
Paper • *Potlatch Karma 100# Dull Coated Text*
Client • *St. Mary's Foundation for Children*

Project Statement
The St. Mary's Foundation for Children annual report is used to recognize and thank the people who, through their support of the foundation, helped better the lives of children with special needs. The report seeks to establish an intimate link between the supporters (4,500 of whom must be listed individually) and the children, who despite their common endeavors, rarely interact. The design uses sparse yet poignant language to provide this link and build a sense of community among the supporters and children.

vitality and personality.

have found fruition in ways both intimate and significant beyond articulation.

Design Firm • *Spangler Associates, Seattle, WA*
Creative Director • *Allen Woodard*
Art Director • *Michael Connors*
Graphic Designers • *Michael Connors,*
Nadine Stellavato, Gabriel Campodonico
Illustrator • *Michael Connors*
Writer • *Michael Connors, Brad Ogura*
Typefaces • *Trade Gothic*
Printer • *Heath Printers*
Paper • *Weyerhaeuser Cougar Opaque*
Client • *NeoRx Corporation*

Project Statement
The challenge was to create a 10-K wrap for a severely reduced budget. At the same time, we needed to show that NeoRx has changed its way of thinking and doing business. In brief, NeoRx looks at things in a new way, beyond the obvious.

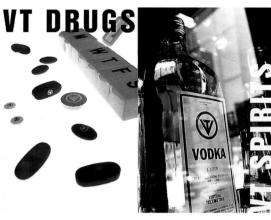

Virtual Telemetrix 1997 Annual Report

Design Firm • *Bielenberg Design,*
San Francisco, CA
Creative Director • *John Bielenberg*
Graphic Designers • *John Bielenberg and*
Chuck Denison
Photographer • *Victor John Penner*
Writer • *Chris Williams*
Typeface • *Helvetica*
Printer • *H. MacDonald Printing*
Paper • *Appleton Utopia Premium*
Blue White Silk 100# Text
Client • *Virtual Telemetrix*

Project Statement
In 1991, Bielenberg Design, under the pseudonym
Virtual Telemetrix, Inc. (VT), began a continuing series
of self-initiated creative projects that address issues related
to the practice of graphic design and the role of image-
making within our culture. Previous pieces in the series
include: a book, a 1993 annual report, a poster, a product
direct-mail catalogue, a T-shirt, and a website at
www.virtualtelemetrix.com. The VT corporate mission
statement is: "Design as a means of propagating corporate
myth to infiltrate consumer psychology."

As corporations have moved to replace church or state
in shaping our culture and behavior, the Virtual Telemetrix
1997 annual report hopes to illustrate this phenomenon.
The theme of the 1997 report is "A Brand New Year."
This report is designed to take a satiric look at corporate
branding and brand extension, as well as parody the annual
report as a communication vehicle. Virtual Telemetrix
has branded itself in these areas: products, media, culture,
sports, the workplace, communications, and politics.

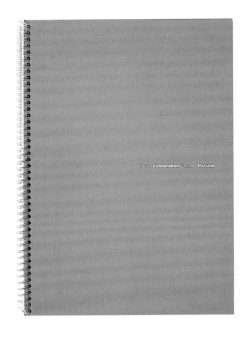

Volvo C70 Global Advertising Kit

Design Firm • *Messner Vetere Berger McNamee Schmetterer, New York, NY*
Creative Director • *Phil Silvestri*
Graphic Designers • *Warren Elwin and Todd Wilcox*
Photographer • *Albert Watson*
Writer • *Rich Roth*
Typeface • *Volvo Sans*
Printer • *Print Technical Group*
Paper • *16 Pt. Carolina Coated Cover, 80# Northwest Cover (Text)*
Client • *Volvo*

Lionel Classic Catalogue 1998

Design Firm • *Fitch, Inc., Worthington, OH*
Art Director • *Kwok C. Chan*
Graphic Designer • *Kian Huat Kuan*
Photographer • *Mark Steele*
Copywriter • *Michelle Geissbuhler*
Typefaces • *Futura and Rotis*
Printer • *Wintor Swan*
Paper • *Utopia Dull White*
Client • *Lionel LLC*

Project Statement

The Lionel Classic Catalogue 1998 showcases Lionel electric trains and related products for both retailers and collectors. Lionel asked us to give their catalogue a more contemporary look and also to combine two previously separate catalogues. Fitch updated the catalogue style by using creatively lighted and staged studio photography with sepia-toned location shots. Typography and layout are sophisticated, yet present information in easy to understand hierarchies. The 1998 catalogue has a dynamic new look while preserving the romance and nostalgia of the Lionel brand — appealing to the "pretender" train operators and avid hobbyists who collect and display model trains. A special collector's edition catalogue was produced that was serially numbered, slipcased, and featured an embossed cover with copper rail bindings as well as a special wraparound timeline chronicling significant events in Lionel's history.

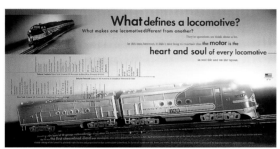

Michael Ray Charles Catalogue Series

Design Firm • *Rigsby Design, Houston, TX*

Art Director • *Lana Rigsby*

Graphic Designer • *Amy Wolpert*

Illustrator • *Michael Ray Charles*

Photographers • *Patrick Demarchelier and Sharon Seligman*

Writers • *Spike Lee, Don Bacigalupi, and Marilyn Kern-Foxworth*

Printer • *H. MacDonald Printing*

Paper • *Fox River Starlight Vicksburg*

Publisher/Client • *Laffer Gallery, University of Houston*

IBM Customer Reference CD-ROM

Design Firm • *Waters Design Associates,*
New York, NY
Creative Director • *John Paolini*
Graphic Designer • *Rob Pietri*
Senior Producer • *Deborah Velick*
Associate Producer • *Sheila Dehner*
Programmer • *John Scilipote*
Client • *IBM S/390*

Project Statement
For IBM, Waters Design produced an interactive customer reference CD-ROM to be used by S/390 Division sales representatives. The CD-ROM promotes a valuable yet underutilized sales resource, a customer information database that resides on the IBM intranet. Encouraging the sales team to participate by contributing their own customer profiles and success stories to the database, the CD-ROM highlights the range of resources available in the database and how they can be used as marketing and relationship enhancement tools. Designed and programmed by Waters Design using Macromedia Director, the CD's graphic design and easy-to-use interface help make the IBM customer reference CD-ROM both a valuable tool and a pleasure to use.

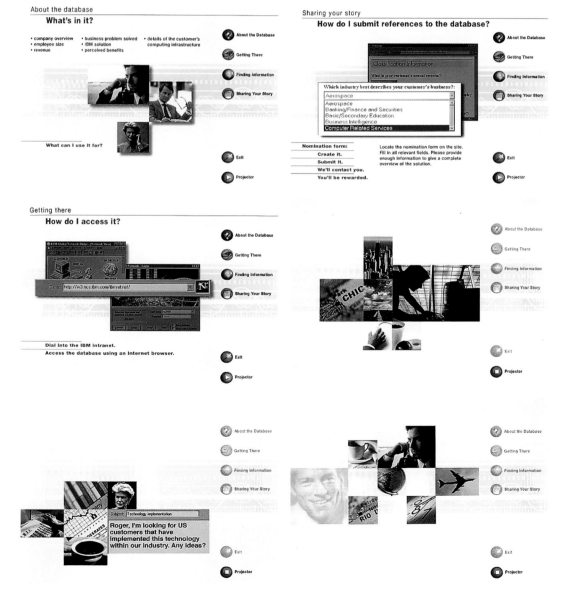

Unionbay Sportswear "The Flow" Video

Design Firm • *Toth Design & Advertising,*
Concord, MA
Creative Director • *Michael Toth*
Graphic Designer • *Jason Skinner*
Director • *Dewey Nicks*
Copywriter • *Risa Mickenberg*
Digital Video Producer • *John Duffin*
Cinematographer • *Jim Fealy*
Editor • *Haines Hall*
Production Company • *Reactor Films*
Client Union Bay

Project Statement
The target audience of Unionbay's "Generations" campaign is young adults age sixteen to twenty-four. The purpose of the campaign is to reinforce Unionbay as a brand of alternative sportswear/casual wear for teens and young adults. The strategy of the "Generations" campaign is to continue to associate Unionbay with a positive message and imagery of teens and young adults. The video uses words of wisdom from older kids to emphasize the opportunity of youth. The message is that life moves very fast, and we should experience and enjoy all that the present has to offer.

The value of Unionbay advertising in the fashion industry is Unionbay's uniquely positive reflection of teens and young adults: happy, healthy, confident individuals.

"Don't Go Changing" Tommy Hilfiger Jeans Video

Design Firm • *Toth Design & Advertising,*
Concord, MA
Creative Director • *Michael Toth*
Agency Producer • *Liza Gurall*
Director • *Dewey Nicks*
Digital Video Producer • *John Duffin*
Cinematographer • *Lance Accord*
Editor • *Sloan Klevin*
Production Company • *Reactor Films*
Client • *Tommy Hilfiger*

Project Statement

The "In the Jeans" campaign promotes designer Tommy Hilfiger's denim sub-brand. The television spot juxtaposes the words "jeans" and "genes" and features the children of actors and musicians describing the traits they inherited from their famous parents. The spots were filmed on location and the footage is framed by the signature Tommy Hilfiger navy logo bars to create an animated version of the Hilfiger brand logo.

The spots were used to target jeans customers in a relevant environment (MTV) while still maintaining the look and feel of the overall brand campaign, which generally occurs in print and outdoor venues.

MTV 10 Spot

Design Firm/Client • *MTV Networks,*
New York, NY
Art Director • *Romy Mann*
Graphic Designer • *Jenny Rask*
Producer • *Mikiko Gill*

Project Statement

The purpose of the MTV 10 Spot was to encompass all of MTV's programs within one time slot beginning at 10:00 pm. The design is uniquely iconographic, which made the packaging and the promos stand out from those of other channels and commercials. The simplistic design and sexy audio from the 10 spot quickly familiarized the viewer with a time slot and location on the channel.

Vertivision

Design Firm • *MTV Networks,*
New York, NY
Creative Directors • *Jim Spegman and*
Matthew Duntemann
Graphic Designer/Illustrator • *Edgeworx*
Writers • *Laura Belgray and Rick Orlando*
Programmer • *Rick Orlando*
Client • *Nick at Nite/TV Land*

Project Statement
"Vertivision" was designed to promote a twelve-hour weekend marathon of one specific show. Through the inspiration of institutional science films and with the addition of a retro 3-D electronic feel, we explain the "scientific" process by which the marathon episodes are selected. The target audience is television fans age eighteen to forty-nine.

3-D Nogglevision Promises

Design Firm • *MTV Networks,*
New York, NY
Creative Directors • *Linda Walsh*
and Agi Fodor
Animators • *Rocketship International*
Writers • *Richard Barry and Anastasia Kedroe*
Digital Video Producers • *Richard Barry,*
Anastasia Kedroe, and Linda Walsh
Client • *Nickelodeon On-Air*

Project Statement
The creative challenge was to enhance Nickelodeon's brand during a 3-D promotional event — with the added challenge of producing spots that could air beyond the event.

Strategically, we created station messages that supported Nickelodeon's brand. We challenged ourselves to find a 3-D technology that didn't distort the image, thereby allowing kids to view our spots with or without the 3-D glasses and after the event. The spot's narrative and graphic style communicate a new way to watch Nickelodeon to an audience age six to eleven. The campaign reflects the imagination and playfulness of being a child.

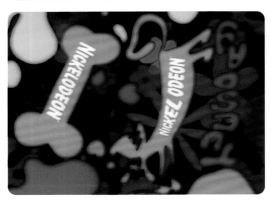 

Nickelodeon Fall Campaign End Pages

Design Firm • *MTV Networks,*
New York, NY
Creative Directors • *George Guzman*
and Agi Fodor
Animator • *Chris Gilligan*
Writer • *McPaul Smith*
Digital Video Producer • *Adam Idelson*
Client • *Nickelodeon On-Air*

Project Statement
The creative strategy was to create specialized end
pages that support the spirit and campaign message of
Nickelodeon's new fall campaign — "You're never
done doing Nickelodeon." We created approaches that
enable kids to interact with our logo in a variety of
ways. Hence, Nickelodeon is in their hands. It's the
network for kids. As a result, the end pages reflect the
imagination and playfulness of Nickelodeon's audience,
kids age six to eleven.

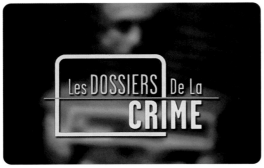 

13th Street Network Launch

Design Firm • *Hatmaker, Watertown, MA*
Creative Director • *Tom Corey*
Producers • *Marianna Gracey and Susan Archer*
Director • *Scott Greig*
Designers • *Haig Bedrossian and John Duffy*
Animator/Editor • *Austin Wallender*
Illustrator • *Ted Smykal*
Film/Photography • *Reid & Walsh*
Client • *Universal Studios Television*

Project Statement

13th Street is an action and suspense channel launched by Universal Studios in France and Germany. It's a channel about place, but not a specific place. From the bumpers to the IDs to the menus, 13th Street is a state of mind.

We needed to convey a sense of place first through the channel logo, so a street sign was a natural fit. It can contain any number of languages and can therefore travel to numerous international markets, which was essential. Elements of danger, suspense and an urban sensibility were integral to creating the on-air look of 13th Street. Through the use of live action and animation, the channel blossomed into one with a unique look and feel. The final result: "The most dangerous address on television."

Skate School Video

Design Firm • *Nike, Inc., Beaverton, OR*
Art Director • *Dan Richards*
Graphic Designers • *Dan Richards*
and James Parker
Illustrators • *Dan Richards and James Parker*
Animator • *James Parker*
Writer • *Neil Webster*
Typeface • *Franklin Gothic Modified*
Client • *Nike Equipment*

Project Statement

The Skate School video was created to teach sales reps and clerks about the unique features of the Nike inline skates. It is a technical video, but is presented in a low-tech, entertaining way. Low-tech animation and simple type were used to tell the story and compliment the genre (and the budget). I feel that this project was successful because the simplicity stands out in the current craze of high-tech, fast-moving, layered visuals.

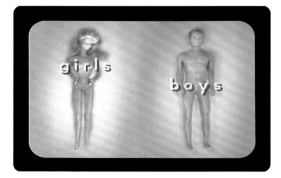

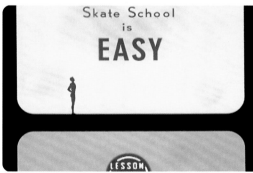

David Brenner Cartoon Animation

Design Firm • *J. J. Sedelmaier Productions, Inc.,*
White Plains, NY
Creative Director • *J. J. Sedelmaier*
Graphic Designer/Animator •
David Wachtenheim
Writer • *Robert Smigel*
Digital Video Producer • *Rob Issen*
Sound Editor • *Michael Fisher*
Client • *NBC/Saturday Night Live*

Project Statement
This piece is one of a series of cartoons created for
NBC's *Saturday Night Live*. The audience age ranges
from early teens through adult. Satirical comedy through
animated celebrity characterization defines its purpose
and creative strategy. The parameters are only defined
by legal/censorship standards as they apply to satire.
Here, the design and animation were purposely kept stiff
to enhance the use of actual audio pulled from previous
broadcast of a David Brenner interview. He has been put
in absurd situations in direct contrast to his mundane story.
It demonstrates a clever and effective use of animation.

Nick Jr. "Monsters" ID

Design Firm • *MTV Networks, New York, NY*
Creative Directors • *George Guzman,*
Agi Fodor, and Linda Walsh
Animators • *Funline Animations*
Writers • *Anastasia Kedroe*
Digital Video Producer • *Anastasia Kedroe*
Client • *Nickelodeon On-Air*

Project Statement
The creative strategy was to create a station ID supporting
Nick Jr.'s brand message, which reflects and encourages
the nurturing relationships between a caregiver and a child.
The big monster in the spot represents the parental figure
and demonstrates a playful, nurturing relationship with
the child-size monster. The design parameters consisted of
using organic materials familiar to a preschooler. The spot's
narrative and graphic style communicate Nick Jr.'s image
to an audience of preschoolers age two to five, and their
caregivers. The result is a spot that is both entertaining and
effective as a station ID.

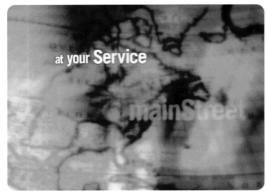

GTE Mainstreet

Design Firm • *GibbsBaronet, Dallas, TX*
Creative Director • *Willie Baronet*
Graphic Designers • *Meta Newhouse,*
Craig Anderson, and Jonathan Ingram
Photographers • *Dick Patrick and Photonica*
Editor • *Dave Laird*
Copywriter • *Lee Sanders*
Typefaces • *Century Schoolbook, Orator,*
and Trade Gothic
Digital Video Producer • *Video Post*
Client • *GTE Mainstreet*

Project Statement
GTE Mainstreet is an interactive cable television channel that is geared toward computer-shy, small-town audiences that want some of the benefits that the Internet may offer without having to own a computer. Each spot highlights a specific benefit the channel provides: an interactive encyclopedia, story time for children, and updated stock quotes on demand. Budget did not allow for live-action film, so we produced everything using still photography scanned onto CDs and went direct to finish in Henry edit suite. Design considerations included matching the colors of these spots with the color coding of subject matter on the Mainstreet channel itself. The typography movement in these spots was designed to foreshadow the exciting interactivity viewers would be able to have right on their own TV. What makes these spots stand out from the clutter of other low-budget TV spots is the witty use of typography in combination with the smart conversational-style copy.

1997 MTV Video Music Awards

Design Firm/Client • *MTV Networks, New York, NY*
Art Director • *Romy Mann*
Graphic Designer • *Jenny Rask*
Animators/Hal Artists • *Betsy Brydon and Karen Perrine*
Producer • *Greg Buyalos*

Project Statement
The challenge this year was to create a new look for our biggest show. Our media-savvy audience has very high expectations of the visuals that are presented to them on our channel, so it is really necessary that we constantly reinvent ourselves in design. This year we created a packaging environment that was completely integrated. The theme for the MTV Video Music Awards this year was "fetish," so the imagery was mainly influenced by Japanese erotica, the design influenced by sophisticated Japanese sensibilities.

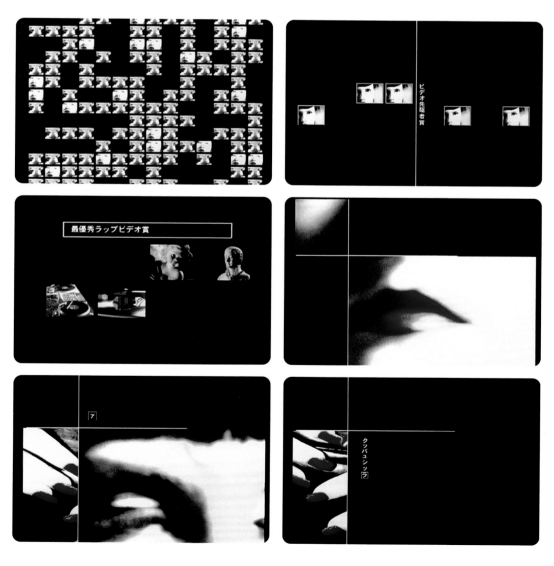

Creative Director/Executive Producer •
Amy Friedman
Graphic Designers • Byron Glaser
and Sandra Higashi
Animator • Pixar
Director • Bob Peterson
Producers • Kori Rae, Essie Chambers,
Karen Fowler
Composers/Sound Design • Lukasz Gottwald
and Tony Widoff
Client • Nickelodeon for UNICEF

Project Statement
Nickelodeon created and produced "The Right to Express
Yourself" as a pro bono project for UNICEF's Rights of
the Child global initiative. The graphic open was created
specifically for Nickelodeon's audience of American and
international six- to eleven-year-olds. The creative goal was
to introduce the animated vignette and communicate its
message to as culturally diverse an audience as possible. The
use of the world's alphabets, accents, and enhancement of
hand-signing were brought together to create a unique and
extremely effective piece of graphic communication.

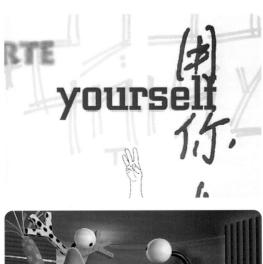

Nike "I Can Play"

Production Firm • *Imaginary Forces,*
Los Angeles, CA
Executive Producer • *Peter Frankfurt*
Creative Director • *Kyle Cooper*
Art Director • *Adam Bluming*
Graphic Designers • *Adam Bluming,*
John Choi, Grant Lau, and Eric Cruz
Advertising Agency • *Weiden & Kennedy*
Agency Producer • *Henry Lu*
Agency Creative Directors • *John Jay*
and Jamie Barrett
Agency Art Director • *Joe Shands*
Agency Copywriters • *Mike Folino*
and Mike Smith
Client • *Nike*
Typeface • *Bell Gothic*

Project Statement
All of the type was shot on 35mm film with various textures and filters and different types of animation. Selected
pieces of this animation were then editorially reconfigured
to suggest staccato movement.

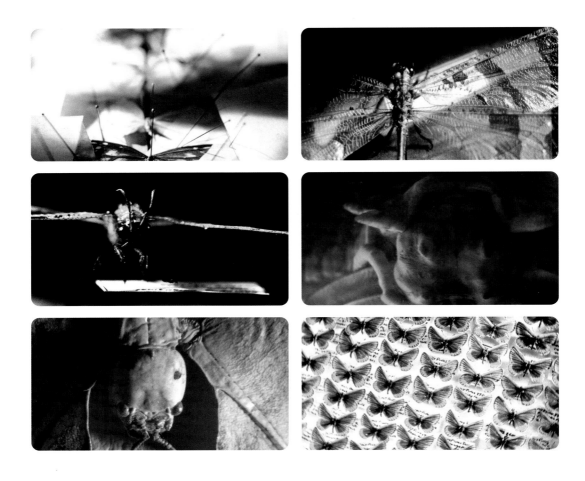

"Mimic" Title Sequence

Director • *Kyle Cooper*
Art Director • *Karin Fong*
Graphic Designers/Model Makers •
Karin Fong, Dana Yee, Kimberly Cooper,
and Scarlett Kim
Editor • *Fred Fouquet*
Executive Producer • *Chip Houghton*
Producer • *Debra Kaufman*
Director of Photography • *Juan Ruiz Anchia*
Digital Photographer • *Keith Cooper*
Feature Director • *Guillermo Del Toro*
Client • *Dimension Films/Miramax*
Typeface • *American Typewriter*

Project Statement

Mimic is a horror film about cockroaches that are quickly evolving into humans. The title refers to the way insects survive by imitating other species. The main title had to tell the film's back story: a terrible plague, spread by cock-roaches, is spreading through New York City, killing young children. In addition, the sequence sets up the film's suspense by evoking constant fear of insect evolution and infestation.

Production Company • *Imaginary Forces,*
Los Angeles, CA
Executive Producer • *Chip Houghton*
Director • *Kyle Cooper*
Graphic Designer • *Geoff Kaplan*
Animator • *Vince Abogado*
Advertising Agency • *Houston Herrstek Favat*
Agency Producer • *Lisa Sulda*
Agency Art Director • *Dan Bryant*
Agency Copywriter • *Maureen Begley*
Client • *Massachusetts Department of*
Public Health
Typeface • *DIN Engschrift*

Project Statement
Words become smoke in this footage, which was meant
to graphically illustrate all the toxins and potential hazards
contained in cigarette smoke.

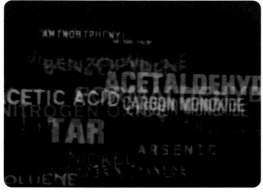

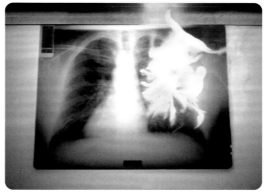

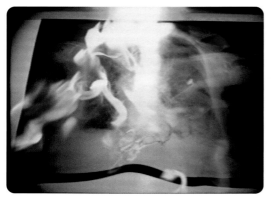

Art Director • *Mikon VanGastel*
Editor • *Kurt Matilla*
Animator • *Ben Lopez*
Client • *American Center for Design*
Typeface • *Headline*

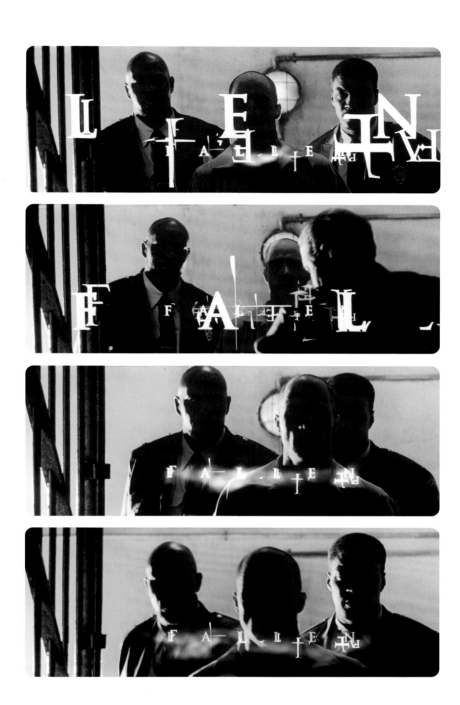

"Fallen" Title Sequence

....

Director • *Kyle Cooper*

Art Director • *Scarlett Kim*

Graphic Designer • *Adam Bluming*

Animators • *Scarlett Kim and Vince Abogado*

Editor • *Jeff Consiglio*

Producer • *Tim Thompson*

Optical Lineup • *James De Rin*

Feature Director • *Gregory Hoblit*

Clients • *Warner Bros., Atlas Entertainment*

Typefaces • *Mixture of Trajan and Mason
(Altered)*

Project Statement

The film is about a demon who moves from one body
to another and takes it over. The animation shows a credit
fading up whole and then transforming into mist, which
then forms another credit. This leaves behind the skeleton
of the once-whole credit that existed there previously.

"Donnie Brasco" Title Sequence

Director • *Kyle Cooper*
Editor • *Kurt Mattila*
Designers • *Adam Bluming, Olivia D'Ablis,*
and Kurt Mattila
Feature Director • *Mike Newell*
Client • *TriStar Pictures,*
Mandalay Entertainment
Typeface • *Bell Gothic*

Project Statement
The film director, Mike Newell, wanted to suggest the obsessive nature of the main character, an outsider and a predator. He had spent three years prior to the first scene of the movie on the streets, in bars, clubs, and lounges following Al Pacino's character and looking for an opening into this criminal family. Instead of shooting live-action footage of Johnny Depp, the existing unit production stills were animated editorially to create this quality, which is intrinsic to the film.

TV Land Roadside "Gunsmoke" Bumper

Design Firm • *MTV Networks,*
New York, NY
Creative Directors • *Jim Spegman and*
Matthew Duntemann
Graphic Designer • *Mitch O'Connell*
Animator • *Tom Cushwa*
Writer • *Tom Hill*
Sound Editor • *Tom Pomposello*
Client • *Nick at Nite/TV Land*

Project Statement
TV Land bumpers are used as :05 second visuals to signal when the channel is going in or out of a specific show and into or out of a commercial break. Building on the idea of TV Land as a place, we deliver the show specific information as one might see it translated through roadside pop culture icons. The target audience is television viewers, primarily age eighteen to forty-nine.

Wert & Company Website

Design Firm • *i/o 360 Digital Design,*
New York, NY
Creative Director • *Dindo Magallanes*
Interface Designer • *Casey Reas*
Project Manager • *Chris Beard*
Website Production • *Jack Biello*
Writers • *Julie Moline and Malcolm Abrams*
Typefaces • *Bembo, Futura, and Scala Sans*
Client • *Wert & Company*

Project Statement
Wert & Company is an international recruitment agency specializing in executive searches within the creative community. The site provides users with background information about the company and their services and contains an extensive list of links to Wert & Company's talent pool. Through the site, potential clients can request further information, while job candidates can submit their resumes and complete a form containing all the necessary information to get them into Wert & Company's database.

The graphic language of the site (large areas of flat color, circles, ampersands, and a visible grid) evolved out of Wert & Company's existing identity. I/o 360 further developed this visual language through a series of animated sequences that form a decodable analogy to Wert & Company's business.

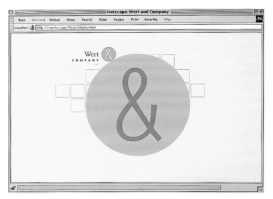

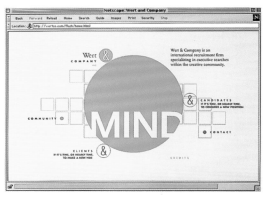

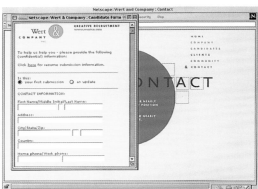

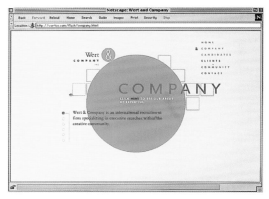

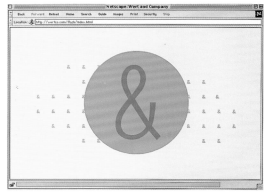

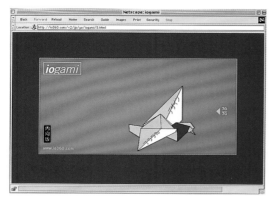

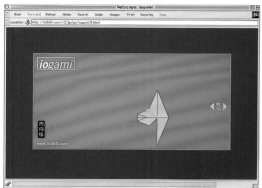

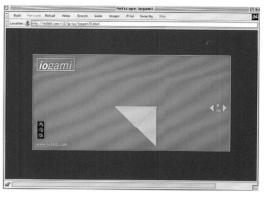

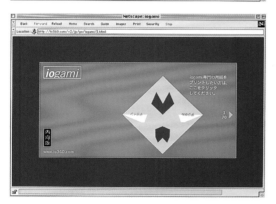

Iogami Website

Design Firm • *i/o 360 Digital Design,*
New York, NY
Creative Directors • *Ralph Lucci,*
Casey Reas, and Nam Szeto
Interface Designer • *Casey Reas*
Translation • *Naomi Moriyama and*
Jocelyn Hayashi
Typeface • *Trade Gothic*
Client • *i/o 360 Digital Design*

Project Statement
Traditional origami transmits culture and tradition through the transformation of paper squares into myriad three-dimensional forms. Iogami captures the spirit of this traditional craft and educates through motion. By displaying the interim forms created by the folding paper, Iogami eliminates the need for explanatory text and allows users to control the pace of the folding process.

Brigham Young University Website

Design Firm • *Brigham Young University,*
Provo, UT
Art Director • *Linda Sullivan*
Graphic Designers • *Linda Sullivan,*
David Groom, and David Meredith
Interface Designer • *Ryan Bailey*
Photographers • *Bradley Slade and*
David Meredith
Writer • *Joyce Janetski*
Typefaces • *News Gothic and Mrs Eaves*

Project Statement
All prospective and current students in the department
of visual arts are directed to this website. It contains over
100 "pages" of current information about our fourteen
major/minor programs as well as information about scholar-
ships, gallery and other facilities, study-abroad opportunities, and admissions procedures. The webite provides
downloadable forms for entering freshmen as well as links
to many other university sources. The site will continue
to grow, with a virtual gallery, current examples of faculty
work, and student portfolios from the department's 800
students.

1185 Design Website

Design Firm • *1185 Design, Palo Alto, CA*
Art Director • *Peggy Burke*
Graphic/Interface Designers • *Mehdi Anvarian,*
Peggy Burke, Peter Casell, Julia Foug, Ross
Geerdes, Ben Kam, Rachel Kirby, John Milly,
Nhut Nguyen, Dave Prescott, Melissa Shimmin,
Ann Sison, and Jennifer Sweeting
Programmer • *Paul Erskine, Jimmy Patrick,*
and Ed Struzenberg

Project Statement

1185 Design is a graphic design firm specializing in creating print and electronic corporate identities. One of our greatest assets is our client list, which we decided to showcase on our home page. The navigation is designed to allow our current and potential clients, as well as prospective employees, easy access to our work. The site is a valuable tool in demonstrating our ability to build very creative and efficient websites while showcasing pieces from our portfolio. Each section is specifically designed to engage our visitors with relevant and interactive imagery for print and/or electronic media. It's a dynamic, ongoing project with no creative limitations. A designer's dream project — if only we could figure out a way to pay ourselves for producing it!

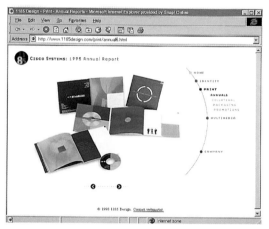
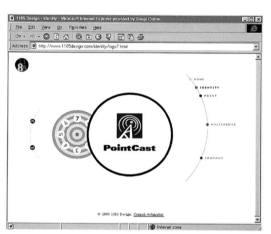

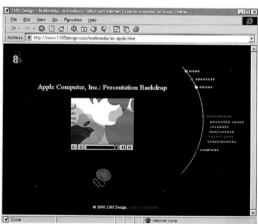
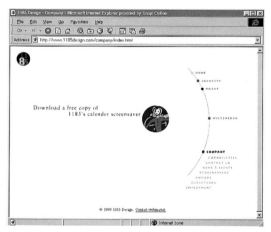

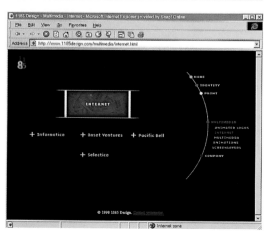

Aptar Group 1996 Annual Report Website

Design Firm • *SamataMason, Dundee, IL*
Art Directors • *Pat Samata*
Graphic Designer • *Kevin Krueger*
Photographers • *Sandro, SamataMason*
Writer • *Ralph Polterman*
Typeface • *Trade Gothic*
Programmer • *Lynch2*
Client • *Aptar Group*

Project Statement
Aptar Group is a international supplier of convenience dispensing products for the fragrance/cosmetics, personal care, pharmaceutical, household, and food markets. Through the use of type and photography, we displayed the broad range of these products, which are part of every consumer's daily life.

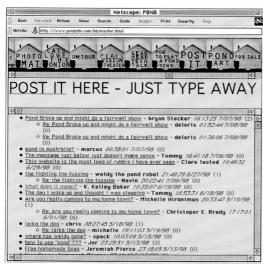

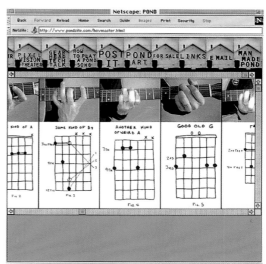

Pondsite (Full of Tiny Men) Website

Design Firm • *Sony Music Creative Services,*
Santa Monica, CA
Art Director • *Mary Maurer*
Graphic Designers • *Mary Maurer*
and Brandy Flower
Photographer • *John Clark*
Producers • *Peter Anton and*
Chris Cunningham
Programmer/Graphic Artist •
Chris Cunningham
Client • *Work Records*

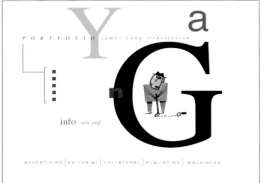

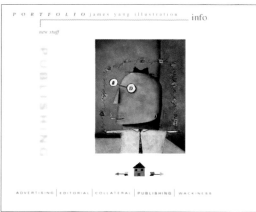
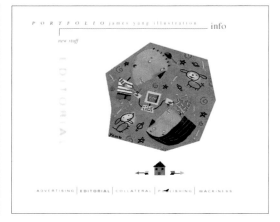

James Yang Illustration Website

Design Firm • *Particle, Rockville, MD*
Art Director/Interface Designer • *Chris Noel*
Illustrator/Client • *James Yang*

Project Statement
The audience for this website is anyone in the business
of purchasing creative services, particularly illustration. The
site is intended to be an online portfolio that lets clients
view samples of recent work. The design objective was to
create a quick, simple, elegant, and easy-to-use graphic
interface that would not distract users from the artwork.

Design Firm • *The Blahaus Group,*
Brooklyn, NY
Creative Director • *Jason Pearson*
Graphic/Interface Designer • *Walt Grouper*
Typeface • *Blahaus*

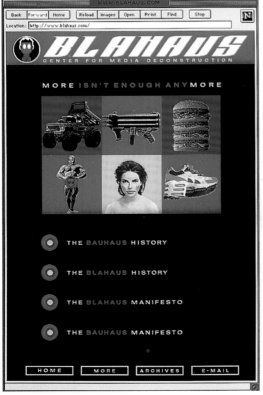

Apple Trade Show Exhibit Reuse Program

Design Firm • *Mauk Design,*
San Francisco, CA
Art Director • *Mitchell Mauk*
Graphic Designers • *Adam Brodsley,*
Mitchell Mauk, and Tim Mautz
Photographer • *Julie Chase*
Typefaces • *Apple Garamond and*
Helvetica Black
Fabricator • *General Exhibits and Displays*
Client • *Apple Computer*

Project Statement
Apple's Mainframe trade show exhibit, a flexible, Lego-like system, was killing them in inventory, set-up/tear down, and refurb costs. Our objectives included reusing the effective components of the system, reducing parts, and improving function.

The solution was a simple "X"-shaped floor plan that could be lengthened and shortened as needed, from 20' x 30' to 110' x 120'. The redesign saved Apple $6 million in new exhibit costs and extended the life of the system for up to eight years. Powder coating eliminated airborne paint emissions, and a reduction in physical mass eliminated the need for three trucks, reducing gas consumption, air pollution, and wear and tear on the infrastructure.

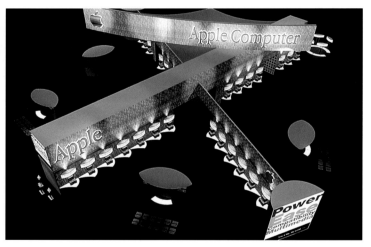

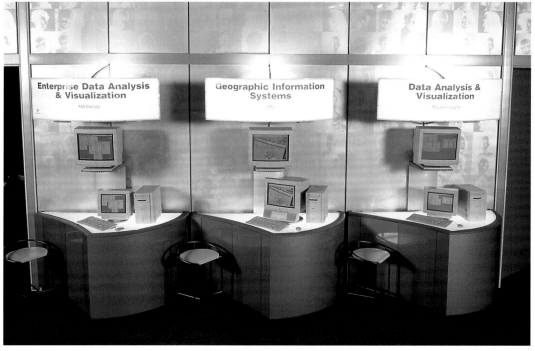

Grand Central Terminal Construction Barricades

Design Firm • *Two Twelve Associates,*
New York, NY
Creative Director • *Ann Harakawa*
Art Director • *Colleen Hall*
Graphic Designer • *Patricia Kelleher*
Illustrator • *Maira Kalman*
Typefaces • *Filosofia Unicase, Trade Gothic*
Printer • *Mega Art*
Client • *Grand Central Terminal Ventures*

Project Statement

Grand Central Terminal, the exquisite New York City rail and transportation hub, is undergoing a $175 million renovation to restore the landmark building to its original glory. Envisioned as more than a railway station, the terminal will now house more than 100 new retail stores and restaurants.

The barricades erected during construction inform pedestrians about the renovation and provide a medium for creative graphic presentations. Grand Central Terminal Ventures commissioned Two Twelve to design a system that expressed the near completion of construction and gave pedestrians a sense of what was to come.

Two Twelve developed the concept for the barricades using the unique style of Maira Kalman, an illustrator well known for her *New Yorker* covers and children's books. The new barricade design is bright, cheerful, and warm. We presented five different subjects that highlighted the renovated facilities — the Grand Central Market, Vanderbilt Hall, the Main Concourse, and the Dining Concourse. We designed graphic intermediate separation panels that alert pedestrians to wayfinding and construction conditions. The panels were also used to acknowledge participants in the renovation and sponsors of the barricades.

Texas Instruments Sundial

Design Firm • *Donovan and Green,*
New York, NY
Art Director • *Michael Donovan*
Graphic Designers • *Adrian Levin*
and Michael Donovan
Photographers • *Nick Merrick,*
Hedrich Blessing Phototgraphy
Writer • *Claudia Clay*
Fabricator • *ASI Sign Systems*
Client • *Texas Instruments*

Project Statement
Addressed to its technologically sophisticated clients, and
as a symbolic entry to Forest Lane, one of the largest,
most precise solar clocks in the world was conceived and
designed by Donovan and Green. The sundial, with a solar
projection of a world map at its center, combines ancient
and modern technology and serves as a reminder of Texas
Instruments' global presence and commitment to reduce
time to market. The twelve surrounding plinths represent
Texas Instruments' key technological developments, while
the shadow-casting gnomon points to the celestial pole.

Levi's Jeans for Women Shop

Design Firm • *Morla Design,*
San Francisco, CA
Creative Director • *Brian Collins*
Art Directors • *Jennifer Morla and Eric Rindal*
Designer • *Jennifer Morla*
Photographers • *Sheila Metzner*
and Cesar Rubio
Copywriter • *Suzanne Finamore*
Fabricators • *Fun Display, Bentley Carpets*
Client • *Foot, Cone & Belding*

Project Statement
The Levi's Jeans for Women Shop is a 3,200-square-foot in-store boutique designed to appeal to women between the ages of fifteen and thirty. The design concept is based upon shape. Fixtures curve like a woman's body: mannequin dress forms are in different body sizes; laminated glass walls curve convex and concave to create hallways; and photographic murals show the female body against curvaceous sandstone rocks. Black and cream custom carpeting has cursive writing based on entries from a woman's journal. The floating ceiling of the focus area accents custom seating, furniture, and softly fluted lighting fixtures.

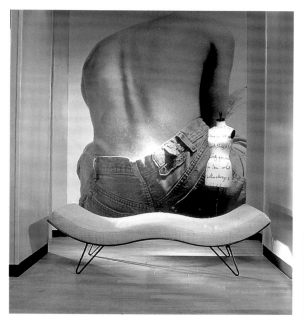

Gratefish Storm Drain

Design Firm • *Mauk Design,*
San Francisco, CA
Creative Director • *Mitchell Mauk*
Graphic Designers • *Mitchell Mauk*
and Laurence Raines
Client • *Grate Drains*

Project Statement
Problem: People pour old motor oil and other toxic chemicals down storm drains. The current solutions are spray-painted warnings and hefty fines. Unfortunately, the paint wears off (into the drain), incurring an ongoing maintenance cost, and the fines are applied only after the fact. Moreover, the warnings are usually in English and don't work in multilingual communities.

The Gratefish drain uses a universally understandable symbol to communicate the consequences of pouring motor oil (or other chemicals) down storm drains. The playful shape of the fish communicates the message with a positive tone.

Volkswagen Exhibit

Design Firm • *Mauk Design,*
San Francisco, CA
Creative Director • *Mitchell Mauk*
Graphic Designers • *Adam Brodsley,*
Laurence Raines, and Michael Minn
Photographer • *Andy Caulfield*
Typeface • *Futura Heavy*
Fabricators • *Exhibitworks*
Client • *Volkswagen of America*

Project Statement
Exhibit Primary's objective was to communicate
Volkswagen's brand essence in a car show environment,
through the experience of the space. The exhibit showed
not just the brand's rational mind, but also the emotional
soul of the product. It was intended to go beyond kicking
the tires, by adding another level of fun and intelligence
to the exhibit, without adding more bucks. It used low-
tech interactivity, simple video, clean shapes, and straight-
forward finishes.

Beaulieu Exhibit

Design Firm • *i.e., design, Canton, GA*
Art Director/Graphic Designer • *i.e., design*
Photographers • *Greg Slater and Steve Hall*
Fabricators • *EDE Corp.*
Client • *Beaulieu Commercial*

Project Statement
The Beaulieu traveling exhibit was designed to introduce the commercial carpet manufacturer to architects and designers at various industry trade shows. Although the company is the largest privately owned carpet manufacturer in the world, they were relatively unknown to the critical customer base. As part of an overall identity launch, the exhibit was designed to communicate the company's capabilities and showcase their products in a museum-quality atmosphere. One of the primary goals in identity development for Beaulieu involved teaching the audience how to pronounce the corporate name. Accordingly, the design featured a phonetic pronunciation for Beaulieu.

Henry Dreyfuss Exhibition Design and Graphics

Exhibition Design • *Architectural Research Office*

Creative Director • *Adam Yarinsky*

Project Manager • *Josh Pulver*

Graphic Designer • *Jen Roos, Cooper-Hewitt, National Design Museum*

Exhibition Team (Architectural Research Office) • *Stephen Cassel, Elena Moutsopoulos and Wendy Weintraub*

Exhibition Team • (Cooper-Hewitt, National Design Museum) *Brent Rumage and Christine McKee*

Exhibition Curator • *Russell Flinchum*

Project Statement

The installation for the Henry Dreyfuss exhibition was created for the Cooper–Hewitt, National Design Museum. Six case studies of the industrial design work of Henry Dreyfuss and Associates were featured, including the John Deere tractor of 1941 and the Honeywell round thermostat of 1953.

The design presents a wide range of information with an economy of means, in harmony with Dreyfuss's overall approach to design. Simply proportioned white panels display the objects, removing them from the dark interiors of the nineteenth-century Andrew Carnegie mansion that houses the National Design Museum. Sketches by Dreyfuss retrieved from microfilm were silkscreened on the walls to highlight his design process. The exhibition graphics use the typeface Nobel and reflect a period feeling while emphasizing Dreyfuss's favorite geometric form, the circle.

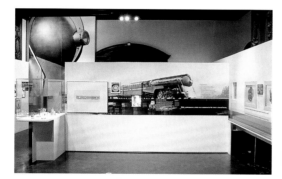

"Sound Off: CD 100" Traveling Exhibition

Design Firm • *AdamsMorioka,*
Beverly Hills, CA
Art Directors • *Sean Adams*
and Noreen Morioka
Graphic Designers • *Sean Adams,*
Noreen Morioka, and Anna Dolan
Photographer • *Jennifer Krogh*
Copywriters • *Gabriela Mirensky*
and Moira Cullen
Typefaces • *Folio and Monotype Grotesque*
Fabricators • *AAA Banners, StatHouse,*
AdamsMorioka, PlasticMart
Paper • *Appleton Utopia Photo Seamless Paper*
Project Coordinator • *Gabriela Mirensky*
Clients • *American Institute of Graphic Arts,*
Appleton Papers

Project Statement
This traveling exhibition contains 100 CDs, books, posters, interactive media, and special packaging. In order to reach as wide an audience as possible, the exhibition needed to travel intact, with little setup needed and flexibility for venue requirements.

The pink curtain is vinyl with clear pockets to hold the 100 CDs in the exhibition. Other materials include plastic retail connectors, lamination, and grommets.

The concept for the exhibition incorporates the idea of reproduction, consumerism, artificiality, and accessibility. The materials and colors (plastics and fluorescence) reinforced these ideas. The exhibition has traveled, thus far, to fifteen cities with great success. The message has remained consistent and the quality of materials has not been compromised.

Garden of Samsung Electronics Exhibition

Design Firm • *The Burdick Group,*
San Francisco, CA
Creative Directors • *Bruce Burdick*
and Susan Burdick
Exhibition Designers • *Bruce Lightbody,*
Jerome Goh, Cory Covington, and
Raphael Henry
Video Program Designers • *John Binninger*
and Michelle Koza
Video Photographer • *Rich Wise,*
The Image Bank, The Stock Market
Fabricators/Editors • *Design and Production*
Digital Video Producer • *The Burdick Group*
Sound Editors • *The Burdick Group,*
Disher Music & Sound
Client • *Samsung Electronics*

Project Statement
This exhibition communicates about Samsung Electronics'
capabilities in a natural and indirect way, avoiding static
product displays common to corporate settings. Our solution: an environment that is art, information, and technology combined. Stylized garden areas were created in whose
abstracted foliage are planted 150 flat-screen LCD monitors.
Video programs in each garden convey different aspects
of Samsung's capabilities, which relate metaphorically to
that area. The monitors within the Spring Garden's green
grasses communicate about Samsung's environmental programs, the monitors nestled in the garden tree's branching
layers of gold-colored aluminum leaves communicate
about Samsung's global reach and those within the flower-
ing summer garden communicate about the blooms of
product innovation.

Ciba Specialty Chemicals Precision Poster

Design Firm • *Gottschalk & Ash*
International, Toronto, Ontario
Graphic Designers • *Hélène L'Heureux,*
Heather Lafleur, and Stuart Ash
Typeface • *Stone*
Printer • *Bowne of Toronto*
Paper • *Utopia Premium*
Blue White Silk 100# Text
Client • *Ciba Specialty Chemicals*

Project Statement
The poster is one in a series devoted to communicating the meaning behind the Ciba Specialty Chemical's corporate logo — the butterfly symbol — to company employees and the general public. The featured image represents the precise design and superlative technical expertise of Ciba's chemical processes. The logical structure of the symbol underpins the company's dedication to quality and perfection in all its operations. As part of a unified design program for Ciba, this poster demonstrates excellence through its clear, concise, and powerful design, dedicated to a single, high-impact message. In addition, the identity positions the new Ciba Specialty Chemicals as assertive and strong, self-confident, youthful, international, and alive, and refocuses its culture toward high performance in the wake of the merger/demerger from its former parent.

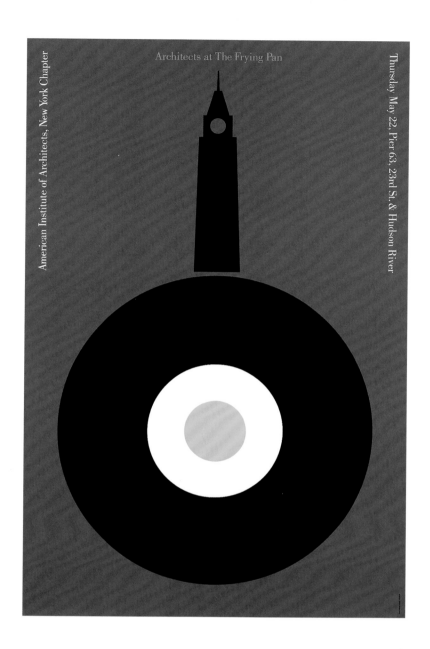

Architects at the Frying Pan Poster

Design Firm • *Pentagram, New York, NY*
Graphic Designer • *Michael Gericke*
Typeface • *Bodoni*
Printer • *Ambassador Arts*
Client • *American Institute of Architects*

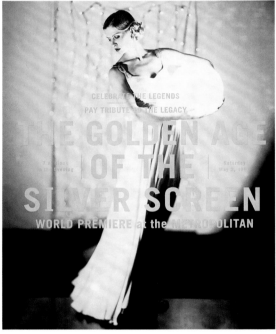

The Golden Age of the Silver Screen Posters

Design Firm • *Carmichael, Lynch & Thorburn,*
Minneapolis, MN
Creative Director • *Bill Thorburn*
Graphic Designer • *Chad Hagen*
Photographer • *Bill Phelps*
Writer • *Jonathan Sunshine*
Printer • *General Litho Service*
Client • *Children's Health Care of Minneapolis*

Project Statement
The Golden Age of the Silver Screen identity system is
an event-related promotion for the Association of
Children's Health Care of Minneapolis. The pieces in the
system celebrate the mood of that time period through
typography and imagery. The four-color, black & white, and
a run of silver give it vibrant and rich tone, yet maintain
a quiet monotone presence. The communication comes
through in the allure of its elegance and sophistication. The
campaign was meant to engage the participant to step back
to a time when life seemed much more grand.

San Francisco Performance 1 and 4 Posters

Design Firm • *Jennifer Sterling Design,*
San Francisco, CA
Art Director/Graphic Designer • *Jennifer Sterling*
Typographer • *Jennifer Sterling*
Copywriter • *Corey Weinstein*
Typefaces • *Garamond 3, Keedy*
Printer • *Belle Air Displays*
Paper • *Simpson White*
Client • *San Francisco Performances*

Project Statement
These are from a series of posters and bus shelters
designed for San Francisco Performances that announces
upcoming performances. The series and performances
feature quite different elements of dance, so the individual
posters needed to reflect the works of these various dance
companies. The companies had little or no photography
to work with (compounded with a limited budget) so
the typography became responsible for evoking the dance
or experience of each performance.

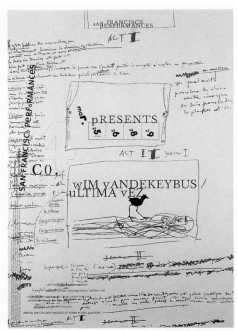

Design Firm • *James Victore Inc.,*
New York, NY
Art Director • *Koichi Yano*
Graphic Designer • *James Victore*
Typeface • *Lefty*
Printer • *Dai Nippon*
Client • *DDD Gallery*

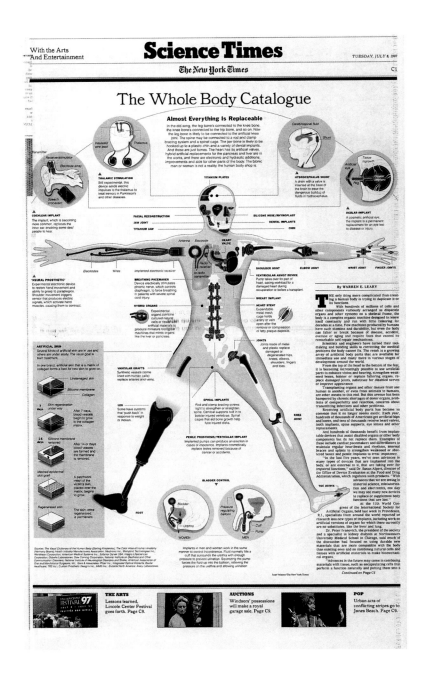

The Whole Body Catalogue

Design Firm • *The New York Times,*
New York, NY
Art Director • *Michael Valenti*
Graphic Designer/Illustrator • *Juan Velasco*
Client/Publisher • *The New York Times*

Design Firm • *Pentagram Design,*
New York, NY
Graphic Designer • *Woody Pirtle*
Printer • *Ambassador Arts*
Paper • *French Speckletone 80# Cover*
Client • *Hampton Day School*

Immigrant Theater Festival 1997 Poster

Design Firm • *Luba Lukova Studio,*
New York, NY
Art Director/Graphic Designer/Illustrator •
Luba Lukova
Typeface • *Sancho*
Printer • *Izmo*
Paper • *Fabriano Tiziano*
Client • *Immigrant Theater Project*

Project Statement
In designing a poster for the 1997 Immigrant Theater
Festival at the Henry Street Settlement in Manhattan's
Lower East Side, I was looking for an image that would
speak in a simple way about the positive aspects of immi-
gration. I depicted the immigrant as a growing, grafted
person, not an alien.

Virgil Poster

Design Firm • *Luba Lukova Studio,*
New York, NY
Art Director/Graphic Designer/Illustrator •
Luba Lukova
Typeface • *Quixote*
Printer • *Izmo, New York*
Paper • *Fabriano Tiziano*
Client • *Affinity Productions*

Project Statement
A poster for a production at the Theater for the New
City, New York. This is the story of a Vietnam veteran
who looks at his past through the eyes of his Chinese-
American wife.

Manga Restaurant Poster Series

Design Firm • *Rigsby Design, Houston, TX*
Art Director • *Lana Rigsby*
Graphic Designers • *Lana Rigsby and
Thomas Hull*
Illustrator • *Roichi Ikegami*
Writer • *Lana Rigsby*
Printer • *Mercury Signs, Inc.*
Client • *Manga*

Project Statement
Series of limited-edition silkscreened and letterpress posters
promoting Manga, an Asian diner.

Freak Poster

Design Firm • *Spot Design, New York, NY*
Creative Director • *Drew Hodges*
Graphic Designer • *Kevin Brainard*
Illustrator • *Ward Sutton*
Printer • *Infiniti Color Graphics*
Clients • *Airlle Teppek, Bill Haber,*
Gregory Mosher

Pentagram: The Brand Poster

Design Firm • *Pentagram Design, Inc.,*
Austin, TX
Art Director • *Lowell Williams*
Graphic Designers • *Bill Carson,*
Jeff Williams, and Marc Stephens
Typeface • *Hand-Made Custom Type*
Printer • *Grover Printing*
Client • *Pentagram Design, Inc.*

Project Statement
This poster was created to promote a lecture by the
U.S. Pentagram partners in Austin, Texas. The lecture was
intended to show how Pentagram branded itself in the
design marketplace. Thus, we created a "brand" for each
letter in the name "Pentagram." The audience was the
creative community of Austin.

CCAC 18th Annual Design Lecture Concept Symposium Poster

Design Firm • *Jennifer Sterling Design,*
San Francisco, CA
Art Director/Graphic Designer •
Jennifer Sterling
Photographer • *Marko Lavrishka*
Typeface • *Garamond*
Printer • *Bel Air Display*
Client • *California College of Arts and Crafts*

Project Statement
The poster was printed on see-through plastic and hung from the ceiling in the gallery. The poster can be seen from both sides in the student area. Vellum was used to depict the views and insights from the various speakers, including Chee Pearlman, editor of *I.D.* Magazine, Michael Mabry of Michael Mabry Design, No. 17, and Sharon Werner of Werner Design Werks. A screen print of the poster is featured in the middle to depict process to students.

Literacy Poster

Design Firm • *Haley Johnson Design Co.,*
Minneapolis, MN
Art Director • *Haley Johnson*
Graphic Designers • *Haley Johnson and*
Richard Boynton
Typefaces • *Futura, Remington Typewriter,*
circa 1945
Printer • *Gopher State Litho*
Paper • *French Paper Dur-O-Tone 50#*
Newsprint
Client • *AIGA/Colorado*

Project Statement
The intent was to bring attention to the problem of
illiteracy. Two recognizable icons — the television and the
book — were chosen and morphed into one memorable
image to communicate the simple message of placing books
and reading first, before TV.

Design Firm • *Open, New York, NY*
Art Directors • *Scott Stowell and Chip Wass*
Graphic Designer • *Scott Stowell*
Illustrator • *Chip Wass*
Copywriters • *Scott Stowell and Chip Wass*
Typefaces • *Chippies by Wassco, Futura,
and Trade Gothic*
Paper • *Lithofect Venetian 70# Text*
Client • *Wassco*

Project Statement
Chippies by Wassco is a new dingbat font designed by
illustrator Chip Wass and distributed by T–26. The Periodic
Table of Chippies (Wassco Wal-Chart CBW-01, Revised
9/97) raises public awareness about Chippies while providing vital information to Chippies users. The chart shows
where each symbol can be found on the keyboard, as well
as categorizing the symbols into extremely helpful cate-
gories such as "plants," "people (and animals acting like
people)," and "Polynesian Interlude." There are 108
Chippies in all — at last count, there were 105 elements in
the periodic table. This was just too good to pass up. Plus,
printed on funky textured paper, it looks good on
any designer's office wall.

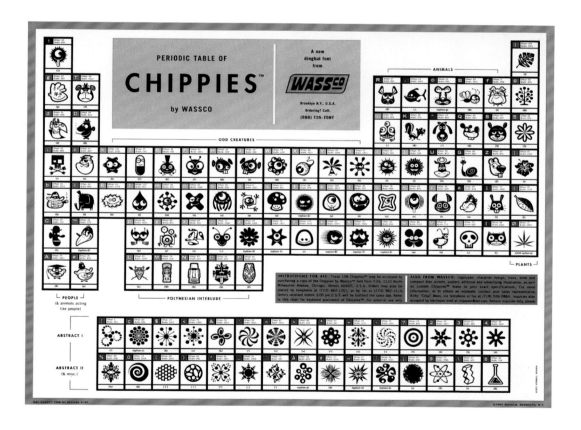

Design Firm • *Johnny Vitorovich,*
New York, NY
Art Director/Graphic Designer •
Johnny Vitorovich
Illustrator/Photographer • *Johnny Vitorovich*
Screen Image • *Archive Films*
Copywriter • *Johnny Vitorovich*
Typefaces • *Georgianna and Blackoak*
Paper • *French Butcher Off White*
Client • *Bengies Drive-In Theater*

Project Statement

This campaign is intended to generate new interest in and heighten awareness of Maryland's oldest surviving drive-in theater. Each poster was designed to reach a specific audience — those searching for a fun family night out, couples looking to rekindle a romance, and any adult who remembers the magic of a summer night on the grass watching a movie.

Because of the interest and nostalgia the posters have generated, all the printing, stock, and foil stamping were donated by multiple vendors. What started out as a personal quest to photo-document this drive-in over two years ended up as a poster series. I think the posters succeed because they capture the romance, the sounds, smells, texture and Americana that is/was the drive-in theater.

Raise 'Em Right Poster

Design Firm • *Johnny Vitorovich,*
New York, NY
Art Director/Graphic Designer •
Johnny Vitorovich
Illustrator/Photographer • *Johnny Vitorovich*
Copywriter • *Johnny Vitorovich*
Typeface • *Addled*
Printers • *Colorcraft of Virginia,*
Artisan II (Foils)
Paper • *French Butcher Off White*
Client • *Bengies Drive-In Theater*

Be 10 Again Poster

Design Firm • *Johnny Vitorovich,*
New York, NY
Art Director/Graphic Designer •
Johnny Vitorovich
Illustrator/Photographer • *Johnny Vitorovich*
Screen Image • *Archive Films*
Copywriter • *Johnny Vitorovich*
Typefaces • *Blackoak and Rosewood*
Printer • *Colorcraft of Virginia,*
Artisan II (Foils)
Paper • *French Butcher Off White*
Client • *Bengies Drive-In Theater*

John Cale Concert Poster

Design Firm • *Eye Noise, Orlando, FL*
Graphic Designer • *Thomas Scott*
Typefaces • *Geometric Stab,*
Franklin Gothic, Akzidenz Grotesk, Latiara,
and Latin Exra Condensed
Printer • *Chad's Screen Printing Services*
Paper • *Neenah Classic Linen Cover*

Project Statement
These concert posters do not serve as the primary advertising medium. Rather, they are intended to reinforce awareness of the upcoming performance and create a memorable image for fans of the artist. Screen printing allows for a larger poster when producing a limited quantity for a low budget. We also opted for two-color screen printing on a linen stock, which enabled the printer to hold detail well.

This piece is meant to work on different levels. Although there are a number of elements, they are united into a single, simple design that works best on the street. The eccentric typography is representative of Cale's reported idiosyncracies. The symbolism would be clear to his fans — his then most recent recording is entitled *Walking on Locusts*, and the heraldic symbols of Great Britain and the Prince of Wales refers to Cale's Welsh nationality.

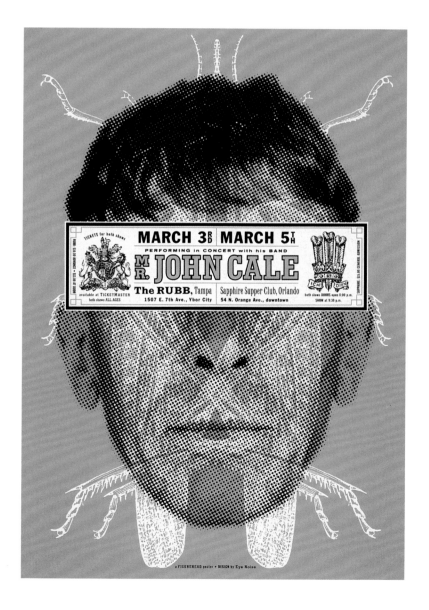

Design Firm • *Fahrenheit, Boston, MA*
Art Director • *Paul Montie*
Graphic Designers • *Paul Montie and*
Jennifer Alden
Printer • *Sam Johnson and Sons*
Paper • *Preprinted Florist Paper*
Client • *C. Walsh Theatre, Suffolk University*

Project Statement
The challenge was salvaging a low-budget poster when we hated the illustration provided by the client. First, we chopped up the illustration and put it back together in a more appealing collage. Then, because the play was set in a flower shop, we used preprinted florist paper and silkscreened it with one ink color. The result is just ugly enough to make it interesting.

Texas State of the Arts Poster

Design Firm • *Eisenberg and Associates,*
Dallas, TX
Creative Director • *Saul Torres*
Graphic Designer • *Larry White*
Illustrator • *Larry White*

Project Statement
The Dallas Theater Center came to us to design a
poster/invitation for the Texas State of the Arts exhibition.
I wanted the visual to suggest both Texas and the arts, so
I selected pieces of famous art to create a cowboy. I think
the poster succeeds because of the freedom the client gave
us and because it communicates the message quickly and
simply — like a herd of cattle at feeding time.

Burton 3-D Letter Advertisement

Design Firm • *Jager Di Paola Kemp Design,*
Burlington, VT
Creative Director • *Michael Jager*
Art Director • *Jim Anfuso*
Graphic Designers • *Jim Anfuso and*
Byron O'Neill
Client • *Burton Snowboards*

Project Statement
We chose to create an image with the Burton name that
would visually incorporate the brand with the excitement
of snowboard action photography while, at the same time,
cutting through stock editorial images in the publications.
We were careful to balance the brand presence with respect
for the sport, a crucial consideration for this youthful core
audience. This piece demonstrates excellence with unique
honesty and individuality.

Isaac's First Swim

Design Firm • *Emerson Wajdowicz Studios, Inc.,*
New York, NY

Art Director • *Jurek Wajdowicz*

Graphic Designers • *Lisa La Rochelle and*
Jurek Wajdowicz

Photographer/Writer • *Larry Towell*

Printer • *Active Graphics, Inc.*

Paper • *Bravo Dull 100# Text and Cover*

Client • *E.B. Eddy Paper/Island*

Paper Mills Division

Project Statement

This is the center tritone double-page spread from the
"BravoTowell" brochure. The brochure is part of the
Bravo Photo Masters Series published by E.B. Eddy Paper,
which presents the best photojournalism in the world.
Here, the strikingly beautiful photography of Larry Towell,
showing his children, is merged in a subtle way with the
poignant typography of Larry's own poetry to create serene,
distinctive, and memorable pages.

Humane Village Posters

Design Firm • *Concrete Design*
Communications, Inc., Toronto, Ontario
Art Directors • *Diti Katona and John Pylypczak*
Graphic Designer • *Nick Monteleone*
Illustrator • *John Pylypczak*
Printer • *C.J. Graphics*
Client • *International Council of Societies of*
Industrial Design

Project Statement

The poster series was designed for the 20th Congress of the International Council of Societies of Industrial Design. Marshall McLuhan's quote "It's not about the world of design, it's about the design of the world" was the conference theme. We thought that the use of 1960s iconography and design styles would be appropriate for the McLuhan-esque topics being discussed. But at the same time, the happy face would provide a bit of whimsy to counterpoint the weighty intellectual tone these conferences can take on. We knew that people who took themselves too seriously would hate it. And we liked that.

Images, Politics, and Cross-Pollination Poster

Design Firm • *James Victore Inc.,*
New York, NY
Art Director • *Debra Bandelin*
Graphic Designer • *James Victore*
Printer • *Rosepoint*
Client • *Syracuse University*

Colorado International Poster Symposium

Design Firm • *James Victore Inc.,*
New York, NY
Art Director • *Linny Frickman*
Graphic Designer • *James Victore*
Printer • *Rosepoint*
Paper • *French*
Client • *CIIPE*

AIGA Conference Poster

Art Director/Graphic Designer •
Stefan Sagmeister
Illustrators • *Kazumi Matsumoto,*
Peggy Chuang, Stefan Sagmeister, and
Raphael Rudisser
Photographer • *Bela Borsodi*
Writers • *Janet Abrams, Stefan Sagmeister*
Paint Box: Dalton Portella/Magic Graphics, Inc.
Printer • *Williamson Printing Corporation*
Paper • *Mohawk 70# Matte Coated*
Client • *AIGA*

Project Statement
As it reads in the tiny squiggly type on the top corner of this poster for the National Design Conference of the American Institute of Graphic Arts in New Orleans: Why a headless chicken? Is it a metaphor for the profession? Should we stop running around like one and sign up for this very interesting conference? Is it a Voodoo symbol? Anti-technology? Will a mixture of telephone scribbles and turn-of-the-century Art Brut really be the hot new style replacing wood veneer, itsy-bitsy type in boxes, and round corners? Wasn't New Simplicity supposed to come first? Euro-Techno?

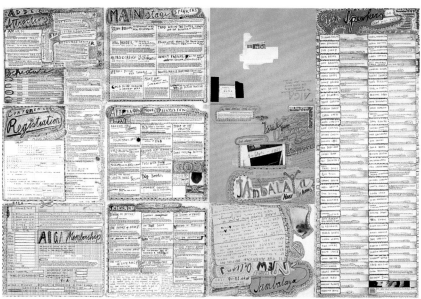

1997

50 Books/50 Covers of 1997

September 10–October 4, 1998

The Strathmore Gallery at the AIGA

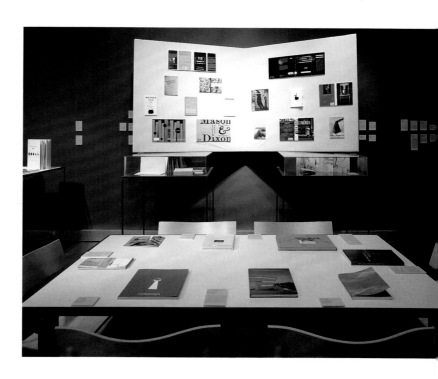

Two Essays by Jessica Helfand

50 Books/50 Covers

William Drenttel CHAIR

William Drenttel is a designer and publisher who works in partnership with Jessica Helfand in Falls Village, Connecticut. He is president emeritus of the AIGA and chairman of both the AIGA's Literacy Initiative and the *50 Books/50 Covers* book show. He is actively involved in literacy projects around the country and is a board member of the Poetry Society of America.

Title *Paul Rand: American Modernist*
Design Firm *Jessica Helfand/ William Drenttel, Falls Village, CT*
Art Directors *Jessica Helfand and William Drenttel*
Graphic Designer *Jeffery Tyson*
Typeface *Filosofia*
Printer *Red Ink Productions*
Paper *Mohawk Options*
Publisher *William Drenttel Editions*

Title *Chapbooks for Learning*
Design Firm *Jessica Helfand/ William Drenttel, Falls Village, CT*
Art Director *William Drenttel*
Graphic Designer *Jeffery Tyson*
Photographer *John Dolan*
Writers *James Traub and Students at P.S. 89*
Printer *Red Ink Productions*
Editors *William Drenttel and Sam Swode*
Paper *Mohawk Superfine*
Publishers *Chapbooks for Learning/Mohawk Paper Mills*

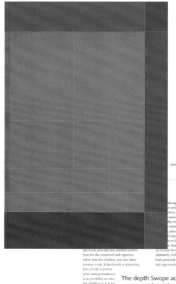

The depth Swope achieves comes not from the book itself, but from the way he uses the book as the organizing instrument of a writing curriculum. The broader academic point is that children are capable of much more serious intellectual work than they normally perform; we have to know how to evoke it.

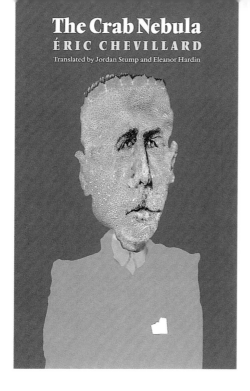

Richard Eckersley

Richard Eckersley is a graduate of
Trinity College, Dublin, and the
London College of Printing. After
polite refusals from Henrion, Schleger,
and Schmoller, he started out as a
design assistant with Lund Humphries,
the publisher of *Typographica* and
the *Penrose Annual*. He moved
to Ireland and the Kilkenny Design
Workshops in the 1970s; his work
there ranged from a silver trophy
for the tidiest hydroelectric station
to an identity for the National
Film Studios. He then emigrated to
America, teaching at Tyler for a
year before joining the University
of Nebraska Press, where he has
remained ever since.

Title *The Crab Nebula*
Author *Eric Chevillard*
Design Firm *University of Nebraska Press, Lincoln, NE*
Graphic Designer/Illustrator *Richard Eckersley*
Typeface *Vendôme*
Paper *Glatfelter 55# Natural*
Printers *Bookcrafters and U.N. Printing Services*
Publisher *University of Nebraska Press*

Title *Dangerous Virtues*
Author *Ana Maria Moix*
Design Firm *University of Nebraska Press, Lincoln, NE*
Graphic Designer/Illustrator *Richard Eckersley*
Typeface *Koloss, Minion*
Printers *Bookcrafters and U.N. Printing Services*
Paper *Glatfelter 55# Natural*
Publisher *University of Nebraska Press*

Title *Choral Works*
Authors *Jacques Derrida and Peter Eisenmann*
Editors *Jeffrey Kipnis and Thomas Leeser*
Graphic Designer *Thomas Leeser*
Publisher *The Monacelli Press*

Jonathan Galassi

Jonathan Galassi, editor-in-chief and executive vice president of Farrar, Straus & Giroux, is a poet, translator, and editor who has been awarded both the P.E.N./Roger Klein Award for Editing (1984) and the LMP Editors Award (1990). After graduating from Harvard College and Cambridge University — earning two baccalaureate degrees as well as a master's — he began a dual career as a trade book editor and poet/translator/anthologist. His poems have appeared the *Paris Review, Atlantic, The Nation, New Republic, Ploughshares and Poetry,* and in the anthology *Ten American Poets,* edited by James Atlas (1974). He served as poetry editor of the *Paris Review* for ten years and was the translator and editor of numerous collections of poetry. His grants include two Ingram Merrill Foundation Fellowships and a Guggenheim. Before beginning his tenure at Farrar, Straus & Giroux, he was an editor at Houghton Mifflin Company as well as Random House.

Gianfranco Monacelli

Gianfranco Monacelli is president and publisher of The Monacelli Press. Born in Italy, he first came to New York in 1965 to study music. At the same time, he started to work at the legendary Rizzoli bookstore on 55th Street and Fifth Avenue. He quickly became manager of the bookstore and oversaw its expansion throughout the United States. Subsequently, Monacelli founded Rizzoli International Publications, which during his tenure became one of the country's most renowned publishers of illustrated books. In 1994 he started his own publishing house, The Monacelli Press, with the goal of originating books of the highest graphic and textual quality. The press has published more than 100 books and has received significant recognition and numerous awards.

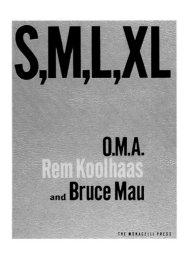

Title *S, M, L, XL*
Authors *Rem Koolhaas and Bruce Mau*
Design Firm *Bruce Mau Design, Inc., Toronto, Ontario*
Graphic Designers *Bruce Mau and Kevin Sugden*
Photographer *Hans Werlemann*
Publisher *The Monacelli Press*

Title *Closing: The Life and Death
of an American Factory*
Authors *Bill Bamberger and
Cathy N. Davidson*
Graphic Designer *Molly Renda*
Photographer *Bill Bamberger*
Typeface *Danson*
Printer *Tien Wah Press*
Paper *135 gsm Allegro Demi Matte*
Publishers *W.W. Norton and
DoubleTake*

Closing chronicles the final months
and shutdown of a 100-year-old
furniture factory, and weaves the
stories of six former employees into a
larger discussion of the postindustrial
world we live in. The design needed
to accommodate a full text that would
be comfortable to read, and black-
and-white and color photographs that
were intended to appear as art rather
than illustration. Photos and text were
arranged to tell one story through two
voices without subordinating either
to the other. The publisher's commitment to ensuring that this book
reached a broader audience required
a trim size that would fit on a standard bookstore shelf with a jacket that
announced itself boldly.

Molly Renda

Molly Renda is the executive
editor for design and production of
DoubleTake magazine, which is published by the Center for Documentary
Studies at Duke University. A fine
arts graduate of the School of Visual
Arts, Renda has designed the magazine since its launch in 1995 and
also acts as design and production
manager for DoubleTake Books,
published in association with W. W.
Norton. Before joining the staff of
DoubleTake, she ran her own studio
in Durham, North Carolina. Clients
included Algonquin Books, Duke
Press, University of Chicago Press,
and the Carnegie Museum of
Natural History. Her work has
received awards for design excellence
from the AIGA, American Center
for Design, Society of Publication
Designers, and *Communication Arts*
magazine. *DoubleTake* magazine
received the 1998 National Magazine
Award for General Excellence.

Title *French Lessons: A Memoir*
by Alice Kaplan
Design Firm *Molly Renda
Graphic Design, Durham, NC*
Graphic Designer *Molly Renda*
Typefaces *Joanna, Gill Sans*
Paper *Glatfelter*
Publisher *University of Chicago Press*

The design needed to reflect the
clarity and intimacy of the author's
voice without veering into pre-
ciousness. The result is a small, slim
volume with a narrow text page set
in Eric Gill's slightly quirky, highly
legible Joanna.

Central to the jacket design is
a photograph of prosecutors at the
Nuremberg trials, one of whom
is Kaplan's father. This, along
with other elements, was collaged,
photographed, and collaged again
in the printing process to illustrate
the confluence of memory and
meaning.

Susan Sellers

Susan Sellers received a B.F.A. in graphic design from Rhode Island School of Design in 1989. After earning a master's degree in American Studies from Yale University, she went on to teach, lecture widely, and publish articles in *Eye, Design Issues, Visible Language,* and other journals. She is currently a critic in the graphic design department at Yale University School of Art. After holding positions in several studios, including Total Design and UNA in Amsterdam, Sellers founded the multidisciplinary studio 2x4 in New York City in 1995, with partners Michael Rock and Georgianna Stout. The studio's clients include Knoll, Vitra, the New York Times, National Geographic, the Whitney Museum of American Art, Rem Koolhaas/Office for Metropolitan Architecture (OMA), Architecture New York (ANY), Philip Johnson FAIA, Princeton School of Architecture, P.S.1 Center for Contemporary Art, and many others.

Title *[Reflecting] Philip Johnson's Glass House*
Author *Toshio Nakamura*
Design Firm *2 x 4, New York, NY*
Art Directors
Michael Rock and Susan Sellers
Graphic Designer *Penelope Hardy*
Photographer *Michael Moran*
Printer *Grafisches Zentrum/Godfried Bühler Drucktechnik*
Publisher *YKK*

This book began as a conversation between designers, photographer, and writers about the relationship between the space of a building and the space of a page. How might a book convey an experience of place? It was not until we visited Philip Johnson at the Glass House and spent time wandering the grounds that we came to a resolution. On Johnson's estate, walking not only transports you to different buildings but to different architectural moments, programs, sites, fantasies. The Glass House itself is a central staging area for those extended forays. The book is an expression of that experience; it is book imagined as wandering. We designed a series of aesthetic locations, each containing new, or old, ways to imagine the place. Those locations have their own special character while sharing something of the whole. *Reflecting: Philip Johnson's Glass House* is in itself a reflection of the place, and a series of graphic reflections on how a place in the world is rendered as a place on the page.

Title *Charrette [MOMA]*
Design Firm *2 x 4, New York, NY*
Art Directors *Michael Rock and Susan Sellers*
Graphic Designers *David Israel, Chin Lien Chen, William Morrisey, Hitomi Murai*
Photographer *Steven Ahlgren*
Printing *Docutech, Indigo Printing*
Publisher *Self-Published, Limited Edition of 150*

This book was produced as Office for Metropolitan Architecture's entry for the MoMA Urban Expansion Competition in the spring of 1997. The book is a rumination on the state of the modern museum and urbanism rather than the faithful presentation of an architectural project. The project is the polemic. It is a collaboration between architects, designers, photographers, and archivists from all over the world — conceived, written, assembled, designed, and produced over the course of eight days. It was inexpensively produced in an edition of 150 using digital printing (Docutext and indigo) and Smythe-sewn by a local New York bookbinder. Like a film or play, it is the work of many people who contributed expertise, critique, and craft to the final product.

Title *The Adventures of Telemachus*
Author *Louis Aragon*
Design Firm *Exact Change,*
Boston, MA
Designer *Naomi Yang*
Printer *Thomson-Shore*
Publisher *Exact Change*

This is an example of the books I design for Exact Change. The program of the press is to reissue literary works of the avant-garde. In order to create a library of classics, all the books match in format (6 x 8 inches) and specifications (4/c covers, a solid PMS color in the inside covers, and acid-free paper).

For the covers, I usually use artwork or photography from the era in which the book was written. In this case, I used a Max Ernst drawing from 1922, which is in fact the year the book was first published in French; Ernst and Aragon were both members of a Surrealist group at the time.

For the design of the interior, I drew upon the typography of the French first edition. It is by no means a scientific reproduction of the original, but I tried to match it in spirit, as well as in a few specific details.

Naomi Yang

Naomi Yang graduated from Harvard/Radcliffe College in 1986, and attended the Harvard Graduate School of Design in Architecture from 1986 to 1989, but did not complete the degree. In 1989, Yang started a publishing house, Exact Change, with her partner, Damon Krukowski. Located in Boston, Exact Change reprints classics of experimental works of literature and has published twenty books to date, including titles by Gertrude Stein, Giorgio de Chirico, John Cage, and Leonora Carrington. Yang designs all the books and related ephemera. From 1987 to 1991, Yang also played bass in the rock band Galaxie 500; currently, she continues her musical career as half of the duo Damon & Naomi. Yang also maintains a painting studio, and in 1994 had her first one-person show.

Title *The Galaxie 500 Box Set*
Design Firm
Exact Change, Boston, MA
Designer *Naomi Yang*
Production Manager *Traci Swartz*
Paper *French Speckletone Pepper*
Client *Rykodisc*

The Galaxie 500 Box Set is a repackaging of three out-of-print records by my former band, with a previously unreleased fourth compact disk of outtakes and a 52-page booklet of photographs and essays. I chose not to reuse the original artwork of the individual albums, which I had also designed, because I wanted to give the whole package a new and unified look. It was important to me that the boxed set be a coherent object, rather than a collection of individual CDs inside a slipcase.

I opted to use only two colors on the packaging, blue and silver, in order to save the rest of the budget for a heavy slipcase, and as much four-color printing inside the booklet as possible. The illustrations are seventeenth-century astronomical engravings, because although the band's name was taken from a 1960s Ford car, I always enjoyed its more poetic associations.

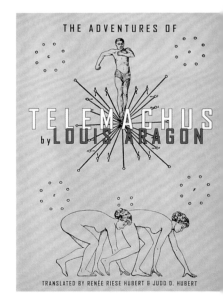

Introduction • *Paul Goldberger*
Foreword • *Joseph Rosa*
Design Firm • *Bureau, New York, NY*
Art Director • *Bureau*
Graphic Designer • *Claudia Brandenberg*
Typefaces • *Officina and Frutiger*
Printer • *Tien Wah Press*
Paper • *150# Nimola Matte*
Publisher • *Rizzoli International Publications*

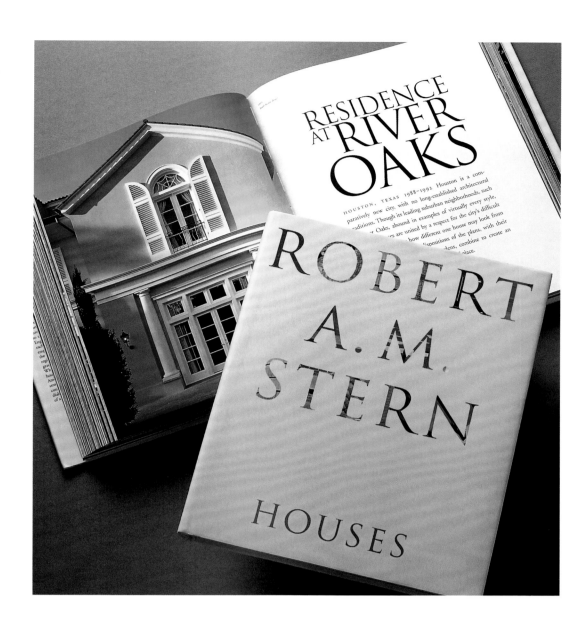

Robert A.M. Stern Houses

Author • *Robert A.M. Stern*
Design Firm • *Pentagram Design,*
New York, NY
Art Director • *Michael Bierut*
Graphic Designers • *Michael Bierut*
and Esther Bridavsky
Client/Publisher • *The Monacelli Press*

Project Statement
Houses is the second of two books on the work of architect
Robert A.M. Stern. This edition focuses on residential projects, while the first featured offices, hotels, and institutional
buildings. Pentagram's design is meant to reflect Stern's
architectural approach: the contemporary interpretation of
classical forms in a confident, even monumental form.

Suffragettes to She-Devils

Author • *Liz McQuiston*
Design Firm • *Pentagram Design,*
New York, NY
Art Director • *Paula Scher*
Graphic Designers • *Lisa Mazur,*
Esther Bridavsky, and Anke Stohlman
Client/Publisher • *Phaidon*

Project Statement
Bold colors and type distinguish this book on the history
of the women's movement, which is illustrated with graphic design ephemera documenting the era.

Bill Viola

Author • *David A. Ross*

Graphic Designer • *Rebeca Méndez*

Photographers • *Kira Pirov and Various*

Typeface • *Franklin Gothic*

Printer • *Dr. Cantz'sche Druckerai,
Ostfildern, Germany*

Paper • *Cover: Igepa Invercote 350 gsm;
Text: Schneidersöhne Luxosamtoffset 150 gsm*

Publishers • *Whitney Museum of American Art
in association with Flammarion, Paris/New York*

Constructions

Author • *John Rajchman*
Design Firm • *MIT Press Design Department,*
Cambridge, MA
Art Director/Graphic Designer • *Jean Wilcox*
Typefaces • *Janson and Franklin Gothic*
Printer • *Quebecor, Kingsport*
Paper • *Glatfelter D57 White*
Client/Publisher • *MIT Press*

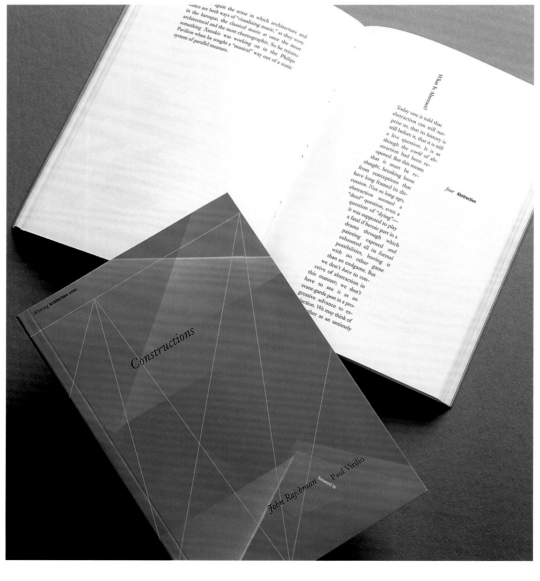

Mark Rothko

Author • *Jeffrey Weiss*
Design Firm • *The National Gallery of Art,*
Washington, DC
Graphic Designer • *Margaret Bauer*
Typefaces • *Minion and Cronos*
Printer • *Arnoldo Mondadori Editore*
Paper • *Gardapat, 135 gsm*
Publisher • *National Gallery of Art*

Dance Ink: Photographs

Design Firm • *Design/Writing/Research,
New York, NY*
Creative Director • *J. Abbott Miller*
Graphic Designers • *J. Abbott Miller
and Paul Carlos*
Photographers • *Various*
Typefaces • *FF Scala and FF Scala Jewels*
Printer • *Toppan Printing*
Publisher • *Chronicle Books*
Client • *The Dance Ink Foundation*

Project Statement
The *Dance Ink Photographs* book assembles the archive of
a quarterly dance magazine into a theatrically sequenced
narrative. The curtain opens with a clown at the beginning
and the "performance" begins, moving through a series of
different dancers, photographers, and color environments.
In the midst of this performance, there are five essays on
choreographers of the modern movement. After the finale,
there is a list of closing credits that identify the performers
in order of appearance.

Introduction • *Pee Wee Kirkland*
Design Firm • *John Jay Design, Portland, OR*
Creative Director • *John C. Jay*
Graphic Designers • *Joshua Berger*
and *John C. Jay*
Photographer • *John Huet*
Typefaces • *Retrospecta and Interface*
Printer • *Toppan Printing Co.*
Paper • *Oji Ok Bright Rough Text*
Publisher • *Melcher Media/Workman Publishing*

Editor • *Christine Normandin*
Design Firm • *Callaway Editions, New York, NY*
Creative Director • *Nicholas Callaway*
Graphic Designer • *Jennifer Wagner*
Illustrator • *Chief Lelooska*
Typefaces • *Mrs Eaves and Mantinia*
Printer • *Palace Press International*
Paper • *140 gsm NPI, Japanese Uncoated Stock*
Publishers • *Dorling Kindersley/Callaway Editions*

Project Statement

Echoes of the Elders is the first in a storytelling series dedicated to preserving the spoken word in book form. I wanted this book to be a tall tale. Its grand size, large type, and silhouetted paintings set against a stark white background were combined to instill a larger-than-life feeling. Passing a story down to a child is a gift that should feel magical to both child and reader. The ligatures in the fonts Mrs Eaves and Mantinia were selected so as to capture the feeling of a secret language, another time and place.

The Jungle ABC

Author • *Michael Roberts*
Design Firm • *Callaway Editions,*
New York, NY
Creative Director • *Nicholas Callaway*
Graphic Designer • *Toshiya Masuda*
Illustrator • *Michael Roberts*
Typeface • *Eagle*
Printer • *Palace Place International*
Paper • *180 gsm NPI, Japanese*
Uncoated Stock
Publishers • *Hyperion Books for*
Children/Callaway

The Brothers Grimm

....

Authors • *The Brothers Grimm*
Design Firm • *Pentagram Design,*
New York, NY
Art Director • *Paula Scher*
Graphic Designers • *Paula Scher*
and Lisa Mazur
Illustrator • *Seymour Chwast*
Printer • *Heritage Press*
Paper • *Text and Cover: 80#*
Mohawk Vellum Text, Warm White;
Endsheets: 80# Neenah Classic Linen Text,
Epic Black
Client/Publisher • *Heritage Press*

Project Statement
For this latest volume in a series of limited editions for
friends of Heritage Press, Paula Scher selected the darkest
fairy tales by the Brothers Grimm and designed the book
with unease in mind. "I wanted a scary children's book,
with the bloodiest stories, the scariest pictures, and big,
nasty type. I was tired of nice, sweet children's books."

The Monster Mash

Author • *Mimi Maxwell*

Design Firm • *Campbell Sheffield Design Inc.,*
Toronto, Ontario

Creative Director • *Mimi Maxwell*

Graphic Designer • *Campbell Sheffield Design Inc.*

Illustrator • *Mimi Maxwell*

Printer • *King's Web Printers*

Paper • *9.6 Matte Cover, 80# Luna Matte #2*

Publisher • *Tumbleweed Press*

Project Statement

Dancing monsters and prancing goblins jump off the page in this funky counting book by designer Mimi Maxwell. This book is a fun little tale about someone trying to go to sleep while the bedroom keeps filling up with mischievous dancing monsters. Although each new page is darkened by the addition of a new monster, *Monster Mash,* with its charming rhymes, is designed to convey the message that monsters in the night aren't so scary after all.

2 little **monsters**
looking at me funny
grinning, scheming
jumping up like bunnies.
creepy, kooky frights
how their tricks **delight**
oh, you little monsters **two.**

The Wind-Up Bird Chronicle

Author • *Haruki Murakami*
Design Firm • *Alfred A. Knopf,*
New York, NY
Art Director • *Chip Kidd*
Graphic Designers • *Chip Kidd*
and Misha Beletsky
Illustrator • *Chris Ware for Acme Novelty*
Productions
Jacket Photographer • *Geoff Spear*
Typefaces • *Iowan Old Style, OCR B,*
Monotype Grotesque, Din Schriften
Printer • *The Haddon Craftsmen/Phoenix Color*
Paper • *50# Sebago MF*
Publisher • *Alfred A. Knopf*

Project Statement

The title character is a ubiquitous bird that lives in the narrator's neighborhood. He hears it all the time but never sees it, and that became the focus of the visual scheme in two ways: as a large photograph and as a mechanical diagram, neither of which can be seen in full by the reader. The relative simplicity of the jacket photo, suggesting a banal exterior, is in direct contrast to the binding diagram's wildly intricate workings, which imply that beneath such serene surfaces all is not what it may seem. Other formal elements echo this — the circle motif in the mechanical diagram is carried through in jacket and front-matter typography, chapter numbers and folios. Winding motion is another theme: it's expressed in the zooming out of the frontmatter titles and the folios, which "travel" around the margins page by page. The variation of the letterspacing and alignment of chapter subtitles also mimic the properties of springs and mechanisms. The crowning touch is the layering of a light silver gloss varnish depicting the diagram directly on top of the matte photo on the jacket, something we had never done before. I think it says to readers, before they ever open the book, that they are in for much more than they expected.

Sea of Buddha

Author • *Hiroshi Sugimoto*
Design Firm • *Matsumoto Incorporated,*
New York, NY
Art Director/Graphic Designer •
Takaaki Matsumoto
Photographer • *Hiroshi Sugimoto*
Editor • *Atsuko Koyanagi*
Typeface • *Garamond*
Printer • *Dai Nippon Printing Co., Ltd.*
Paper • *Text: Van Nouveau 135 gsm,*
Aluminum Cover
Publisher • *Sonnabend Sundell Editions/*
Sonnabend Gallery

Project Statement
This book contains forty-eight photographs of 1,000
Buddha sculptures in the temple of Sanju San-Gen-do,
Kyoto. The book is bound to display the entire panoramic
scene, and is sixty pages long.

Against the Tide

Author • *Randy F. Weinstein*

Design Firm • *The Stinehour Press,
New York, NY*

Art Director/Graphic Designer • *Jerry Kelly*

Typeface • *Janson*

Printer • *The Stinehour Press*

Paper • *Monadnock Dulcet*

Publisher • *Glenn Horowitz, Bookseller*

Project Statement

This book was almost entirely dense, somewhat technical text, with only a handful of illustrations scattered across almost 300 pages, so the main challenge was coming up with an attractive and clear type page that organized the material (which was quite diverse) in an accessible manner. To do this, I put the most technical information — the physical description of the books — in the outer margins, leaving the main text block for the author, title, and interesting running commentary. Frontmatter and backmatter are always a challenge to the designer, and this book — with its two indices, dedication, copious notes, and other ancillary materials — presented myriad opportunities for diverse typographic treatment. The author, Randy Weinstein, worked closely with me on all aspects of the design. The binding design took some convincing, but he also provided much useful input that helped the appearance of this publication.

Bordertown

Authors • *Barry Gifford and David Perry*
Design Firm • *Appetite Engineers,*
San Francisco, CA
Creative Director • *Michael Carabetta/*
Chronicle Books
Art Director • *Martin Venezky*
Graphic Designers • *Martin Venezky*
and Geoff Kaplan
Photographer • *David Perry*
Typefaces • *Scotch Roman, Kabel,*
and Univers Condensed
Client/Publisher • *Chronicle Books*

Project Statement

It is unusual for designers to be asked not just to form the look of a book, but to help create it as well. Under the careful watch of Chronicle Books, *Bordertown* was a collaboration between the author, the photographer, and the designers. We were given the opportunity not only to edit and rearrange the contents, but to contribute to them as well.

Because we are outside of the culture — we don't even speak the language — our outsider status became a catalyst of discovery. We traveled, visited, observed, and collected. Posters, packages, shopping bags, trinkets, fabric. What we could read and what we could only guess at became part of the creative process.

We developed a basic architecture for the book, and within that tight structure, we were able to move freely. We wanted the elements that come together on the pages to react to each other, as if we as designers were standing at a distance. Violence, humor, voices shouting over one another or whispering in our ears. Typography, like walls and windows, sometimes obstructed our view, but sometimes made it safe for us to stare.

We decided to keep the fictional passages absolutely quiet — like an empty dream state, a rest before the turmoil of the day begins.

Which parts of a given spread were brought in by Barry or David, Martin or Geoff? What parts of a child belong to either parent? We hoped that the question of authorship would, in places, mingle and dissolve as the book acquired a character and personality of its own.

Word + Image: Swiss Poster Design, 1955–1997

Authors • *Franc Nunoo-Quarcoo*
and Cynthia M. Wayne
Design Firm • *University of Maryland, Baltimore*
County, Visual Arts Department, Baltimore, MD
Art Director • *Franc Nunoo-Quarcoo*
Graphic Designers • *Franc Nunoo-Quarcoo (text),*
Bruno Monguzzi, Rosmarie Tissi,
and Wolfgang Weingart (cover)
Photographers • *Roderick Topping*
and Dan Meyers
Typefaces • *Akzidenz Grotesk, Futura,*
and Univers
Printer • *Charles McAree, Schmitz Press*
Paper • *McCoy Silk 100# Text*
Publisher • *University of Maryland,*
Baltimore County
Client • *Albin O. Kuhn Library and Gallery*

Project Statement
Word + Image: Swiss Poster Design, 1955–1997 is an exhibition catalogue documenting the brilliance of Swiss poster designers from the Modernist period through the present. To demonstrate the diversity in Swiss design aesthetic, Rosmarie Tissi, Bruno Monguzzi, and Wolfgang Weingart designed covers for the catalogue. The interior of the catalogue was designed to complement all three covers. The 6 x 9 inch format, though unusual for a catalogue, was economical for printing and assembly. The warm red and white covers refer to the official colors of the Swiss flag. The text and images in the catalogue make for a document reflecting the importance and power of Swiss poster design.

Making Architecture

Authors • *Richard Meier, Ada Louise Huxtable,*
Stephen D. Rountree, and Harold M. Williams
Graphic Designer • *Lorraine Wild*
Photographers • *Various*
Typeface • *Syntax*
Printer • *Lithographix*
Fabricator • *Roswell Book Bindery*
Paper • *Text: 80# Dulcet Smooth Book;*
Cover: 100# White Dulcet Smooth
Publisher • *J. Paul Getty Trust Publication Services*

Project Statement
This publication provides a unique record of the design
and construction of one of the most significant building
efforts of this century. The richness of the book lies in the
variety of viewpoints that it presents: from the stark aerial
photography of the construction to the lushly detailed
photographic interpretations of the landscape and construction. The drawings of Meier, Despont, and Irwin illustrate
the varied approaches and aesthetics. The essays of
Rountree and Meier provide point of view of both client
and architect while Huxtable's article takes a broader view
of the meaning of building in the twenty-first century.

Still More Distant Journeys

Author • *Stephanie D'Alessandro*
Design Firm • *studio blue, Chicago, IL*
Creative Director • *Kathy Fredrickson
and Cheryl Towler Weese*
Graphic Designers • *Cheryl Towler Weese
and Joellen Kames*
Typefaces • *Kipp, Clarendon,
Monotype Grotesque, and Franklin Gothic*
Printer • *C&C Offset Printing Co.*
Client • *The Smart Museum of Art,
University of Chicago*

Project Statement
Still More Distant Journeys accompanied a show of the work
of artist Lasar Segall. Segall was born in a Jewish ghetto in
Lithuania, then moved to Germany and later to Brazil. At
the time of each emigration, his work changed decisively in
response to the new locale, culture, and popular images of
that culture.

Because Segall used postcards, magazines, and snapshots
as reference materials for his art, our cover repeats an image
of a steamer from his postcard collection, and includes a
perforated postcard that can be pulled out and used. Inside
the book we continue the theme of coming from and
going to: a horizontal gap divides each page, and a double
collage begins each chapter — representing both Segall's
departure and destination.

Instrumental Form: Words, Buildings, Machines

Author • *Wes Jones*

Design Firm • *Jones: Partners, Architecture, El Segundo, CA*

Graphic Designer • *Doug Jackson*

Typeface • *Helvetica Light, Customized*

Printer • *C&C Offset, Hong Kong*

Paper • *Mitsubishi Matte Art, 105 gsm*

Publisher • *Princeton Architectural Press*

Project Statement

As indicated by the subtitle of this architectural monograph, the design of *Instrumental Form* tends to give equal consideration graphically to the author's text and varied built work, allowing each to contribute synergistically to the discussion of a technological approach to architecture.

The book design therefore eschews the closed method of presentation common to architectural monographs, wherein text is used simply to explain the visual material. Rather, *Instrumental Form* offers the possibility of a more open reading of both the visual and written material, which are presented as contiguous, parallel tracks of information.

This approach allows the reader to participate more actively in the reading of the work, as links within the main body of the text and the adjacent images prompt improved understanding.

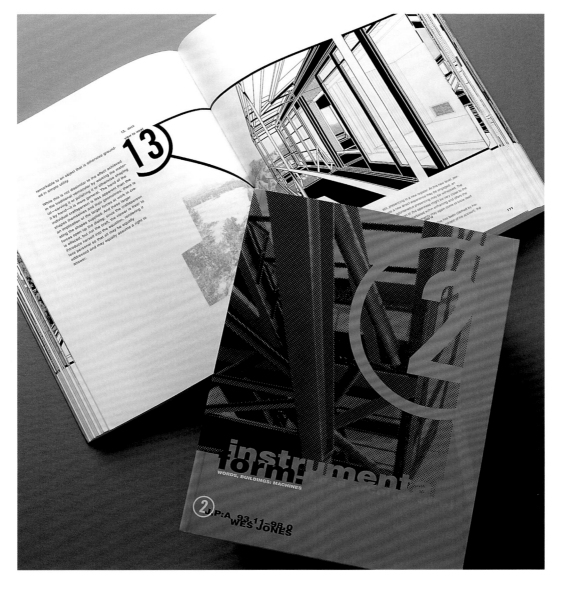

Painting by Numbers

Editor • *Joann Wypijewski*
Design Firm • *Alfred A. Knopf, New York, NY*
Art Director • *Barbara deWilde*
Publisher • *Alfred A. Knopf*

Blackletter: Type and National Identity

Editors • *Peter Bain and Paul Shaw*
Design Firm • *The Cooper Union Center
for Design and Typography*
Art Director • *Mindy Lang*
Graphic Designer • *Stephanie Reyer*
Typefaces • *Berthold Akzidenz Grotesk,
Stempel Garamond*
Printers • *Friesens Printing, Book Division*
Paper • *70# Warren Lustro Dull*
Publisher • *Princeton Architectural Press*

Project Statement
Blackletter: Type and National Identity, which accompanied
an exhibition at the Cooper Union's Herb Lubalin Study
Center for Design and Typography, is an exploration of the
history and contemporary perceptions of blackletter typefaces. The collection of essays ranges from the formal
qualities and nomenclature of the type to the contemporary
stigma reflected in its aesthetics. The challenge in designing
such a monograph was integrating the voluminous text,
the supporting type specimens, and the detailed chronology
of interrelated events into a comprehensive and legible
presentation. Even more difficult a task, however, was mea-
suring up to the scrutiny of a discriminating audience of
typophiles.

San Francisco Ballet 65th Anniversary Book

Author • *Sheryl Flatow*
Design Firm • *Tolleson Design,*
San Francisco, CA
Creative Director • *Steve Tolleson*
Graphic Designers • *Steve Tolleson*
and Michael Verdine
Photographer • *David Martinez*
Typefaces • *Mrs Eaves, Rosewood Fill,*
Filosofia, and Type Embellishments
Printer • *Watermark Press*
Paper • *80# Quest Black Cover,*
120# Lustro Dull Cover, 24# Gilbert Esse White
Green Text Endsheets, 80# Lustro Dull Book Text,
80# Hammermill Accent Opaque Book Text,
80# French Construction Charcoal Brown Cover
(Divider Pages)
Client • *San Francisco Ballet*

On a Balcony: A Novel (Mark Luyten)

Author • *Mark Luyten*
Design Firm • *Walker Art Center,*
Minneapolis, MN
Art Director • *Matt Ellen*
Graphic Designers • *Mark Luyten, Dan Dennehy,*
Glenn Halvorson, and Barb Economon
Typeface • *Mrs Eaves*
Printer • *Wallace Carlson*
Paper • *Cougar 80# Text Smooth, Gilclear Medium*
Publisher • *Walker Art Center*

Project Statement
The intent of *On a Balcony: A Novel (Mark Luyten)* was
to document a two-year commissioned art project, link it
to the resulting exhibition — *On a Balcony: A Cinema
(Mark Luyten)* — and give readers a clear understanding
of both. The process was truly a collaboration (long distance) between the designers and the Belgium-based artist.
Several inspired moments were the result of a narrative
that developed through the handling of fragmented texts,
a huge file of photographs, and a modest budget. Readers
received not only a document, but an artist's book and
artwork in one package.

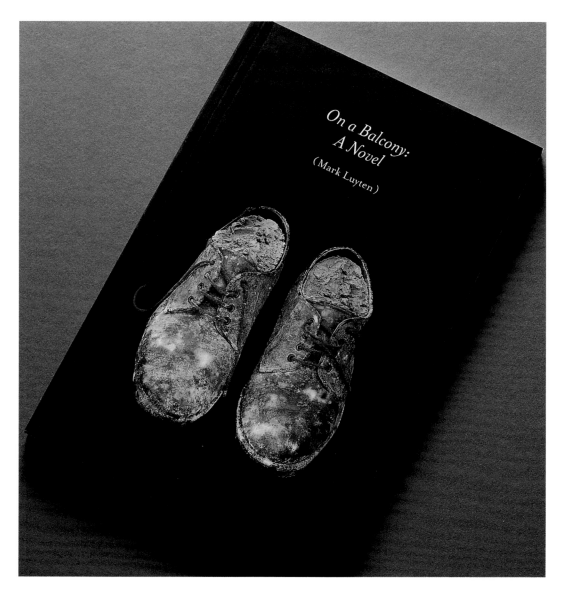

As in Queen (The ABCedarium of a Typophiliac)

Author • *Leda Black*
Design Firm • *Palabra Press, Ithaca, NY*
Art Director/Graphic Designer • *Leda Black*
Typefaces • *Various*
Printer/Binder • *Leda Black*
 (Letterpress, Hand Bound)
Paper • *Somerset Satin 250 gsm,*
Fabriano Ingres Cover, Hahnemühle Ingres
Publisher • *Palabra Press*

Project Statement

The book is an alphabet book of the letter Q. The text is a series of praise poems to this letter. The words form mesostichs (similar to acrostics) in which a word is created by the vertical alignment of horizontal lines, in the middle of the text block. The words thus formed are the name of the typeface of the particular Q, in alphabetical order.

I enjoyed the enviable situation of being both writer and designer (and printer and binder and publisher). I (we?) sought to make the writing and physicality of the work wholly entwined. This is my ideal as a book artist. I tried to keep the cost of materials down, which prompted me to use this intimate page size. The essence of the letters can't be contained on any page, however large. The cropped emphasis on parts of letters dovetails with the fetishism of the words to embody the obsessive gaze of the typophiliac. The whole is text.

The Books of Antonio Frasconi

Author • *The Grolier Club*
Design Firm • *The Stinehour Press,*
New York, NY
Art Director • *Antonio Frasconi*
Graphic Designer • *Jerry Kelly*
Illustrator • *Antonio Frasconi*
Typeface • *Garamond 3*
Printer • *The Stinehour Press*
Paper • *Monadnock Dulcet*
Publisher • *The Grolier Club*

Project Statement
We wanted to convey the beauty of the woodcuts as
well as possible for this catalogue of the work of one of the
major book artists of our time. Fletcher Manley at the
Stinehour Press made excellent color separations from the
35mm slides supplied by the artist, and the Stinehour Press
did their usual exemplary job of printing the color images
on a high-quality uncoated paper (Monadnock Dulcet).
For the typography I chose the slightly bouncy and irregular Garamond 3, which went well with the handmade
woodcuts. All the work was done in close collaboration
with the artist, who deserves a good deal of the credit for
the success of this book. With tireless energy he oversaw
every aspect of the production, including creating a special
two-color image for the catalogue cover. Working with
him was always a pleasure, and cemented a long friendship.

Pages from the Press

....

Author • *The Stinehour Press*

Design Firm • *The Stinehour Press,*
New York, NY

Art Director/Graphic Designer • *Jerry Kelly*

Typefaces • *Zapf Renaissance, and Numerous*
Others for Specimens

Printer/Publisher • *The Stinehour Press*

Project Statement

This book was printed as a specimen book, showing
sample pages from various books I had designed for customers in my capacity as designer and New York representative for the Stinehour Press. We wanted to show
a selection of the assorted books we print and design, so
we included pages from designs that included color on
coated; color on uncoated, duotone, single color offset;
and our special letterpress facilities.

Visual Explanations: Images and Quantities, Evidence and Narrative

Author • *Edward R. Tufte*

Design Firm • *Graphics Press, Cheshire, CT*

Art Director • *Edward R. Tufte*

Design Assistants • *Bonnie Scranton,*
Dmitry Krasny, Weilin Wu, and John Connolly

Typeface • *Monotype Bembo*

Project Statement

The design and printing of this book were intended to exemplify the argument of the text. The highest-quality materials and processes were used in order to enhance the information resolution of the illustrations. Fine substance combined with fine craft; content and design as a coherent whole.

Editor • *Karl Gernot Kuehn*
Design Firm • *University of California Press,*
Oakland, CA
Graphic Designer • *Nola Burger*
Typefaces • *Adobe Granjon and*
Univers Condensed (Light and Bold)
Printer • *Tien Wah Press*
Paper • *135 gsm Matte*
Publisher • *University of California Press*

Project Statement
This collection of powerful images by fifty-five East German photographers demanded a reconsideration of all aspects of the design. The need for duotones and fine paper on a small print run precluded a large-format book. Instead, a 7 x 10 trim was reduced to near-square dimensions, offering an unusual shape and surrounding both horizontal and vertical images with similar blocks of white space. Staggered placement allows the varied images to be viewed independently. Typography adheres to a clean, ordered grid with occasional modern twists, acknowledging the mixed influences of the era from which the photos originate.

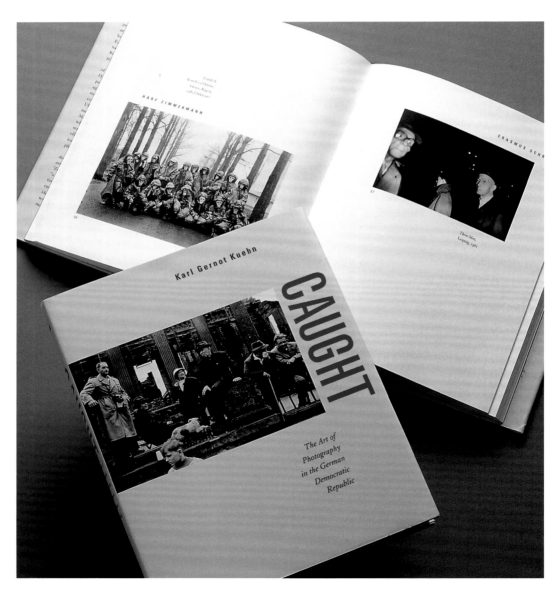

Post-War Literature

Authors • *Glenn Horowitz and Sara Funke*
Design Firm • *The Stinehour Press,*
New York, NY
Art Director/Graphic Designer • *Jerry Kelly*
Typeface • *Walbaum (Monotype and Berthold)*
Printer • *The Stinehour Press*
Paper • *Mohawk Superfine*
Publisher • *Glenn Horowitz Bookseller*

Project Statement

Originally the customer wanted to print an 8.5 x 11 inch catalogue, with an illustration section at the end containing one color image (dust jacket) and one black-and-white (text or inscription page) image per page from each book illustrated. We designed a much smaller catalogue (6 x 9) with inserted four-page sections, each containing a color image on the front and black-and-white inside. This way, we could reproduce the images at about 5 x 8 inches, much larger than two per page on the 8.5 x 11 format; the images would follow sequentially, as in a book; and it would be more economical since we could print the color on one side of a 4/1 sheet. As an added bonus, we fit a color dust jacket for this catalogue on the two sheets that had the color images. We also played off the gloss coated paper for the illustration inserts against an uncoated paper for the text, highlighting the reproductions. The typography was relatively straightforward and clean, using two different "cuts" of the elegant Walbaum typeface (the Berthold drawing, which is weightier and crisper, for display; and the Monotype drawing — based on the smaller sizes of the Walbaum originals — for text).

The Portraits Speak: Chuck Close in Conversation with 27 of His Subjects

Editor • *Joanne Kesten*

Design Firm • *Lausten Cossutta Design,*
Los Angeles, CA

Graphic Designers • *Judith Lausten*
and Renée Cossutta

Typeface • *Gill Sans*

Printer • *Publishers Press*

Paper • *Sterling Matte*

Publisher • *A.R.T. Press*

Project Statement

The book was designed to bring to a broad audience the work of Chuck Close and the artists he painted. To do this, each artist's conversation opens with a visual narrative of full-bleed black-and-white photos showing both the artist and his or her work. These photo-narratives are intended to show connections between the artist's life and work that might otherwise be overlooked. A limited printing budget guided decisions such as the jacketless cover, the 28-page color frontispiece that opens the book, the documentary-like black-and-white body of the book, and the lightweight paper.

A Morning's Work

Author • *Stanley B. Burns, M.D.*
Design Firm • *Twin Palms Publishing,*
Santa Fe, NM
Art Directors/Graphic Designers • *Jack Woody*
and Eleanor Morris Caponigra
Typeface • *Digital Version of Monotype Bulmer*
Printer • *Palace Press, Hong Kong*

Project Statement
We wanted this volume of primarily nineteenth-century images to convey both their time and place within the context of this book design, yet appear clearly contemporary on the surface. By choosing the egg-yolk yellow color for a cover design, we felt its oddness at once transcended the time and place of its contents, yet gave the book object a richness that is timeless.

Author • *Solomon R. Guggenheim Foundation*
Design Firm • *Design/Writing/Research,*
New York, NY
Creative Director • *J. Abbott Miller*
Art Director/Graphic Designer • *Luke Hayman*
Typeface • *HTF Guggenheim*
Printer • *Hull Printing*
Paper • *Warren LOE Dull, Mohawk Superfine*
Publisher • *Solomon R. Guggenheim Foundation*

Project Statement
The Guggenheim has become both famous and infamous for its international scale and impressive building projects. This publication, which is intended to help raise $200 million, is asking donors to expand the resources of the museum and support its growth. The front of the book is handled as a full-color visual dossier, while the financial data in the back is treated as a two-color report. The typography (a custom-designed font called Guggenheim) refers to the Frank Lloyd Wright lettering that is found throughout the Fifth Avenue building. A thumb notch marks the famous spiral ramp of the Guggenheim. The small scale of the book and its modest production deliberately undercut the expectation that everything associated with the Guggenheim is large and costly, offering itself as a sleek, concise document.

Building in Los Angeles

Author • *Southern California Institute*
of Architecture
Design Firm • *Greimanski, Los Angeles, CA*
Graphic Designer • *April Greiman*
Printer • *Foundation Press*
Publisher • *Southern California Institute*
of Architecture

Project Statement
Building in Los Angeles collects residential, commercial,
and institutional projects in the area designed by SCI-Arc
faculty and alumni. Originally published in 1994 for an
annual meeting of the AIA in Los Angeles, this updated
version features a cover that folds out to become a poster-
sized "map" of the region. The poster uses the topographic
language of the Raven map and separates the geographic
area into eight sections. Intended for recruitment, the
publication had to be inexpensive to produce, yet include
187 projects. The audience includes those who want to
use the guide to research new work in Los Angeles as well
as high school students in other parts of the country who
might be attracted by the bold, colorful poster design.
As part of a celebration of the school's twenty-fifth anniversary, the publication demonstrates how both the faculty
and the alumni have contributed to and changed the built
environment of Los Angeles.

Important Design: The Life of Piero Fornasetti

Design Firm • *Christie's Creative Services,*
New York, NY
Creative Director • *Lynda Havell*
Graphic Designer • *Lynn Fylak*
Photographer • *Dave Schlegel*
Typefaces • *Simoncini Garamond and Helvetica*
Printer • *White Brothers*
Publisher • *Christie's Inc.*

Author • *Maurice Berger*

Design Firm • *University of Maryland, Baltimore County, Visual Arts Department, Baltimore, MD*

Art Director/Graphic Designer • *Franc Nunoo-Quarcoo*

Photographers • *Various*

Typefaces • *Janson and Trajan*

Printer • *H&N Printing*

Paper • *Mohawk Vellum 80# Text*

Publisher • *University of Maryland, Baltimore County*

Client • *Fine Arts Gallery*

Project Statement

The design of this book, a theoretical primer for an exhibition about minimal art, plays on the show's exploration of the interconnection between form and ideology. *Minimal Politics* examines the leftist political concerns lurking in the industrial cubes and plinths of the century's most abstract and pared-down aesthetic movement. The design expands on the exhibition's historical, aesthetic, and social issues, elegantly subverting the formal vocabulary of book design: the cover slyly conceals much of its "content" under its cool, metallic surface; the pages play with and against the modernist grid, continually testing our preconceptions about typography and composition.

Typographia Polyglotta

Authors • *George Sadek and Maxim Zhukov*

Design Firm • *Association Typographique Internationale*

Graphic Designer • *Maxim Zhukov*

Typefaces • *Frutiger 57 and Various*

Typositor • *Spectrum Multilanguage Communications*

Printer • *The Stinehour Press*

Paper • *80# Mohawk Vellum Text, Warm White*

Publisher • *Association Typographique Internationale*

Project Statement

In designing the layout of the book, priority was given to presenting the language exhibits, which constitute the centerpiece of this study. Decisions on the typographic formatting of the language exhibits were made first: the typography of the text was both coordinated to it and subordinated to it. Where the language extracts were set in a justified serif font, black on white, the text was set in an unjustified sans serif, dark gray on light gray. Thus, the light gray exhibit pages ended up sandwiched between the white pages of the front and back matter. The page layout of the book (the column measure, the margins, and the unit grid in general) is built around the typographic parameters of the language exhibits. A square "window" in the tinted background is sized to the length of the "control" language exhibit (all English); it provides for a quick visual reference to the extent of a given language sample.

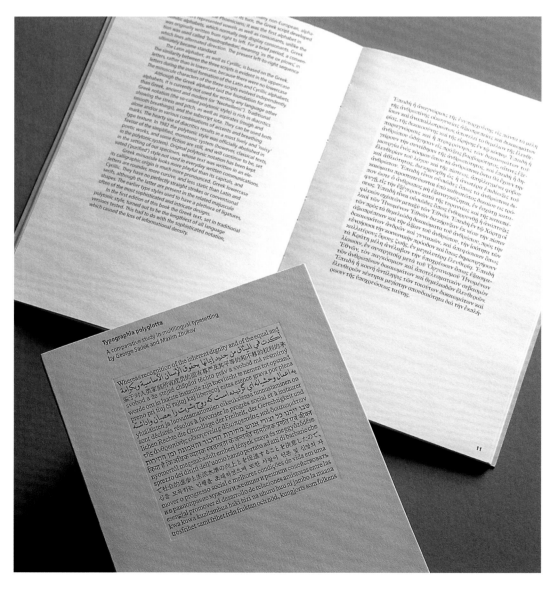

Burning with Desire

Author • *Geoffrey Batchen*
Design Firm • *MIT Press Design Department,*
Cambridge, MA
Graphic Designer • *Ori Kometani*
Typeface • *Engravers Gothic*
and Monotype Garamond
Printers • *Phoenix Color*
and Quebecor Printing, Kingsport
Publisher • *The MIT Press*

Still Rooms & Excavations

Authors • *Richard Barnes and Douglas Nickel*
Design Firm • *Tenazas Design,*
San Francisco, CA
Art Director • *Lucille Tenazas*
Graphic Designer • *Kelly Tokerud*
Photographer • *Richard Barnes*
Typefaces • *Bauer Bodoni*
Printer • *The Studley Press*
Paper • *Mohawk Superfine White,*
Warren Lustro Dull Enamel Cream
Publisher • *Richard Barnes*

Project Statement
Still Rooms & Excavations was a collaborative effort with
my husband, Richard Barnes. This catalogue (and the traveling exhibition it accompanies) documents the seismic
excavation of the DeYoung Museum in San Francisco and
the ensuing discovery of a potter's field underneath the
museum. In designing *Still Rooms*, my desire was to highlight the photographs in a way that was both provocative
and understated, allowing the images to speak for themselves. My own intervention was minimal, out of respect
both for Richard's work and for those buried beneath the
DeYoung. The size of *Still Rooms and Excavations* reflects
the enormity of the project itself, a project that literally
delved beneath the surface. Like the site it documents, this
piece has a tactility and emotional draw that are nearly palpable. The pacing of *Still Rooms* is as quiet as the title suggests: hushed and measured, almost to the point of stillness.

Author • *Andreas Vesalius*
Design Firm • *Norman Publishing,*
San Francisco, CA
Graphic Designer • *Steve Renick/Anselm Design*
Typefaces • *Bembo, Centaur/Monotype*
Typography Ltd.
Electronic Typesetter • *Paul Benkman/*
Tiki Bob Publishing and Design
Printer • *Thomson-Shore, Inc.*
Paper • *Mohawk Superfine Softwhite Eggshell 80#*
Publisher • *Norman Publishing*

Project Statement
At 12 x 16.5 inches, the Latin version of *On the Fabric of the Human Body* contains hundreds of marginal references and several full-page woodcuts. The design challenge for this first English translation was to create a format that was both legible and economical to print, while essentially conserving the look of the original. The 9 x 12 inch standard trim allowed us to print almost all the illustrations at full size, include the marginal references, and add new scholarly references. Printed on acid-free Mohawk paper, this limited edition provides an essential and lasting contribution to Renaissance, medicine, and art scholarship.

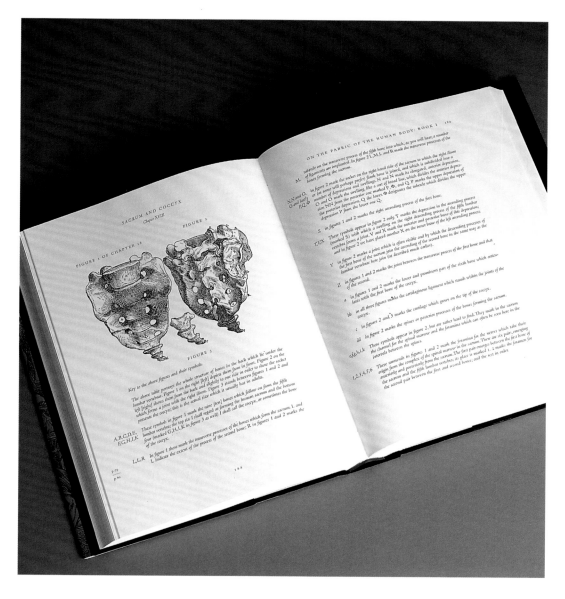

Author • *R.O. Blechman*
Design Firm • *R.O. Blechman, Inc.,*
New York, NY
Art Director • *Amanda Freymann*
Graphic Designer/Illustrator • *R.O. Blechman*

Project Statement
The Book of Jonah began as a project commissioned by
Harper & Row as a children's book, but it soon became
clear to the publisher and to me that the material was more
adult oriented. I lost interest in the project and abandoned
it until several years later, when the Gulf War broke out.
My strong feelings about that conflict made me take up the
project again when I projected myself as the protagonist,
Jonah, and our government and President Bush as an Old
Testament Jehovah.

The picture and hand-written format is something I first
did back in 1952, when I wrote and illustrated *The Juggler of
Our Lady*. Coincidentally, it was selected as one of the Fifty
Books of the Year.

Puppies

....

Author • *William Wegman*
Design Firm • *Doyle Partners, New York, NY*
Creative Director • *Stephen Doyle*
Graphic Designer • *Gary Tooth*
Photographer • *William Wegman*
Typefaces • *Trade Gothic and Scala*
Publisher • *Hyperion Books*

Project Statement
This is the sixth book we've created with William
Wegman, but the first we've designed for all ages (the
other books were primarily for kids). Beginning with
Wegman's first weimaraner puppy, Man Ray, the book
traces the personalities and adventures of several generations of weimaraners, revealing the relationships they
have with each other, with Wegman, and with his ubiquitous camera.

Shaped Poetry

Authors • *Various*
Design Firm • *Archetype Press, Pasadena, CA*
Art Director • *Vance Studley*
Graphic Designers • *Jennifer Case, Haejin Cho,
Erik Flippo, Daniel Garcia, Amanda Margolis,
Kate Rivinus, Teri Weber, Lies Wihono,
Gregory Chapuisat, Aaron Delesie, Volker Durre,
Marie Gauthier, Alison Green, Seungmin Ji,
Allen King, Tito Sanpaolesi, Julio Alcantar,
Johnny Chen, Jill Franks, Thomas Kendzie,
Marilyn Prado, Pascal Wever, Jacob Atmodjojo,
Scott Matz, Karen Orilla, Brian Paumier,
Bang H. Pham, Alex Yang*
Typeface • *53 Foundry Metal Fonts
and Hamilton Wood Type*
Printer • *Archetype Press, Art Center
College of Design*
Paper • *Strathmore 24# Text*
Publisher • *Archetype Press, Art Center
College of Design*

Project Statement
The book is a concerted effort by student designers to use
foundry type to create a purely typographic statement about
the essence of a poem and the overall form it assumes.
Foundry type and letterpress printing enable the designer to
both manually manipulate type and experience letterforms
in visual communication.

Golden Cockerel Type

Authors • *John Dreyfus, Sebastian Carter,*
and James Mosley
Design Firm • *The Stinehour Press,*
New York, NY
Art Director/Graphic Designer • *Jerry Kelly*
Illustrator • *Eric Gill*
Typographers • *Jerry Kelly and Lissa Dodington*
Typeface • *ITC Golden Cockerel*
Printer • *The Stinehour Press*
Paper • *Text: Simpson Teton; Jacket:*
Hahnemuhle Bugra
Publisher • *International Typeface Corporation*

Project Statement

Printing a specimen for a type company has its challenges and rewards. Type manufacturers tend to give designers more leeway in producing specimens that will show off their fonts, but of course there are pressures and restrictions involved. In today's wild market for typefaces, economics are key, and such materials must be produced on tight budgets. This book was printed in black ink only through-out (with a second color only behind the illustrations), but printing it letterpress (for the text) helped to set it apart from the average job. A careful selection of good papers for the text (Simpson Teton) and jacket (imported Hahnemuhle Bugra) was a key element. Lissa Dodington and I worked carefully on the typesetting, using unusually tight word spacing and occasionally careful adjustment of the kerning to show this somewhat weighty, unusual type to best advantage. Again, it was a pleasure working with a sympathetic client who is also a good friend (Mark Batty). The excellence of the texts he procured for this publication enhanced the project greatly, in my opinion.

A Commonsense Guide to Your 401(k)

Author • *Mary Rowland*
Design Firm • *Don Morris Design,*
New York, NY
Creative Director • *Don Morris*
Graphic Designers • *Don Morris*
and Josh Klenert
Photo-Illustrator • *Heidi Merscher*
Typeface • *Thesis, Bureau Agency*
Printing • *Quebecor Printing*
Paper • *Matrix 100# C2S*
Publisher • *Bloomberg Press*

Project Statement

Bloomberg LLP, a high-tech news-gathering service with its own dedicated computer network and television programming, was interested in getting into the book business. They commissioned our studio to create a book series on personal finance. These books needed to feel modern and current, but also remain fresh-looking as the series expanded. *A Commonsense Guide to Your 401(k)* is the sixth book in this series.

Since personal finance can be rather dry and unexciting, we wanted to evoke the human side with lush color and soft, sensual lighting. Heidi Merscher did the photo-illustration, shooting many objects herself and digitally rendering the rest to create gravity-defying still lifes. They hint at the high-tech authority of Bloomberg, but bring it into a human context that is understandable and appealing. The main typeface, Thesis, presents the title directly and concisely, yet its curved letterforms project a warmth that is personal rather than institutional. The monochromatic palette of the book cover changes with each new book, building a spectrum of color as the series continues.

Luminous Code: Photo-Based Artworks Catalogue

Curator • *Jennifer Blessing*
Design Firm • *Marc English: Design,*
Austin, TX
Creative Director/Graphic Designer •
Marc English
Photographer • *Andrew Yates and Various*
Typefaces • *Monaco and Meta*
Printer • *The Lithoprint Company*
Paper • *Jacket: Neenah UV Ultra II #17,*
Catalogue: S.D. Warren Patina Matte
70# Text and 80# Cover
Publisher • *Texas Fine Arts Association*

Project Statement

The title of this exhibition catalogue of photo-based art
served as my inspiration. A translucent cover came to
mind immediately when I heard the word "luminous."
For "code," I drew upon camera F-stop settings and developing instructions — all codes to those who understand
them, namely photographers. The stuff of the photographic
process was also used in my introductory collages: silver
tape, masking tape, Polaroid prints, a Hasselblad, and
viewfinders.

The display typography apes F-stops. Inks are metallic.
The display of the exhibition pieces places the artists' work
at the fore, as it should be, with supporting text, though
somewhat stylized, kept to a minimum. The remaining
cover and supplementary spreads I have tried to approached
as my own version of "photo-based art." The printer
did a great job printing on both sides of the translucent dust
jacket, marrying it with the actual cover images. Every-
body's happy.

Dutch Journal

Author • *Malcolm Cochran*
Design Firm • *D. Betz Design, Seattle, WA*
Graphic Designer • *David Betz*
Illustrators • *David Betz and Malcolm Cochran*
Photographers • *Various*
Typefaces • *Sabon and Bureau Agency*
Printer • *McLile Printing*
Paper • *Starwhite Vicksburgh Archival Text,*
Champion Benefit Cover
Client • *Malcolm Cochran*

Project Statement
Dutch Journal is a collaboration between designer David
Betz and artist Malcolm Cochran. The goal was to produce
a compelling object that documented the artist's work and
experience in the Netherlands.

All of the decisions about the look and feel of this
limited edition grew out of a shared aesthetic of the designer and artist. Sizing the book to fit the artist's tastes as well
as press size, ganging the four-color work on one form,
and having the artist sign and place the cover labels were all
cost-saving measures that allowed this book to be produced
within tight budget constraints. This understated design
(no Photoshop!) supports the artist's narrative about this
period in his life.

Hours

Author • *Kenneth A. Lohf*
Design Firm • *Kelly/Winterton Press,
New York, NY*
Art Director • *Jerry Kelly*
Typeface • *Centaur*
Printer • *Omega Litho*
Binder • *Judi Conant*
Paper • *Arches Text Laid*
Publisher • *Kelly/Winterton Press*

Project Statement

Ken Lohf, former president of the Grolier Club and head
of special collections at Columbia University, is also a poet
who publishes his work occasionally. Being an avid book
man, he takes the physical appearance of books seriously.
His first publications were printed by the Janus Press and
Bembo Typographers, but for the past few years I have
had the honor of printing his books. He has always allowed
me to do more or less as I wished in designing his books,
always in close consultation with him, and often leading to
fine papers, bindings, etc. For this book I was immediately
struck by the underlying religious nature of the text. The
title referring to medieval Books of Hours, gave me a clue
to treat this text with ruled borders in the manner of the
early printed and manuscript Books of Hours.

A Sculptor's Fortunes

Author • *Walter Hancock,*
with Edward Connery Lathem
Design Firm • *The Stinehour Press,*
New York, NY
Graphic Designer • *Dean Bornstein*
Jacket Photo • *Tony King*
Typefaces • *Adobe Jensen and Monotype Castellar*
Printer • *The Stinehour Press*
Binder • *Acme Bookbinding*
Paper • *Mohawk Superfine Softwhite Eggshell*
Publisher • *Cape Ann Historical Association*

Project Statement
This memoir introduces the 97-year-old sculptor Walker
Hancock to a new audience and recognizes his important
contribution to art and culture. This modest and quiet
memoir of a truly monumental figure is complemented
by an equally understated and elegant book design. The
materials chosen are of the highest quality and permanence
(acid-free stock, for example) and the reproductions are
300-line duotone to best reproduce detail and tonal range.

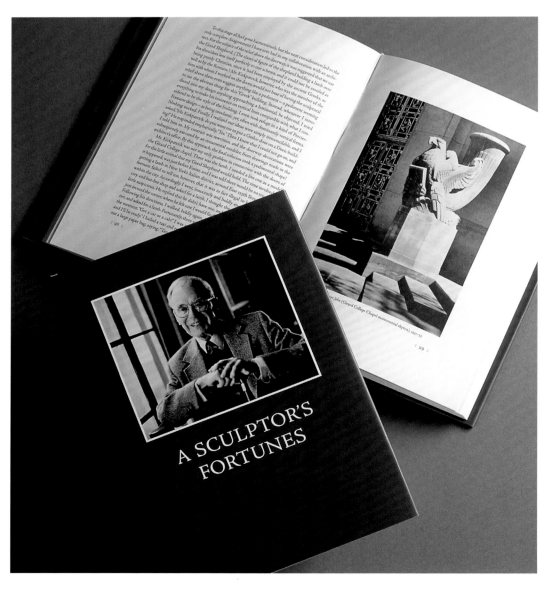

Inspiring Reform: Boston's Arts and Crafts Movement

Curator • *Marilee Boyd Meyer*
Design Firm • *Design/Writing/Research,*
New York, NY
Creative Director • *J. Abbott Miller*
Art Director • *Paul Carlos*
Graphic Designer • *Paul Carlos*
Typefaces • *FF Quadraat and Emigre Whirligigs*
Printer • *The Studley Press*
Paper • *Mohawk Superfine, 50/10 Vellum*
Publishers • *Davis Museum*
and Cultural Center/Harry N. Abrams

Project Statement
This exhibition catalogue evokes the Arts and Crafts tradition in design and bookmaking, but in a contemporary manner. Produced to accompany an exhibition, which we also designed, the book used contemporary fonts (Quadraat) in ways that refer to the ideal book traditions of the Arts and Crafts movement. In place of the dense floral ornamentation of Arts and Crafts books, we have used copious footnotes as a kind of organic, textural frame to the two columns of text. The book interleaves color plates into the uncoated text pages, creating lush interludes within the typographic environment of the historical essays.

Author • *Russell Flinchum*
Design Firm • *Hahn Smith Design,*
Toronto, Ontario
Art Directors/Graphic Designers • *Alison Hahn*
and Nigel Smith
Photographer • *Dennis Cowby*
Typefaces • *Kaufman, Scala, and Abadi*
Printer • *Worzala*
Paper • *80# Repap Matte*
Publishers • *Rizzoli International Publications/*
Cooper-Hewitt, National Design Museum,
Smithsonian Institution

Project Statement
This book was published as a companion to an exhibition at the Cooper-Hewitt Museum in New York as well as for sale to the outside public. Although Dreyfuss is relatively unknown outside design circles, his work is familiar to many. Our primary objective was to create a compelling object that would get people involved in this fascinating and very readable account of a man whose work revolutionized industrial design principles.

Dreyfuss always wore a brown suit and was reputed to own a brown tuxedo, thus the brown jacket. The Big Ben alarm clock on the front and back covers and typography of the title evoke the aura and era of a 1940s detective novel. We lifted some of this typographic detailing from Dreyfuss's own work.

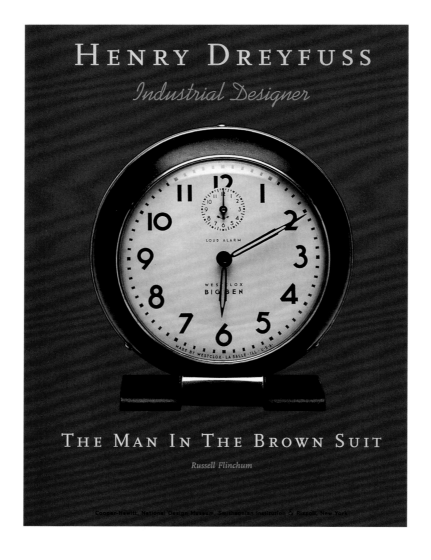

Pragmatism

....

Author • *Louis Menand*

Design Firm • *Vintage Books, New York, NY*

Art Director/Graphic Designer • *John Gall*

Photographer • *Katherine McGlynn*

Typefaces • *Trade Gothic and Centaur*

Printer • *Phoenix Color*

Publisher • *Vintage Books*

LISA PALAC   THE EDGE OF THE BED
HOW DIRTY PICTURES CHANGED MY LIFE

The Edge of the Bed

Author • *Lisa Palac*

Design Firm • *Little, Brown & Company,*
New York, NY

Creative Director/Graphic Designer •
Michael Ian Kaye

Photographer • *Melissa Hayden*

Typeface • *Helvetica Bold*

Printer • *Jaguar Advanced Graphics*

Paper • *80# Simpson Bright White C/1/S*

Publisher • *Little, Brown & Company*

Project Statement
A literal interpretation of the title becomes the symbol
for this memoir of sexual enlightenment.

Editor • *Colin Westerbeck*
Design Firm • *The Art Institute of Chicago,*
Publications Department, Chicago, IL
Art Director/Graphic Designer • *Sam Silvio*
Typeface • *Futura*
Printer • *Meridian Printing Co.*
Paper • *Quintessence*
Publishers • *The Art Institute of Chicago/*
Bulfinch Press, Little, Brown & Company

In 1995, Irving Penn donated his professional archives to the Art Institute of Chicago, along with a set of prints representing his life's work. This catalogue accompanied the exhibition of the same name and celebrates Penn's gift to the museum.

The cover is a revealing example from the archival materials donated. This contact sheet assemblage, *Unpublished Variants for the Christmas Cover of Vogue, November 15, 1949*, demonstrates Penn's working process. With its grease pencil markings, the image exposes not only the artist's material practice but his visual thinking.

Author • *Carole Klein*
Design Firm • *Little, Brown & Company,*
New York, NY
Creative Director • *Michael Ian Kaye*
Graphic Designer • *Leslie Goldman*
Typeface • *Univers*
Printer • *Phoenix Color Corp.*
Paper • *Phoenix 80# Truwhite*
Publisher • *Little, Brown & Company*

The type solution for this biography of Doris Lessing is straightforward, with rigid lines separating the title from subtitle and author. This is juxtaposed over a shadow that is blurred and fades in an untypical way, to symbolize Lessing's fondness for breaking rules and ignoring social convention.

MIRROR WOMEN, SURREALISM, AND IMAGES
SELF-REPRESENTATION

WHITNEY CHADWICK
EDITED BY

Mirror Images

Editor • *Whitney Chadwick*
Design Firm • *MIT Press Design Department,
Cambridge, MA*
Art Director/Graphic Designer • *Jean Wilcox*
Photographer • *Claude Cahun*
Typefaces • *Trade Gothic and Bell Gothic*
Printer • *Phoenix Color*
Paper • *Zanders Mirricard*
Client/Publisher • *MIT Press*

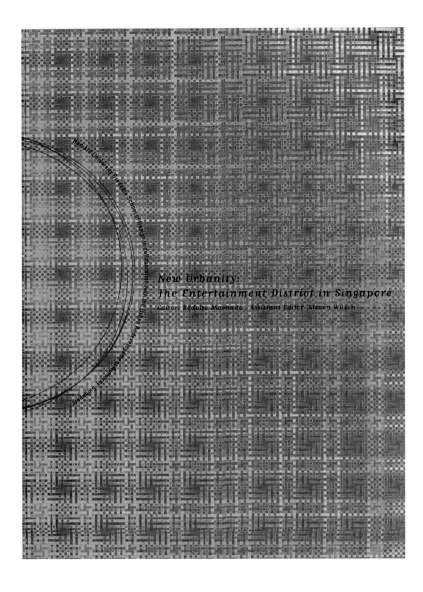

New Urbanity:
The Entertainment District in Singapore
Editor: Rodolfo Machado , Assistant Editor: Steven Wilson

New Urbanity: The Entertainment District in Singapore

Editors • *Rodolfo Machado and Steven Wilson*
Design Firm • *Nassar Design, Boston, MA*
Graphic Designer • *Nelida Nassar*
Illustrator • *Margarita Encomienda*
Photographers • *Harvard Graduate School of
Design Faculty and Students*
Typeface • *Matrix*
Printer • *Bolder Publications / Creative Printing*
Paper • *Holoplaid .015 by Pennsylvania
Pulp & Paper*
Publisher • *Harvard University Graduate
School of Design*

Project Statement
New Urbanity: Entertainment in Singapore documents the
research undertaken by Harvard graduate faculty and students in the field of urban design and planning. The book
is meant to encapsulate their research efforts in the most
efficient and eloquent format for a wide audience. Potential
readers range from experts in government agencies to
students in the field and individuals who have a marginal
interest in contemporary issues of urbanism.

The aim was to embody the spirit of the book in the
making of the cover. A sense of entertainment was thus
realized with unusual materials and new printing methods
that broke through the conventions of graphic design.
Typical of Nassar Design's work is the daring blend of genres and sensibilities: classical typography and design layouts
with avant garde materials, colors, and printing materials.
The result is a compelling hybrid that engages the viewer
without losing sight of the issues of legibility, efficiency,
and sobriety in the delivery of the message.

Author • *Southern California Institute*
of Architecture
Design Firm • *Greimanski, Los Angeles, CA*
Graphic Designer • *April Greiman*
Design Assistant • *Lorna Turner*
Typefaces • *Mrs Eaves Italic, Meta,*
Egyptian 505, and Monaco
Printer • *Pozzo Gros Monti*
Publisher • *The Monacelli Press*

Project Statement
From the Center: Design Process at SCI-Arc, a 224-page
compendium of projects by fifty-two of SCI-Arc's faculty,
documents the design thinking or process behind a variety
of built and theoretical projects. The work includes an
art museum website, a Beverly Hills dentist's office, a Sioux
university, Swiss propeller factory renovation, a daycare
center at a Metro stop, clothing boutiques, residences,
restaurants, and urban design schemes for Havana and
North Hollywood. The simulated chipboard paper cover
slips off to reveal the actual chipboard cover underneath,
with its hieroglyphic printed spine. Concealed spiral binding completes the feel of a working sketchbook. The
cover design integrates the two-dimensional moving hand,
an icon designed for the school's twenty-fifth anniversary
materials, with a softly illusionistic geometric space.

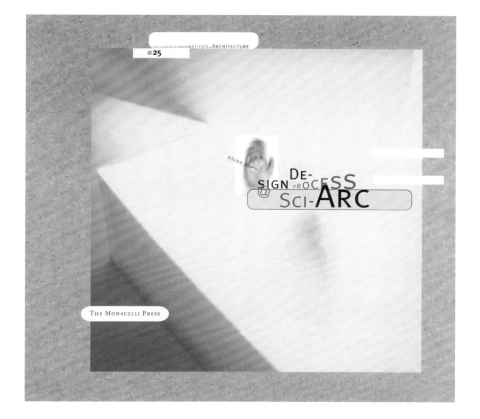

Author • *Patrick Chamoiseau*
Design Firm • *Royce M. Becker Design,*
New York, NY
Art Director • *Marjorie Anderson*
Graphic Designer • *Royce M. Becker*
Illustration (Painting detail) •
Marie Guilhelmine Benoist
Additional Digital Illustration •
Royce M. Becker
Typeface • *Handscript One, Felix Titling*
Publisher • *Pantheon*

Project Statement
This epic novel chronicles 150 years of post-slavery
Carribbean history, as told through the many individual
stories of Marie-Sophie, daughter of a slave and spokes-
woman for the shantytown the book is named after. The
challenge was to design an elegant and contemporary cover
that in structure reflected the book's immense complexity,
and at the same time honored its clarity. The cover's success is largely due to the beauty and timelessness of its
central image, a detail from a painting ("Portrait of a Black
Woman") that hangs in the Louvre. Through the wonders
of Photoshop, I was able to integrate the painting thematically with some visually unrelated images I felt were vital
to evoke both the book's mystical dimensions as well as
its factual historical content. Hence, the amorphous tropical
greenery, which gives a sense of environment, and a
yellowed antique map that establishes time and place.

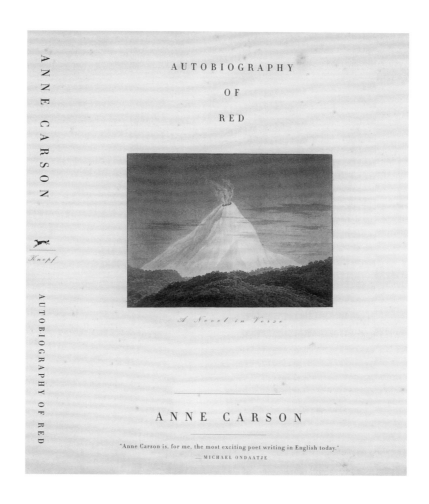

Autobiography of Red

Author • *Anne Carson*
Design Firm • *Alfred A. Knopf, New York, NY*
Art Director/Graphic Designer •
Carol Devine Carson
Typeface • *HTF Didot*
Printer • *Coral Graphics*
Publisher • *Alfred A. Knopf*

Project Statement
When many book jacket designs seem directed by marketing or author egos, and you have a chance to design a jacket for a book that is a deceptively simple novel in verse written by a prize-winning author — with quotes from not only Michael Ondaatje but Susan Sontag — it means you can use very small type.

Che

Author • *Jon Lee Anderson*
Design Firm • *Grove Press, New York, NY*
Art Director/Graphic Designer • *John Gall*
Illustrator • *Paul Davis*
Typeface • *Opti Morgan Two*
Printer • *Coral Graphics*
Publisher • *Grove Atlantic*

Author • *Patrick Smith*
Design Firm • *Kathleen DiGrado Design,*
New York, NY
Art Director • *Marjorie Anderson*
Graphic Designer • *Kathleen DiGrado*
Typeface • *Hanseatic (Swiss 924)*
Printer • *Coral Graphic Services, Inc.*
Publisher • *Pantheon Books*

Project Statement
To quote the author, "The reader is invited to hold this book, see it for what it appears to be, and then remove its surface layer to discover it is something else. This is exactly what the book is intended to do for its subject."

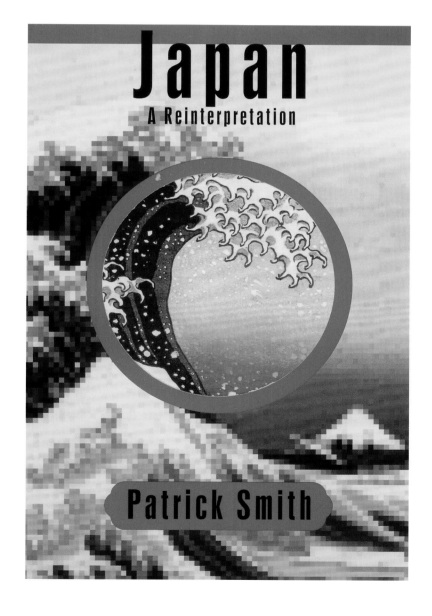

Author • *Knut Hamsun*
Design Firm • *Farrar, Straus & Giroux,*
New York, NY
Art Director • *Susan Mitchell*
Graphic Designer • *Rodrigo Corral*
Illustrator • *Donna Mehalko*
Typefaces • *Futura Bold Condensed,*
Futura Medium Condensed
Printer • *Phoenix Color*
Paper • *Mohawk White 80#*
Publisher • *Noonday*

Project Statement
A gripping portrait of an artist struggling for integrity,
Hunger mirrors the dire straits of the author's own life.

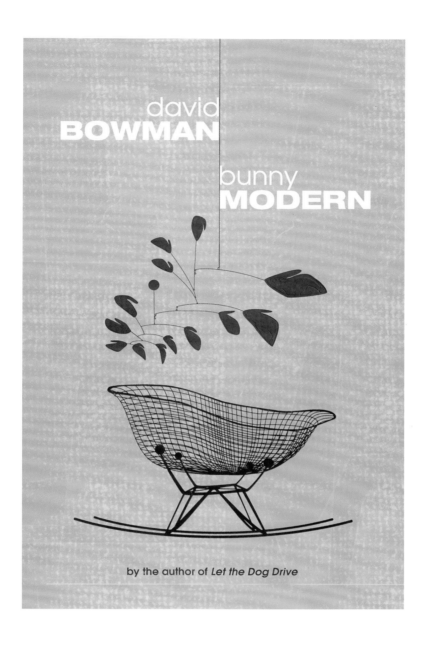

david
BOWMAN

bunny
MODERN

by the author of *Let the Dog Drive*

Bunny Modern

Author • *David Bowman*
Design Firm • *Little, Brown & Company,*
New York, NY
Creative Director • *Michael Ian Kaye*
Graphic Designer/Illustrator • *Stuart Patterson*
Typeface • *ITC Avant Garde Gothic*
Printer • *Phoenix Color Corp.*
Publisher • *Little, Brown & Company*

Project Statement
In the text, Bunny Modern is the brand name of a line of
baby accessories, including cribs and mobiles. The protagonist describes the logo of these items as a bunny face with a
safety helmet. This was the first choice for the cover image,
but I found it to be too limiting, and perhaps too juvenile.
"Bunny Modern" sounded slightly more classic to me —
largely because "modern," the adjective, was placed second.
Images of mid-century modern, I thought, would be more
appropriate, and definitely more attractive. Also, with the
late '90s obsession with '50s and early '60s icons and motifs,
I felt the cover would appeal to a hipper audience.

To keep the images tied to the narrative, I included a
baby mobile and a crib and illustrated these items as if they
had been designed by Calder and by Charles and Ray
Eames, respectively. Perfect for the spine would be a tall,
slim bunny reference to Giacometti.

SURREALIST
ART

THE LINDY AND EDWIN BERGMAN COLLECTION
AT THE ART INSTITUTE OF CHICAGO

Surrealist Art: The Lindy and Edwin Bergman Collection

Author • *Dawn Ades*

Design Firm • *studio blue, Chicago, IL*

Art Directors • *Kathy Fredrickson and Cheryl Towler Weese*

Graphic Designers • *Cheryl Towler Weese, Gail Wiener, JoEllen Kames*

Typefaces • *Scotch Roman, Metro, Chevalier, and Torino*

Typographers • *Paul Baker Typography and studio blue*

Printers • *LS Graphic Inc./Grafica Comense*

Publishers • *The Art Institute of Chicago and Thames and Hudson, Inc.*

Project Statement

Surrealist Art: The Lindy and Edwin Bergman Collection documents a gift of over 100 works of surrealist art to the Art Institute of Chicago. In designing the book, we tried to walk a fine line between the museum's serious scholarship and our own desire to create a book that feels surrealist — one that plays upon surrealism's oblique humor and use of appropriated materials in its structure, imagery, and typography.

Author • *Thomas Mann*
Design Firm • *Alfred A. Knopf, New York, NY*
Art Director • *Carol Devine Carson*
Graphic Designer • *John Gall*
Typefaces • *Fraktur and Centaur*
Publisher • *Alfred A. Knopf*

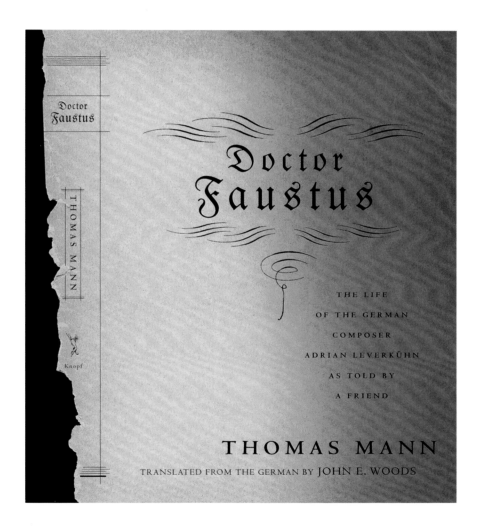

Twenty Questions

Author • *J.D. McClatchy*
Art Director/Graphic Designer • *Chip Kidd*
Photographer • *Max Aguilla-Helwig*
Typeface • *Electra*
Client/Publisher • *Columbia University Press*

Project Statement

Sometimes the process of selecting a piece of art to represent a book's subject matter is so intuitive, the only explanation you can offer for your motives is the book itself, and even then people often walk away scratching their heads. For this poet's collection of literary essays about reading and writing, I found the mystery of the disembodied mouth somehow "spoke" to the nature of raw inquiry, so that the very nature of questioning is questioned. It wouldn't be exaggerating, I think, to suggest that the jacket plays a certain game with the viewer.

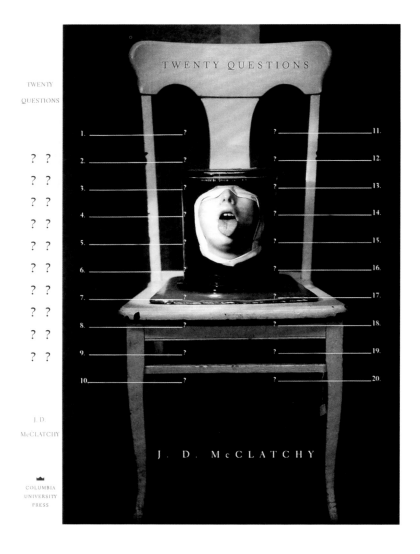

The Boys of My Youth

Author • *JoAnn Beard*
Design Firm • *Alfred A. Knopf, New York, NY*
Art Director • *Barbara DeWilde*
Publisher • *Alfred A. Knopf*

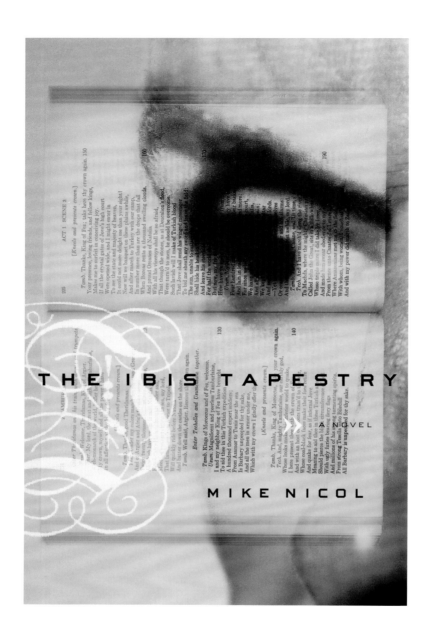

The Ibis Tapestry

Author • *Mike Nicol*
Design Firm • *Evan Gaffney Graphic Design,*
New York, NY
Art Director • *Carol Carson*
Graphic Designer • *Evan Gaffney*
Photographers • *Kate Swan and Jason Beaupré*
Typeface • *Sackers Square Gothic*
Publisher • *Alfred A. Knopf*

Project Statement
The Ibis Tapestry is an intense and abstract thriller chronicling a bored writer's accidental murder investigation of a troubled arms dealer plagued by horrific dreams of Christopher Marlowe's Tamburlaine the Great (and that's the simple version).

Author • *Helen Dunmore*

Design Firm • *Little, Brown & Company,*
New York, NY

Creative Director • *Michael Ian Kaye*

Graphic Designer • *John Fulbook*

Cover Photograph • *Betty Hahn*

Typefaces • *Palace Script and ITC Newtext*

Printer • *Jaguar Advanced Graphics*

Paper • *Jaguar 10 pt C/1/S*

Publisher • *Back Bay Books/Little,*
Brown & Company

Project Statement

The simulated botanical print that Betty Hahn created seemed appropriate for this mystery about a family, and the death of an infant, located in a cottage in the English countryside with many gardens.

Slow Learner

Author • *Thomas Pynchon*
Design Firm • *Little, Brown & Company,*
New York, NY
Creative Director/Graphic Designer •
Michael Ian Kaye
Typeface • *ITC Century*
Printer • *Phoenix Color Corp.*
Paper • *Phoenix Coated One Side, 10 pt.*
Publisher • *Back Bay Books/Little,*
Brown & Company

Project Statement
A collection of writings from an early stage in Pynchon's
career is reflected by a cover that is not yet fully formed.

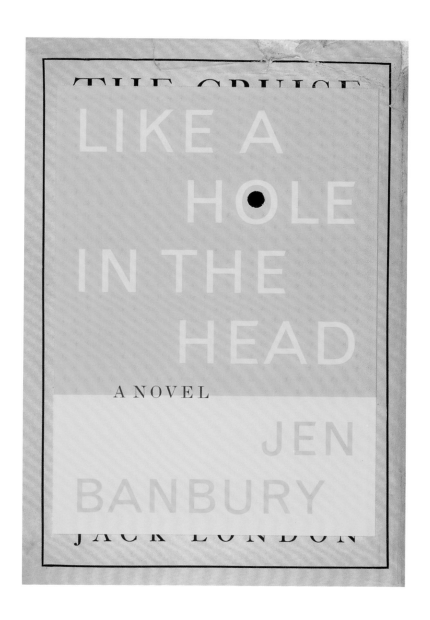

Like a Hole in the Head

Author • *Jen Banbury*
Design Firm • *Little, Brown & Company,*
New York, NY
Creative Director/Graphic Designer •
Michael Ian Kaye
Typeface • *Monotype Grotesque*
Printer • *Phoenix Color Corp.*
Paper • *Phoenix 100# Truwhite*
Publisher • *Little, Brown & Company*

Project Statement
A rollicking novel about a rare book is the impetus
for this modern book jacket, which surprints the book
described in the novel. The book's humor and darkness
are meant to be reflected by the juxtaposition of these
two elements. The die-cut hole, while playing literally
off the title, is also intended to represent the bullets that
fly in the narrative.

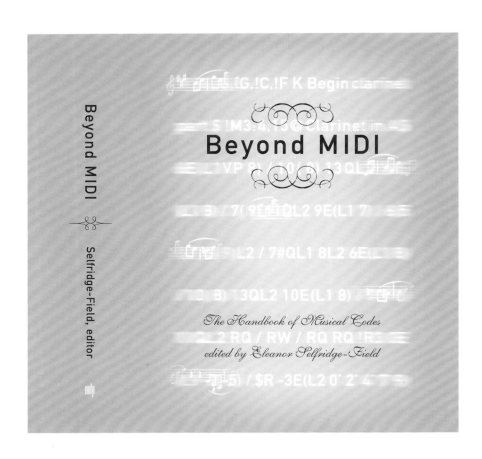

Beyond MIDI

....

Editor • *Eleanor Selfridge-Field*
Design Firm • *MIT Press Design Department,*
Cambridge, MA
Graphic Designer • *Ori Kometani*
Typefaces • *DIN and Shelley*
Printer • *Henry N. Sawyer Company*
Paper • *S. D. Warren Patina Matte Coated 70#*
Publisher • *The MIT Press*

Editors • *Emmanuel Roche and Yves Schabes*
Design Firm • *MIT Press Design Department,*
Cambridge, MA
Graphic Designer • *Jim McWethy*
Typeface • *Syntax*
Printer • *Henry Sawyer Co.*
Paper • *Warren Lustro Offset Enamel Gloss*
Client/Publisher • *MIT Press*

Project Statement

I still don't understand what the book is about. It's heavy-duty computer science theory. Fortunately, I didn't need to understand the content to design the book jacket. In the interior, the authors use finite-state graphs to help illustrate the tech talk. I used the same style of graph on the cover. "Incomplete states" (white circles that mean nothing alone) are connected by lines (yellow squiggly) to form "complete states" (a bunch of white circles that mean something when connected).

I've taken some standard elements on a book jacket and merged them into a complete state that means something. The squiggly lines add some playfulness to an otherwise dry subject.

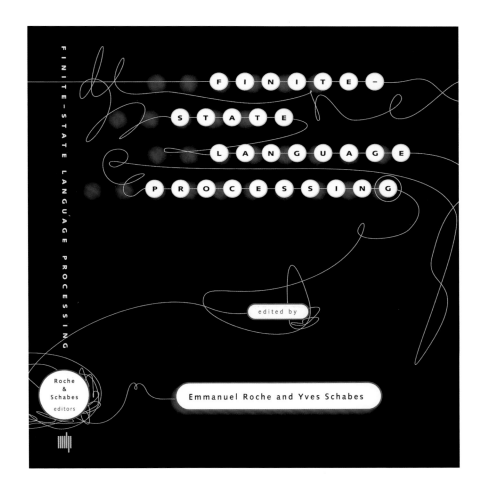

Author • *Thomas Lynch*
Design Firm • *Alfred A. Knopf, New York, NY*
Art Director • *Barbara DeWilde*
Publisher • *Alfred A. Knopf*

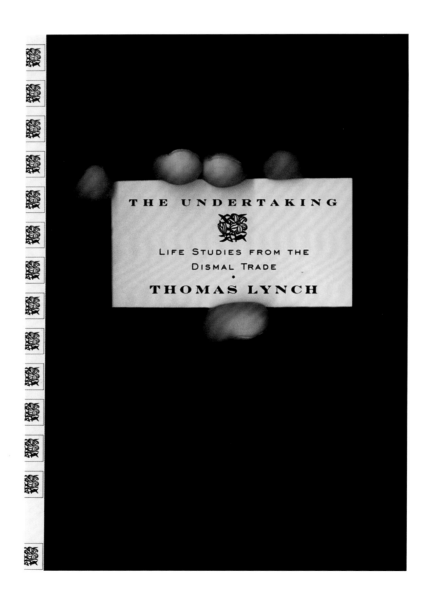

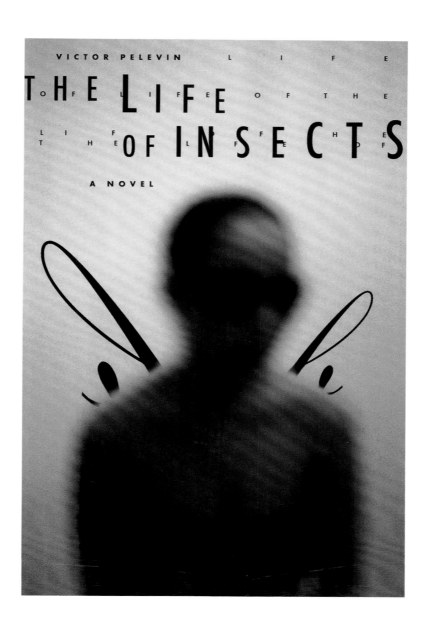

The Life of Insects

Author • *Victor Pelevin*
Design Firm • *Farrar, Straus & Giroux,*
New York, NY
Art Director • *Susan Mitchell*
Graphic Designer • *Rodrigo Corral*
Photographer • *Frederick S. Schmitt*
Typeface • *Univers*
Printer • *Phoenix Color*
Paper • *Phoenix White*
Publisher • *Farrar, Straus & Giroux*

Project Statement
The characters are depicted alternately as human beings and as insects: now they are humans with buggy qualities, now they are insects that walk and talk. I found it to be a great opportunity to put Gina Torres on a jacket.

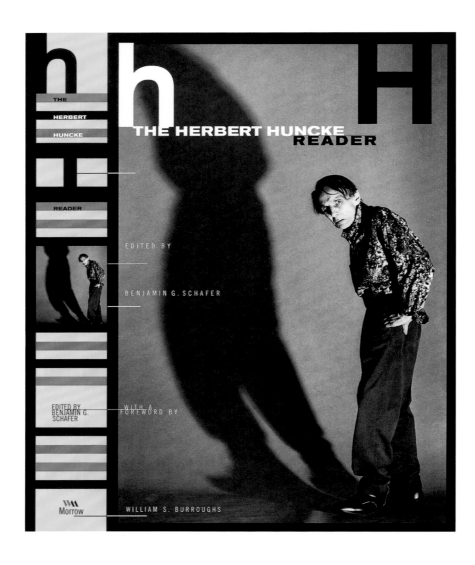

The Herbert Huncke Reader

....

Editors • *Benjamin G. Schafer*
Design Firm • *Carin Goldberg Design,*
Stanfordville, NY
Art Director • *Richard Aquan*
Graphic Designer • *Carin Goldberg*
Photographer • *Christophe von Hohenberg*
Typefaces • *Helvetica Trade Gothic*
Client • *William Morrow*

Project Statement
Sometimes you get lucky and an art director provides
a really nice image. What I saw in this photograph of
Huncke was the relationship and scale between the dimin-
ished and hunched figure and the towering shadow. The
symmetry of the first letters of Huncke's name inspired
a sort of monogram approach along with mimicking the
large and small in the photo with cap and lowercase letters.
The small type at the lower left was designed to suggest
measurement or increments, again inspired by the scale
in the photo.

Author • *David Dante Troutt*
Design Firm • *Evan Gaffney Graphic Design,*
New York, NY
Art Director • *Hall Smyth*
Photographer • *Matthew Antrobus*
Typefaces • *Franklin Gothic, Fournier, and*
Bureau Grotesque
Publisher • *The New Press*

Project Statement
The Monkey Suit is a collection of fictionalized retellings
of famous legal cases involving African Americans. Stories
of senseless racism are told with the gentle, impressionistic
tone of an oral history. My aim was to create something
both elegant and shocking — to express the charm of the
writing as well as the rage behind it.

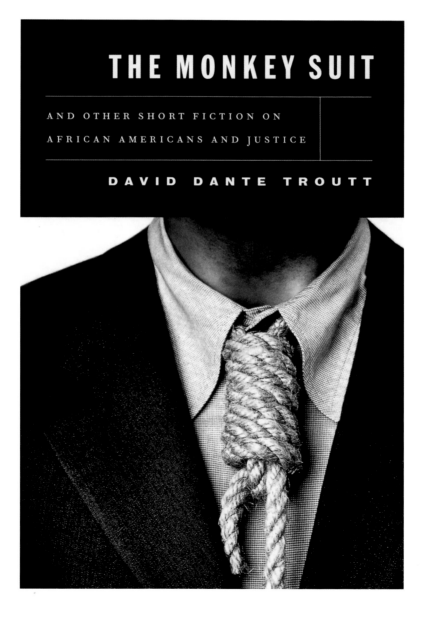

Author • *Paul Hoffman*
Design Firm • *Carin Goldberg Design,*
Stanfordville, NY
Art Directors • *Victor Weaver and Carin Goldberg*
Graphic Designer • *Carin Goldberg*
Illustrator • *Neil Flewellen*
Typefaces • *Helvetica and Clarendon*
Client/Publisher • *Hyperion*

Project Statement
This book is the biography of a very brilliant, yet very eccentric mathematician whose entire existence revolves around numbers. The title is no exaggeration. The connect-the-dots vehicle is meant to imply the literal notion that, in this case, numbers make the man.

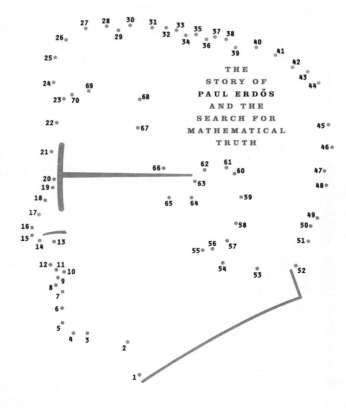

Paul Hoffman

MOTHER
SAID
{POEMS}
BY
HAL
SIROWITZ

Mother Said

Author • *Hal Sirowitz*
Design Firm • *Carin Goldberg Design,*
Stanfordville, NY
Art Directors • *Jim Davis and Carin Goldberg*
Graphic Designer • *Carin Goldberg*
Typeface • *Futura*
Client • *Crown Publishing*

Project Statement

Hal Sirowitz's poems are droll, funny, nutty, and often touching. His writing style is completely dry and straight-forward. Somewhat anti-stylistic. I felt the type should look generic and non-designed without losing the soul or voice of the author. The image of "Mommy's purse" found in a '50s Sears catalogue seemed the right period for the mother in Hal's poems. Metaphorically it represented the psychological baggage between mother and son that the author so humorously portrays.

Dr. J. Zink Raising Emotionally Intelligent Children

UPBRINGING

6 years

5 years

Upbringing

Author • *Dr. J. Zink*

Design Firm • *A Few Creative People,*
Chicago, IL

Creative Director • *Russ Ramage*

Graphic Designers • *Marcus Wiedenhoeft*
and John DeGrace

Photographer • *Jerry Burns*

Typeface • *Franklin Gothic*

Printer • *Consolidated Press, Inc.*

Paper • *Warren Lustro Dull Recycled (Dust Jacket),*
Champion Carnival (Cover)

Publisher • *The Peregrinzilla Press*

Project Statement

Dr. Zink's book is aimed at parents struggling to find solid, no-nonsense advice on how to raise well-adjusted, emotionally intelligent children. The intent of the cover design is to quickly communicate a sense of the subject matter and to position the book as serious, yet accessible, differentiating it from less substantive child-rearing how-to books. The gatefold cover flaps give the book a more substantial feeling than a typical paperback, while still maintaining the production economy required for mass distribution. The cover successfully conveys the quality of the book's content, both visually and tactilely.

Author • *Robin D.G. Kelley*
Design Firm • *Beacon Press, Boston, MA*
Creative Director • *Sara Eisenman*
Graphic Designer • *David J. High*
Typefaces • *Helvetica and Helvetica Condensed*
Printer • *Coral Graphics*
Paper • *Simpson 100# Coated Bright White*
Publisher • *Beacon Press*

Project Statement
The bold typographic jacket design is a fitting solution to this provocatively titled book. Professor Kelley's book is a "bracing blend of biting wit and bold polemic" and so is its cover.

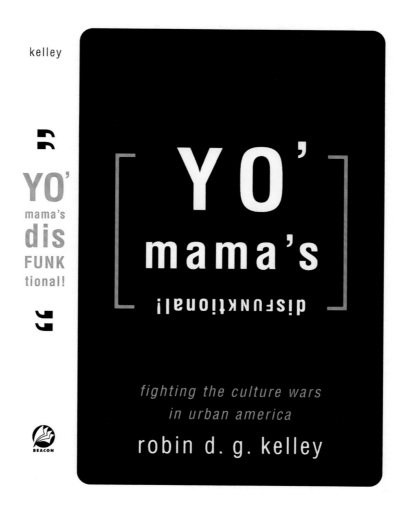

Seven Moves

Author • *Carol Anshaw*
Design Firm • *Carin Goldberg Design,*
Stanfordville, NY
Art Directors • *Michaela Sullivan and*
Carin Goldberg
Graphic Designer • *Carin Goldberg*
Client/Publisher • *Houghton Mifflin*

Project Statement
This novel is more or less about a woman — a photographer — who moves a lot. The cover image and border are meant to imply a contact sheet and photographic negative. The back cover is one more way of emphasizing "move." The type is meant to resemble the monograms often stamped on luggage. In this case, the only demand made by the editor was to make the cover look more feminine, so I suggested we make the suitcase pink — a compromise well worth making, as it saved the cover design from doom.

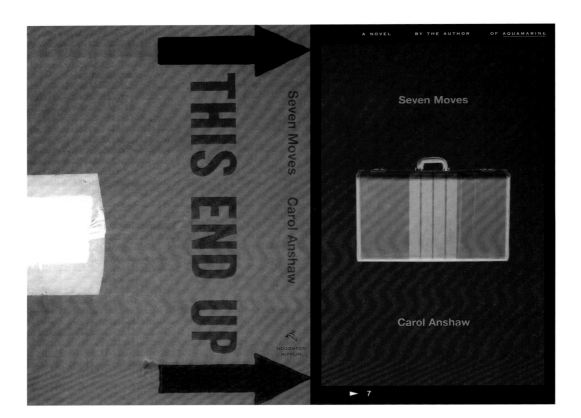

The Disease State Management Tracker

Version 2.1

The Disease State Management Tracker

Author • *Pfizer, Inc.*

Design Firm • *Warhaftig Associates, Inc.,*
New York, NY

Art Director • *Reiner Lubge*

Photographer • *Tigerhill Studios*

Typeface • *Thesis Sans*

Paper • *100# Vintage Velvet*

Client • *Pfizer Inc.*

Project Statement

This software is designed to help clinical pharmacists and physicians integrate complex treatment pathways into their everyday practice. Since the software itself can be rather intimidating, we believe that an important part of our role as designers and writers is to make it intriguing and accessible. It helped to have a client who was willing to go with an idea that is uncharacteristic of the industry, which tends to be very conservative. We liked the cover because it addresses the precise function of the software in a way that is completely unexpected.

Many Strong and Beautiful Voices

Author • *Quinn Eli*
Design Firm • *Running Press Book Publishers,*
New York, NY
Art Director • *Ken Newbaker*
Graphic Designer • *Paul Kepple*
Illustrator • *Charlene Potts*
Typefaces • *Neuland and Univers*
Printer • *R.R. Donnelley*
Paper • *80# Cover Coated One Side,*
70# Glatfelter Antique Text
Publisher • *Running Press Book Publishers*

Project Statement
This collection of quotes celebrates Africans throughout
the world, from America and the Caribbean to Europe and
Africa. Because of the diversity of people represented, we
didn't want to limit the audience by making the faces on
the cover too specific. We felt the cover should be as rich
and warm as the text inside. The hand-lettered type and
color palette hint at heritage, and the African-inspired pattern on the case cover provides a nice surprise.

Author • *Linda Yablonsky*
Design Firm • *Little, Brown & Company*
Art Director • *Michael Ian Kaye*
Graphic Designers • *Michael Ian Kaye*
and John Fulbrook
Cover Photograph • *Michael Ian Kaye*
Arm Model • *Leslie Goldman*
Typeface • *Helvetica*
Printer • *Jaguar Advanced Graphics*
Paper • *Jaguar 10 pt C/1/S*
Publisher • *Back Bay Books/Little,*
Brown & Company

Project Statement
We tried to represent the reality of this gritty New York heroin story by depicting real flesh at the point of entry. The soft quality of the skin reflects the novel's sense of emotion.

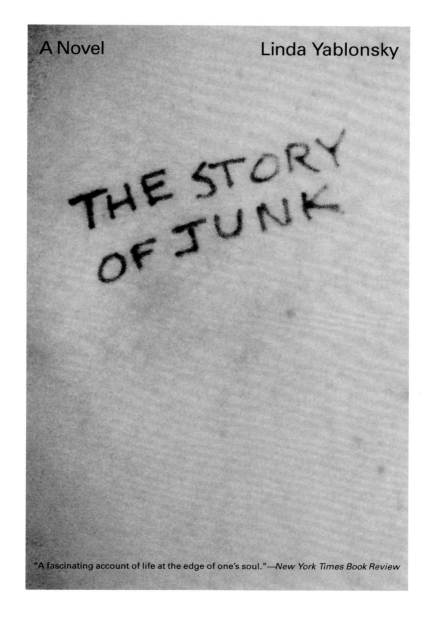

Compiled by • *John Bielenberg*
and AIGA/Colorado
Design Firm • *Bielenberg Design,*
San Francisco, CA
Creative Director • *John Bielenberg*
Graphic Designers • *John Bielenberg*
and Sevia Dyakov
Photographer • *Paul Franz-Moore*
Typeface • *Franklin Gothic Demi Oblique*
Printer • *H. MacDonald Printing*
Paper • *Appleton Utopia One,*
Blue White Dull, 120# Cover
Publisher • *AIGA/Colorado*

Project Statement
In 1997 the AIGA/Colorado board of directors invited designers from across the United States to produce one-of-a-kind posters to promote literacy. This book documents forty-three of those posters. I was perversely interested in the idea of promoting the concept of literacy without actually using any words. The idea for the cover photo came from my two-year-old daughter (shown on the cover) who loves books but shows absolutely no interest in television or any screen-based images. I was trying to illustrate the competition between paper-based books and television for the attention of our children.

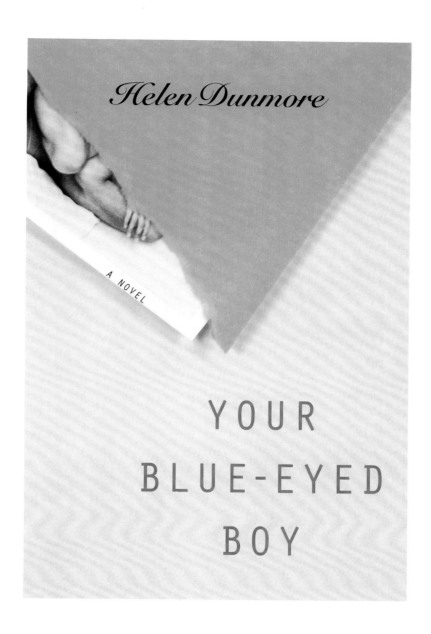

Your Blue-Eyed Boy

Author • *Helen Dunmore*
Design Firm • *Little, Brown & Company,*
New York, NY
Creative Director • *Michael Ian Kaye*
Graphic Designer • *Leslie Goldman*
Typefaces • *Orator, Snell Roundhand, Frutiger*
Printer • *Phoenix Color Corp.*
Paper • *Phoenix 100# Truwhite*
Publisher • *Little, Brown & Company*

Project Statement
This cover had to be feminine and edgy at the same time.
The foil type on an open background with the spot gloss
photo and torn envelope placed diagonally combine to
communicate a slightly disturbing yet intriguing and hope-
fully accessible visual.

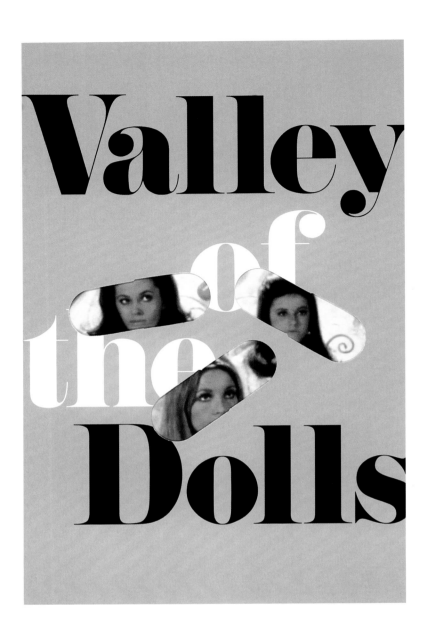

Valley of the Dolls

....

Author • *Jacqueline Susann*
Design Firm • *Grove Press, New York, NY*
Art Director • *Charles Rue Woods*
Graphic Designer • *Evan Gaffney*
Photo • *Courtesy of Neil Peters*
Typeface • *Opti Pirogi*
Printer • *Castlereagh*
Publisher • *Grove Atlantic*

Interviewer • *Gary Indiana*
Design Firm • *Lisa Feldman Design, Inc.,*
New York, NY
Art Director/Graphic Designer • *Lisa Feldman*
Illustrator • *Nancy Chunn*
Typeface • *News Gothic*
Publisher • *Rizzoli International Publications*

Project Statement
This book is intended for news buffs, art lovers, and
political junkies. It presents artist Nancy Chunn's year-long
work *Front Pages*, an illustrated commentary on the front
pages of the *New York Times* for every day of 1996. I set
out to create a cover that would allow the concept of
the artwork to be understood at first glance. This objective
created the challenge of finding a way to make the title
and Nancy Chunn's first name stand out on a busy background.

Five Plays

Author • *Michael Weller*
Design Firm • *Pentagram Design, New York, NY*
Art Director • *Paula Scher*
Graphic Designers • *Paula Scher and Keith Daigle*
Publisher • *Theatre Communications Group, Inc.*

Project Statement

Pentagram designed a new cover for the first Theatre Communications Group edition of *Five Plays*. The book presents five works by Michael Weller from 1971 to 1982.

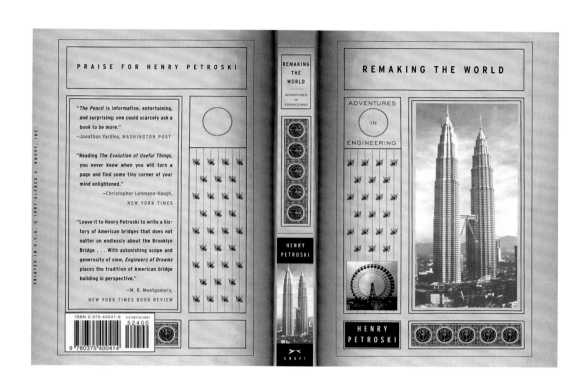

Remaking the World

Author • *Henry Petroski*
Design Firm • *Alfred A. Knopf,*
New York, NY
Art Director/Graphic Designer •
Chip Kidd
Photographer • *J. Apicella/*
Cesar Pelli & Associates
Typeface • *TR1*
Printer • *Coral Graphics*
Publisher • *Alfred A. Knopf*

Project Statement
The title recalls the tone of those "Wasn't Tomorrow Wonderful?" visions of the future from the '20s and '30s, so I wanted the jacket to look like a Utopian textbook from that era. Even though the twin towers pictured on the front look like something out of a Fritz Lang film, they are actually (as of this writing) the world's tallest buildings, the Petronas Towers in Malaysia, designed in 1995 by Cesar Pelli and Associates. Petroski makes you realize that to engineer and build such a complex project, or even one as relatively simple as a Ferris wheel, is something like a miracle.

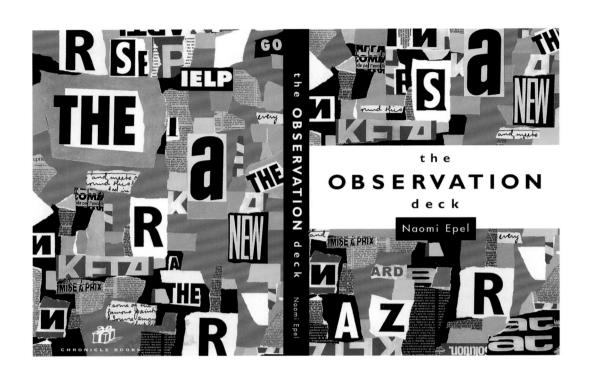

The Observation Deck

Author • *Naomi Epel*

Design Firm • *Doubleugee, Petaluma, CA*

Art Director • *Michele Wetherbee*

Graphic Designers • *Stefan Gutermuth and Michele Wetherbee*

Illustrator • *Stefan Gutermuth*

Typeface • *Gill Sans and Futura*

Client/Publisher • *Giftworks/Chronicle Books*

Project Statement

This book is part of a gift package that includes an outer box and cards. It is intended for sophisticated writers and readers. The artwork combines a love of letterform with observations of environments leading to literary creativity.

Wormholes

Author • *John Fowles*
Design Firm • *Carin Goldberg Design,*
Stanfordville, NY
Art Directors • *Steve Snyder and Carin Goldberg*
Graphic Designer • *Carin Goldberg*
Typefaces • *Futura and Priory*
Client/Publisher • *Little, Brown & Company*

Project Statement

Wormholes are the holes little worms make in old books. In this case I decided to rebel against the obvious, already-done-a-million-times tattered old book/spine solution. Beautiful but tired. So I want the other way and let Quark lead the way. The only demand made on me by the publisher was that the Priory typeface used for the author's name, as was done on the covers of his earlier books. (So what? Very annoying.) Maybe that's why the rest of the design resists the classical approach — I don't like being told which typeface to use.

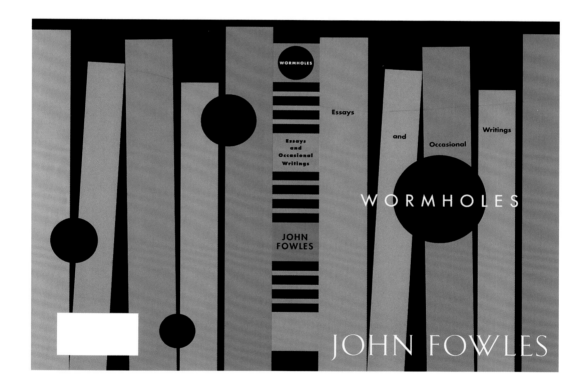

Author • *Ken Hom*
Design Firm • *Alfred A. Knopf, New York, NY*
Art Director • *Carol Devine Carson*
Graphic Designer • *Abby Weintraub*
Typefaces • *Opti Corvinus and Alternate Gothic*
Printer • *Coral Graphics*
Paper • *80# Cover Coated One Side*
Publisher • *Alfred A. Knopf*

On the cover (back):

Give me some cheap sentiment. Give me some sweet pain. Give me some chick-en tonight. Give me your tired, your weary, your huddled masses yearning to breathe free. Give me yr cum, yr piss, yr spit. Give me yr infect-ed blood. Give me yr diseased genitals. Give me yr STDs. Give me yr best make-up tips. Give me yr secrets to clear skin, beauty, success & weight loss. Give me more power Scotty. Give me some sense of empowerment. Give me some sense of security. Give me yr best shot. Give me yr stinking crown. Give me more. Give me. Give me what I ask for & you can take what you want from me.

With scathing humor, brutal honesty, and unflinching detail, award-winning spoken word/performance artist Justin Chin chews through society's limitations and stereo-types of race, desire, and loss through his own life experiences. His work has appeared in *Dissident Song: A Contemporary Asian American Anthology*, *Men on Men 5*, and *Eros In Boystown*.

"Chin embodies the pan-cultural strains that run rampant through the current San Francisco literary scene." — *San Francisco Focus*

"He plugs the stage microphone into the page and lyrically blasts the heart of our fears, rage, and import-export nightmarish dreams." — R. Zamora Linmark, author of *Rolling The R's*

manic D press

ISBN 0-916397-47-5
9 780916 397470
51195>

Gay & Lesbian Studies
Asian Studies
Poetry
$11.95

CHIN BITE HARD MANIC D PRESS

Bite hard.

Justin Chin

Bite Hard

Author • *Justin Chin*
Design Firm • *Blink, San Francisco, CA*
Graphic Designer • *Scott Idleman*
Typeface • *Helvetica*
Paper • *Lustro Dull 100# Cover*
Publisher • *Manic D Press*
Client • *Jennifer Joseph*

Project Statement
Bite Hard is a collection of poetry by Malaysian-born spoken-word artist Justin Chin, whose work explores stereotypes of race, desire, and loss, and is laced with pop-culture references. In approaching this cover, I collected icons representing stereotypical Asian culture, and by digitally juxtaposing the elements, created a literal depiction of biting as well as spoken word becoming printed word. I value *Bite Hard* for its simple visual pun, and for the way I was able to work with the publisher with regard to the unconventional title placement, which we believe conveys the stark flavor of Chin's poetry.

$10.95 ISBN 1-55936-133-6

"This collection has a simple aim: to make matches. You're an actor searching for the right monologue—for auditions or acting class—and here are cuttings from dozens of the most exciting American plays of the last two decades. The material might be said to be searching, too. It's on the lookout for actors who will connect deeply, who have the emotional availability and the craft to deliver these monologues into the world with their complexity intact. It seeks actors who think on their feet, who understand in their bodies the impression contemporary life makes on a character. Like any matchmaker, though, this book offers only an introduction. The work is left to you."
—from the introduction by Todd London

Selected monologues from the works of:

Jon Robin Baitz, Eric Bogosian, Laurie Carlos, Lenora Champagne, Constance Congdon, E.L. Doctorow, Richard Foreman, Maria Irene Fornes, George Furth, Philip Kan Gotanda, David Greenspan, Jessica Hagedorn, William M. Huffman, Tina Howe, Holly Hughes, David Henry Hwang, Judith Alexa Jackson, Adrienne Kennedy, Harry Kondoleon, Tony Kushner, Romulus Linney, Craig Lucas, Eduardo Machado, Emily Mann, Donald Margulies, Robbie McCauley, Marsha Norman, John O'Keefe, Suzan-Lori Parks, Reynolds Price, Aishah Rahman, Ronald Ribman, José Rivera, Rachel Rosenthal, Beatrice Roth, Milcha Sanchez-Scott, Nicky Silver, Stephen Sondheim, Danitra Vance, Paula Vogel and John Weidman

Cover design by Paula Scher
Theatre Communications Group

ISBN 1-55936-133-6
51095
9 781559 361330

TCG

Contemporary American Monologues *for* Women

{ Contemporary American Monologues *for* Women }
Edited by Todd London

$10.95 ISBN 1-55936-134-4

"This collection has a simple aim: to make matches. You're an actor searching for the right monologue—for auditions or acting class—and here are the cuttings from dozens of the most exciting American plays of the last two decades. The material might be said to be searching, too. It's on the lookout for actors who will connect deeply, who have the emotional availability and the craft to deliver these monologues into the world with their complexity intact. It seeks actors who think on their feet, who understand in their bodies the impression contemporary life makes on a character. Like any matchmaker, though, this book offers only an introduction. The work is left to you."
—from the introduction by Todd London

Selected monologues from the works of:

Jon Robin Baitz, Eric Bogosian, Lee Breuer, Constance Congdon, E. L. Doctorow, Richard Foreman, Maria Irene Fornes, Philip Kan Gotanda, Spalding Gray, David Greenspan, William M. Hoffman, Tina Howe, Judith Alexa Jackson, John Jesurun, Adrienne Kennedy, Harry Kondoleon, Tony Kushner, Romulus Linney, Eduardo Machado, Emily Mann, Donald Margulies, Marsha Norman, John O'Keefe, Suzan-Lori Parks, Reynolds Price, Ronald Ribman, José Rivera, Milcha Sanchez-Scott, Nicky Silver, Stephen Sondheim, Paula Vogel and John Weidman.

Cover design by Paula Scher
Theatre Communications Group

ISBN 1-55936-134-4
51095
9 781559 361347

TCG

Contemporary American Monologues *for* Men

{ Contemporary American Monologues *for* Men }
Edited by Todd London

Contemporary American Monologues for Men/for Women

Editor • *Todd London*
Design Firm • *Pentagram Design,*
New York, NY
Art Director • *Paula Scher*
Graphic Designers • *Paula Scher,*
Keith Daigle, and Jane Mella
Client/Publisher •
Theatre Communications Group, Inc.

Project Statement
Each book is a collection of excerpts from plays written during the last two decades, covering a wide range of subject matter. The covers were designed for the first Theatre Communications Group editions.

Author • *Pierre Assouline*
Design Firm • *Alfred A. Knopf,*
New York, NY
Art Director • *Carol Devine Carson*
Graphic Designer • *Archie Ferguson*
Photographer • *Gamma Press Images/*
Gamma Liaison
Typefaces • *Trade Gothic Bold,*
Didot, and Bodoni
Publisher • *Alfred A. Knopf*

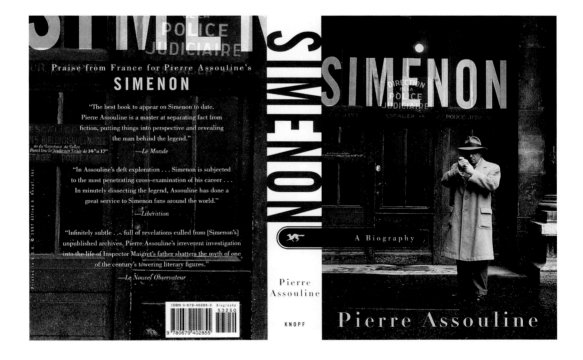

Gentleman Junkie

Author • *Graham Caveney*
Design Firm • *Little, Brown & Company,*
New York, NY
Creative Director • *Michael Ian Kaye*
Graphic Designer • *Leslie Goldman*
Photographer • *Marcia Resnick*
Typeface • *Berthold Akzidenz Grotesk*
Printer • *Butler & Tanner Ltd.*
Paper • *Sequel Gloss 130 gsm Art Paper*
Publisher • *Little, Brown & Company*

Project Statement
The intended audience for this book is fans of William S. Burroughs. I felt that the granddaddy of American counter-culture needed an edgy cover. The purple background feels like a Jimi Hendrix-like purple haze. The type is off to one side. The picture of Burroughs has the added dimension of being art itself, with the use of the border of the negative.

Mason & Dixon

Author • *Thomas Pynchon*
Design Firm • *Henry Holt & Co.,*
New York, NY
Creative Director/Graphic Designer •
Raquel Jaramillo
Typeface • *Unknown (Possibly Caslon)*
Printer • *Phoenix Color Corp.*
Paper • *70# Champion Linen Text Soft White*

Project Statement
I wanted, above all, to comply with the author's wishes that the jacket design be consistent, typographically and stylistically, with the design styles of the eighteenth century, the time period in which the novel is set. After toying with the idea of finding an antique letterpress to set the type, I found a book in an antiquarian bookstore and scanned in a page of the eleven point text. I then created the title words from the letters on the scanned page, enlarging each letter so much that the letters became irregular and rough, and the vague shadows of the hot press type became visible. The paper fiber, blown up so many thousands of times, created a kind of mottled peach effect, which became the background color and texture. Originally, I was going to use the type in a more traditional way, all centered on the front jacket, with some kind of map or graphic element depicting the Mason Dixon line, but as I worked on the letterforms, they seemed so beautiful that I almost couldn't bear to make them small again, to confine them to that 6 x 9 rectangular format of a book cover. I designed it so that they could be as large as possible within the format of an entire jacket, using all the available space allowed from the back and spine and front put together, and even then it didn't quite fit so I made it larger still, bleeding off the page. I was hoping that it would feel as if we had actually taken an old newspaper from that time period, with the headline of Mason & Dixon, and wrapped it around the book. I was so into that concept that I couldn't figure out how to integrate the author's name (the single most important thing about this book, after all!) into the front jacket design without it seeming anachronistic. I kind of liked the idea of those words glaring out at the consumer in a bookstore, "son & xon," without any further explanation. But of course this was entirely unrealistic, in terms of sales and marketing, so the acetate overlay was the perfect solution.

Continental Anchor Touch Show

December 4, 1998 – January 19, 1998

The Strathmore Gallery at the AIGA

Sponsored by Continental Anchor Ltd.

An exhibition of thirty engraved pieces by leading New York graphic designers celebrating the beauty of engraving and fine papers.

WORLD STUDIO FOUNDATION BOARD OF DIRECTORS
SPHERE MAGAZINE &
CHAMPION INTERNATIONAL CORPORATION
INVITE YOU TO A TRIBUTE TO
KEITH HARING
▼

World Studio Foundation: A Tribute to Keith Haring

July 23, 1998

The Strathmore Gallery at the AIGA

Sponsored by Champion International Corporation

A fundraising event to benefit the World Studio Foundation's scholarship program for disadvantaged and minority students of art, architecture, and design. Participants collaborated on a Haring-style painting and bid on works of art by noted artists and designers in a silent auction. Ten percent of the evening's proceeds were donated to the Keith Haring Foundation.

Designers Explore Literacy: The Quest and the Best

March 13–31, 1998

The Strathmore Gallery at the AIGA

Commissioned and presented by AIGA/Colorado

Sponsored by Appleton Papers and xpedex

An exhibition of forty-two posters commissioned by the AIGA's Colorado chapter to promote literacy. The exhibition is one example of how the AIGA, in partnership with the Library of Congress Center for the Book, is working with communities across the country to support literacy.

Concerned Theatre Japan:

The Graphic Art of Japanese Theatre, 1960–1980

June 25–August 22, 1998

The Strathmore Gallery at the AIGA

PRESENTED BY:

Cooper-Hewitt, National Design Museum, Smithsonian Institution

Krannert Art Museum, University of Illinois at Urbana-Champaign

Musashino Art University, Tokyo, Japan

SPONSORED IN PART BY:

Musashino Art University, the Japan Foundation, the National
Endowment of the Arts, the Illinois Arts Council, the Pola Foundation,
Consolidated Communications and McLeod U.S.A., the Center for East
Asian and Pacific Studies, and the Department of East Asian Languages
and Culture at the University of Illinois, Urbana-Champaign

An exhibition of 150 theater posters from the 1960s and '70s, organized
and curated by the Krannert Art Museum. Some of Japan's greatest
designers, including Tadanori Yokoo and Hirono Koga, mixed elements
of Western popular culture with Japanese traditional forms to create innovative theater posters that captured the socially conscious spirit of these
two decades.

Freedom Theatre 自由劇場

1998 AIGA Conferences

AIGA National Student Conference

June 12–14, 1998

California Institute of the Arts, Valencia, California

Major sponsoring partner: Fraser Papers

The first AIGA National Student Design Conference gave one hundred young people a rare opportunity to spend three days exploring design, creativity, and professional practice with some of the country's top designers, paper company representatives, printers, and technology evangelists. Attendees practiced networking, had their portfolios reviewed by giants of the profession, learned the nuts and bolts of being a designer, and got a feel for selecting paper, printing, hardware, and software.

The 1999 AIGA National Student Conference will be held in Baltimore on June 22–24, immediately preceding the AIGA's annual Chapter Leadership Retreat. The AIGA's national board and chapter presidents will be on hand to participate in portfolio reviews and lead workshops.

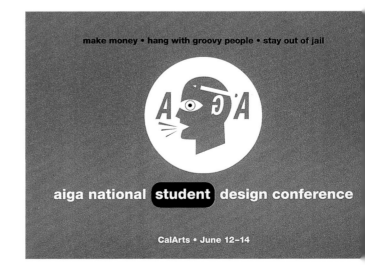

*American Institute of Graphic Arts/Design for Film and TeleVision.Number 1

Brandesign

The AIGA's National Design Business Conference

October 2–4, 1998

New York, New York

A collaboration of the AIGA and the Brand Design Association, the conference explored "branding" — the way a company expresses its personality and core values — and sought to expand participants' definition of what constitutes the business of design and the designer's role within it. Conceived as a limited-attendance event, Brandesign sold out in record time. Speakers provided historical overviews of branding, presented case studies of brands that succeeded or failed, examined the future of branding and consumer trends, and explored the ever-changing, ever-expanding role of technology as it affects branding professionals.

The AIGA's next National Design Business Conference has been tentatively located in San Francisco and will be held in September 2000.

Advance for Design

October 16–18, 1998

Nantucket, Massachusetts

The Advance for Design was intended to begin building a community of new-media practitioners who are challenged to design for a world that is increasingly digital and connected. A core group of interaction design practitioners — design planners and strategists, information designers, interaction designers, product designers, graphic designers, GUI designers, usability specialists, software designers and engineers, web designers, design researchers, and educators — was invited to spend a weekend in Nantucket helping to define the role, reach, and requirements of the designer so that this evolving discipline can continue to make an effective contribution.

The Advance was the first in a series of activities that will define the essential values of interaction design as a profession, with the goal of offering broad public involvement in these issues by the fall of 1999.

Upcoming Conferences

AIGA/DFTV.001

American Institute of Graphic Arts Design for Film and Television Number One
March 12–13, 1999
New York, New York

AIGA/DFTV.001 is the first in a new series of annual AIGA conferences devoted to design for film and television. The two-day conference will take both a critical and a loving look at the visual language being created at the intersection between the film, television and graphic design disciplines.

AIGA National Design Conference

September 29–October 2, 1999
Las Vegas, Nevada

The AIGA's eighth biennial National Design Conference will be held at the Venetian Hotel in Las Vegas. The program will focus on "The Real World."

Renovation of the AIGA

1998 Conclusion

The Capital Campaign renovation of the AIGA National Design Center at 164 Fifth Avenue started five years ago. Now, in 1998, we are concluding the initial phase of the campaign.

We have invested $2.5 million in the center by purchasing it and renovating it during that period, supported by a $1.3 million bond we will pay off over thirty years. The balance was raised from those who believe in the profession and its future, giving sums from $25 to $100,000.

Our most generous donors are now memorialized in steel on the mezzanine of the National Design Center. We want to thank everyone who has supported us and encourage others to contribute to the Capstone Campaign, which we hope will raise the final sums needed over the next eighteen months to complete the building's façade renovation, and the Fund for the Future, which will continue to support new programming initiatives for the profession.

Supporters of these campaigns will also be memorialized on the mezzanine, next to the names of those generous and accomplished designers listed here.

Special Benefactors $100,000

Adobe Systems, Inc.

Strathmore Papers

Benefactors $50,000 +

Champion International Corporation

Digex, Inc.

Pentagram Design, Inc.

Patrons $25,000 +

Apple Computers, Inc.

Crosby Associates, Inc.

The I. Grace Company

Sponsors $10,000 +

Addison Corporate Annual Reports

Harvey Bernstein Design Associates

Brennan Brothers

Chermayeff & Geismar Inc.

Designframe, Inc.

Donovan and Green

Doyle Partners

Fine Arts Engraving Company

Frankfurt Balkind Partners

Gr8

Milton Glaser

Jessica Helfand/William Drenttel

Mirko Ilic

Jet Pak

Steve Liska

Emanuela Frattini Magnusson

Clement Mok

The Overbrook Foundation

Stan Richards

Anthony Russell

Arnold Saks Associates

Siegel and Gale, Inc.

TeamDesign

Vignelli Associates

Wechsler & Partners, Inc.

Donors $5,000 +

Adams/Morioka

Primo Angeli

Appleton Papers

Bass/Yager & Associates

Carbone Smolan Associates

David Cundy

Richard Danne & Associates

GL Lites On

Diana Graham

Hansen Design Company

Hawthorne/Wolfe

Steven Heller

The Hennegan Company

Hornall Anderson Design Works, Inc.

Alexander Isley

Karen Skunta

Robert Star

Sussman/Prejza & Co., Inc.

Typogram, Inc.

Vanderbyl Design, Inc.

Ann Willoughby Design

Weyerhaeuser

Contributors $3,000 +

BlackDog

Doug Byers

Bob Callahan Design

Mark Coleman

Concrete [The Office of Jilly Simons]

Concrete Design Communications, Inc.

Michael Cronan

James Cross

Joe Duffy

Joseph and Susan Feigenbaum

Martin Fox

Georgia-Pacific Papers

Bill Grant

Kent Hunter

Meyer Design Associates, Inc.

J. Abbott Miller

Milocraft, Inc.

Monadnock Paper Mills, Inc.

Elizabeth O'Keefe

Poulin + Morris

Wendy Richmond

Dugald Stermer

AIGA Chapter Leadership Circle $8,000 +

AIGA/Atlanta

AIGA/Boston

AIGA/Chicago

AIGA/Los Angeles

AIGA/New York

AIGA/San Francisco

AIGA/Washington

AIGA Chapter Support

AIGA/Colorado

AIGA/Minnesota

AIGA/Phoenix

AIGA/San Diego

AIGA/Seattle

The American Institute of Graphic Arts (AIGA) is the oldest and largest professional association serving graphic designers in the United States. It is dedicated to the advancement of excellence and professionalism among designers, educators, and students engaged in type and book design, publications design, communications and corporate design, posters, package and branding strategy, interface and web design, and new-media design. Founded in 1914, the AIGA serves over 12,000 members organized in more than forty local chapters, through professional interest groups and on-campus student groups. AIGA activities offer designers the opportunity to develop relationships within the profession, share information, and advance respect for and understanding of the value of graphic design excellence on the part of business and the public. The AIGA conducts a program of competitions, exhibitions, professional seminars, educational activities, and publications to communicate the value of effective design. Publications include *Graphic Design USA,* the annual of the AIGA, which chronicles the work selected in national competitions each year for exhibition by the AIGA; the *AIGA Journal of Graphic Design;* a yearly membership directory; and occasional topical books. The AIGA regularly produces two biennial conferences in alternate years: the AIGA National Design Conference, which celebrates American and international graphic design; and the AIGA Design Business Conference, which focuses on strategic business issues. The AIGA awards the most prestigious award in the graphic design profession — the AIGA Medal — and selects each year's most notable graphic design work in two juried competitions, *Communication Graphics* and *50 Books/50 Covers.*

1997–1998 Board of Directors

Lucille Tenazas, *President*

John DuFresne, *Secretary / Treasurer*

Richard Grefé, *Executive Director*

Paul Montie, *Chapter Presidents'*
Council Chair

DIRECTORS

Sean Adams, Maxey Andress, Michael
Bierut, Meredith Davis, Michael
Donovan, Steff Geissbuhler, Louis
Lenzi, Samina Quraeshi, Lana Rigsby,
Beth Singer, Michael Vanderbyl,
Lorraine Wild

1998–1999 Board of Directors

Michael Bierut, *President*

Richard Grefé, *Executive Director*

Sam Shelton, *Chapter Presidents'*
Council Chair

DIRECTORS

Sean Adams, Maxey Andress,
Bart Crosby, Michael Donovan,
Steff Geissbuhler, Eric Madsen,
Clement Mok, Emily Oberman,
Samina Quraeshi, Lana Rigsby,
Mary Scott, Beth Singer,
Lucille Tenazas, Michael Vanderbyl

AIGA National Staff

Richard Grefé, *Executive Director*

Denise Wood, *Director of Information and Member Services*

Deborah Aldrich, *Director of Corporate Partnerships*

Marie Finamore, *Managing Editor*

Joyce Burgess Horton, *Conference Coordinator*

Gabriela Mirensky, *Program Coordinator*

Rita Grendze, *Chapter Coordinator*

George Fernandez, *Membership Coordinator*

Jennifer Rittner, *Project Coordinator*

Alice Twemlow, *Conference Program Coordinator*

Gary Sisto, *Finance and Administration Associate*

Megan Hackett, *Information Associate*

Christine Fischer, *Gallery and Information Assistant*

Johnny Ventura, *Facilities Assistant*

AIGA Chapters and
Chapter Presidents
1997–1998

Anchorage • Cindy Shake

Arizona • David Rengifo

Atlanta • Bill Grant

Austin • Marc English

Baltimore • Kristin Seeberger

Birmingham • Barry Graham

Boston • Jan Moscowitz

Chicago • Mark Oldach

Cincinnati • Beverly Fox

Cleveland • Kurt Roscoe

Colorado • Rick Griffith

Detroit • Michael Besch

Honolulu • Lynn Kinoshita

Indianapolis • Stacy Kagiwada

Iowa • Steve Pattee

Jacksonville • Jefferson Rall

Kansas City • Deb Lilla

Knoxville • Cary Staples

Los Angeles • Moira Cullen

Miami • Robin Rosenbaum

Minnesota • Dan Woychick

Nebraska • Trish Farrar

New York • Kathleen Schenck Row

Upstate New York • Leslie Lord

Oklahoma City • Sarah Sears

Orange County •
   Anthony Columbini

Philadelphia • Stella Gassaway

Pittsburgh • Kimberly Kalista

Portland • Alicia Johnson

Raleigh • Jim Briggs

Richmond • Frank Gilliam

Salt Lake City • Dave Malone

San Diego • Maelin Levine

San Francisco • Shel Perkins

Seattle • Jesse Doquilo

St. Louis • Scott Gericke

Texas • Jim Mousner

Washington, DC • Samuel Shelton

Wichita • Sherrie Holdeman

AIGA Chapters and
Chapter Presidents
1998–1999

Arizona • David Rengifo

Atlanta • Bill Grant

Austin • Marc English

Baltimore • Kristin Seeberger

Birmingham • MaryAnn Charles

Boston • Jan Moscowitz

Chicago • Mark Oldach

Cincinnati • Tim Smith

Cleveland • Sheila Hart

Colorado • Rick Griffith

Dallas • John J. Conley

Detroit • Michael Besch

Honolulu • Michael Horton

Houston • Shawn Collier

Indianapolis • Stacy Kagiwada

Iowa • Steve Pattee

Jacksonville • Florence Haridan

Kansas City • Deb Lilla

Knoxville • Leland Hume

Las Vegas • Andrew Hershberger

Los Angeles • Moira Cullen

Miami • Maggy Cuesta

Minnesota • Douglas Powell

Nebraska • Trish Farrar

New Orleans • John Barousse

New York • Paula Scher

Upstate New York • Marj Crum

Oklahoma • Sarah Sears

Orange County •
   Anthony Columbini

Philadelphia • Caren Lipkin and
   Steve Williams

Pittsburgh • Bernard Uy

Portland • Susan Agre-Kippenhan

Raleigh • Jim Briggs

Richmond • Donald McCants

Salt Lake City • Dave Malone

San Diego • Maelin Levine

San Francisco • Shel Perkins

Seattle • David Betz and
   Richard Smith

St. Louis • Karen Handelman

Washington, DC • Tamera Lawrence

Wichita • Sherrie Holdeman

Past AIGA Presidents

1914–1915 William B. Howland

1915–1916 John Clyde Oswald

1917–1919 Arthur S. Allen

1920–1921 Walter Gilliss

1921–1922 Frederic W. Goudy

1922–1923 J. Thompson Willing

1924–1925 Burton Emmett

1926–1927 W. Arthur Cole

1927–1928 Frederic G. Melcher

1928–1929 Frank Altschul

1930–1931 Henry A. Groesbeck, Jr.

1932–1934 Harry L. Gage

1935–1936 Charles Chester Lane

1936–1938 Henry Watson Kent

1939–1940 Melbert B. Carey, Jr.

1941–1942 Arthur R. Thompson

1943–1944 George T. Bailey

1945–1946 Walter Frese

1947–1948 Joseph A. Brandt

1948–1950 Donald S. Klopfer

1951–1952 Merle Armitage

1952–1953 Walter Dorwin Teague

1953–1955 Dr. M. F. Agha

1955–1957 Leo Lionni

1957–1958 Sidney R. Jacobs

1958–1960 Edna Beilenson

1960–1963 Alvin Eisenman

1963–1966 Ivan Chermayeff

1966–1968 George Tscherny

1968–1970 Allen Hurlburt

1970–1972 Henry Wolf

1972–1974 Robert O. Bach

1974–1976 Karl Fink

1976–1977 Massimo Vignelli

1977–1979 Richard Danne

1979–1981 James Fogleman

1981–1984 David R. Brown

1984–1986 Colin Forbes

1986–1988 Bruce Blackburn

1988–1991 Nancye Green

1992–1994 Anthony Russell

1994–1996 William Drenttel

1996–1998 Lucille Tenazas

Past Recipients
of the AIGA Medal

Norman T. A. Munder, 1920

Daniel Berkeley Updike, 1922

John C. Agar, 1924

Stephen H. Horgan, 1924

Bruce Rogers, 1925

Burton Emmett, 1926

Timothy Cole, 1927

Frederic W. Goudy, 1927

William A. Dwiggins, 1929

Henry Watson Kent, 1930

Dard Hunter, 1931

Porter Garnett, 1932

Henry Lewis Bullen, 1934

Rudolph Ruzicka, 1935

J. Thompson Willing, 1935

William A. Kittredge, 1939

Thomas M. Cleland, 1940

Carl Purington Rollins, 1941

Edwin and Robert Grabhorn, 1942

Edward Epstean, 1944

Frederic G. Melcher, 1945

Stanley Morison, 1946

Elmer Adler, 1947

Lawrence C. Wroth, 1948

Earnest Elmo Calkins, 1950

Alfred A. Knopf, 1950

Harry L. Gage, 1951

Joseph Blumenthal, 1952

George Macy, 1953

Will Bradley, 1954

Jan Tschichold, 1954

P. J. Conkwright, 1955

Ray Nash, 1956

Dr. M. F. Agha, 1957

Ben Shahn, 1958

May Massee, 1959

Walter Paepcke, 1960

Paul A. Bennett, 1961

Wilhelm Sandberg, 1962

Saul Steinberg, 1963

Josef Albers, 1964

Leonard Baskin, 1965

Paul Rand, 1966

Romana Javitz, 1967

Dr. Giovanni Mardersteig, 1968

Dr. Robert R. Leslie, 1969

Herbert Bayer, 1970

Will Burtin, 1971

Milton Glaser, 1972

Richard Avedon, 1973

Allen Hurlburt, 1973

Philip Johnson, 1973

Robert Rauschenberg, 1974

Bradbury Thompson, 1975

Henry Wolf, 1976

Jerome Snyder, 1976

Charles and Ray Eames, 1977

Lou Dorfsman, 1978

Ivan Chermayeff and
  Thomas Geismar, 1979

Herb Lubalin, 1980

Saul Bass, 1981

Massimo and Lella Vignelli, 1982

Herbert Matter, 1983

Leo Lionni, 1984

Seymour Chwast, 1985

Walter Herdeg, 1986

Alexey Brodovitch, 1987

Gene Federico, 1987

William Golden, 1988

George Tscherny, 1988

Paul Davis, 1989

Bea Feitler, 1989

Alvin Eisenman, 1990

Frank Zachary, 1990

Colin Forbes, 1991

E. McKnight Kauffer, 1991

Rudolph de Harak, 1992

George Nelson, 1992

Lester Beall, 1992

Alvin Lustig, 1993

Tomoko Miho, 1993

Muriel Cooper, 1994

John Massey, 1994

Matthew Carter, 1995

Stan Richards, 1995

Ladislav Sutnar, 1995

Cipe Pineles, 1996

George Lois, 1996

Lucian Bernhard, 1997

Zuzana Licko and
  Rudy VanderLans, 1997

Past Recipients of the

Design Leadership Award

IBM Corporation, 1980

Massachusetts Institute
  of Technology, 1981

Container Corporation
  of America, 1982

Cummins Engine Company, Inc.,
  1982

Herman Miller, Inc., 1984

WGBH Educational Foundation,
  1985

Esprit, 1986

Walker Art Center, 1987

The New York Times, 1988

Apple and Adobe Systems, 1989

The National Park Service, 1990

MTV, 1991

Olivetti, 1991

Sesame Street, Children's
  Television Workshop, 1992

Nike, Inc., 1993